THE WAY OF IMAGINATION

"Alejandro Jodorowsky sees life with the eyes of an eternal soul, living it in synchronicity, mixing reality and dreams, life and death."

YOUSSEF NABIL, ARTIST AND PHOTOGRAPHER

"This book is for everyone to read immediately. It will help all readers understand the complexity of human emotions."

MARINA ABRAMOVIĆ, CONCEPTUAL AND PERFORMANCE ARTIST

PRAISE FOR ALEJANDRO JODOROWSKY

"A man whose life has been defined by cosmic ambitions."

THE NEW YORK TIMES MAGAZINE

"Alejandro Jodorowsky seamlessly and effortlessly weaves together the worlds of art, the confined social structure, and things we can only touch with an open heart and mind."

ERYKAH BADU, SINGER AND SONGWRITER

"A legendary man of many trades, talents, and of passionate sincerity."

ROGER EBERT, AMERICAN FILM CRITIC, FILM HISTORIAN, JOURNALIST, ESSAYIST, SCREENWRITER, AND AUTHOR

"Jodorowsky is today's true Renaissance man—a master of many mediums that all point directly towards a towering and imaginative vision replete with profound insights into the real by way of the surreal."

JOHN ZORN, COMPOSER

"Jodorowsky is a brilliant, wise, gentle, and cunning wizard with tremendous depth of imagination and crystalline insight into the human condition."

DANIEL PINCHBECK, AUTHOR AND
FOUNDER OF THE LIMINAL INSTITUTE

"Alejandro Jodorowsky is a demiurge and an interpreter of our stories, always exploring further the understanding of both the beauty and complexity revealed by humankind."

DIANA WIDMAIER PICASSO, FRENCH ART HISTORIAN
SPECIALIZING IN MODERN ART

THE WAY OF IMAGINATION

From Psychomagic to Psychotrance

ALEJANDRO JODOROWSKY

Translated by Aleksandra Veleno

Park Street Press

Rochester, Vermont

Park Street Press
One Park Street
Rochester, Vermont 05767
www.ParkStPress.com

Park Street Press is a division of Inner Traditions International

Originally published in Spanish in 2022 under the title *De la Psicomagia al Psicotrance: Correspondencia psicomágica: la vía de la imaginación* by Ediciones Siruela, S. A.
First U.S. edition published in 2024 by Park Street Press

Cataloging-in-Publication Data for this title is available from the Library of Congress

ISBN 978-1-64411-801-6 (print)
ISBN 978-1-64411-802-3 (ebook)

Printed and bound in China by Reliance Printing Co., Ltd.

10 9 8 7 6 5 4 3 2 1

Text design and layout by Virginia Scott Bowman
This book was typeset in Garamond Premier Pro and Legacy Sans with Marseille used as the display typeface

Scan the QR code and save 25% at InnerTraditions.com.
Browse over 2,000 titles on spirituality, the occult, ancient mysteries, new science, holistic health, and natural medicine.

Contents

The Birth of Psychomagic

Psychomagic is not an invention created by my intellect. Its birth is not an act of will. It grew little by little in my artistic activities, influenced by the poetry of René Daumal in *Le Contre-Ciel;* the writings of Éliphas Lévi in *The Doctrine and Ritual of High Magic;* an expressionist ballet of Kurt Jooss called *The Green Table; The Surrealist Manifestos:* "Leave the safe for the uncertain"; *The Manifesto of Futurism:* "Poetry is an action"; the theories of Antonin Artaud: "Take the theater out of theater"; Luis Buñuel's movie *Él;* my friendship with Zen master Ejo Takata; the exploration of lucid dreams; the practice of initiatic massage; my meeting with the Mexican *curandera* Pachita; and my psychoanalysis with Erich Fromm.

Psychoanalysis is a therapy of words. Psychomagic is a therapy of actions.

Psychoanalysis prohibits the therapist from touching their patients. Psychomagic recommends that the therapist touch their patients.

Psychoanalysis analyzes dreams as if they were reality. Psychomagic suggests analyzing reality as if it were a dream.

Psychoanalysis has to be paid for. Psychomagic has to be free.

In psychoanalysis when a person has a problem, it's analyzed with words, searching for the trauma causing it. In this modality the patient can talk for six months, ten months, many years, until they realize, for example, that they are holding sexual desires for their mother. But the realization itself does not bring a solution. What can the patient do then to move from words into a healing action?

Salvador Dalí wanted to translate dreams into reality. I follow the reverse path: "You can't teach the unconscious to speak the language of reality. You've got to teach reason to speak the language of dreams." Therefore it is important to clarify the concept of healing.

Our personality has four aspects: intellectual, emotional, sexual, and physical. Every illness is a set of four illnesses.

If we treat one level without considering the others, the patient cannot be healed. One unified energy has to animate and reveal itself through these four languages (words, emotions, desires, and needs) to create a union. That's where the soul appears. If these four energies don't act together, the soul is sick.

What are the soul's diseases? Boredom, sadness, no joy of life, fear of death, permanent dissatisfaction, fatigue, and a lack of enthusiasm. We can't enjoy perfect health if the soul is in darkness. When we agree to heal a person, it implies taking responsibility for healing their entire being and thus becoming a healer of their body, sex, heart, intellect . . . and soul.

I began giving psychomagical consultations as an experiment, through my free readings of the Tarot de Marseille for a large number of people. Back then, I thought we couldn't establish the laws of psychomagic, as psychomagic, being an art, escapes all rules. I once thought I was the only one who could practice it, but over time I've come to feel that I could codify certain laws and establish a scientific basis to allow the transmission of psychomagic to others.

The first of these laws I call "pulling the donkey by the tail." When someone has a problem, we must force them to enter it in order to find a way out. I was inspired by an anecdote from an American psychoanalyst, Milton Erickson. In Texas, he had a donkey that didn't want to go into its enclosure. Everyone was trying to push it in there. Erickson, on the other hand, pulled the donkey in the opposite direction, away from the enclosure. The donkey rushed into his stall.

Before creating psychomagic, when someone would come to see me with a problem, I would realize that trying to boost their morale would make no difference. However, if a person has a fear of the void and we meet them in a room in total darkness, we immerse them in the depths of their phobia and the experience allows them to heal. Seeing the neurosis as an ally allows us to find the solution.

If a patient's lover suffers from premature ejaculation, the first thing to tell the patient is that she chose this man out of convenience. The second is that, by neglecting her sexually, her lover is indirectly expressing his anger against women. Therein lies the source of his premature ejaculation. But the woman nourishes her own anger toward men through this lover, by choosing a partner who doesn't satisfy her. Of course, the woman will object, but the fact remains that she continues to endure the relationship. This situation suits her, and if we accept that the unconscious is all-knowing, she's complicit in a way with what happens to her. I advised the lady whose husband couldn't hold out longer than twenty seconds before ejaculating to make love with a chronometer to know exactly at what instant her husband would have an orgasm. This was the first step. The woman then had to order her husband to make love with a condition: "You have to ejaculate in ten seconds, not in twenty seconds." This was meant to put him in a state of constraint where he had to ejaculate sooner than usual. Following this order, as soon as he started to penetrate her, she began to insult him, allowing herself to expel her anger against men. Her husband was ordered to ejaculate as soon as possible, but he wouldn't do it in order to not satisfy his wife. As a result he lasted for half an hour before ejaculating.

Incest is a constant that shows up in a number of family trees. Generally speaking, one of the partners in a couple reenacts the behaviors of their father or mother. The subtlety lies in the fact that sometimes the man can repeat the behavior of his mother and not his father, and vice versa for the woman. I've often seen women who married men with the name of their favorite brother, or their father. These women are often frigid because they remain fixated on the guilt caused by this incestuous desire. I advised one patient to steal her father's dirty laundry and put it on her partner to make love to him. She would resolve her frigidity through her lover by accepting the need for her incest with her father without actually committing the act, but by metaphorically reenacting it. The woman would stop fighting it and instead, in a therapeutic context, assume it in full consciousness that would include its realization in a metaphoric sense. In case her father had passed away, I would ask her to print a picture of him on a shirt that would serve as her lover's clothes.

I also use cemeteries a lot in psychomagic. In the case of a patient who couldn't express all his rage at the deceased, I dared him to defecate on their tombstone. This act is experienced as liberation of rage and everything left unsaid. Here's a letter from a patient, who had an act to perform on her abusive grandmother's grave, which took place in a small village in Bretagne where she was a chatelaine.

> "I told myself that if there was anyone passing by while I was defecating, I would go directly to prison. When I arrived, there were plenty of people at the cemetery, small elderly women putting flowers on the tombstones, but fifteen minutes later I found myself alone to do my act."

Once the act has been decided upon, a transformation takes place in the patient. Even if they don't think themselves able to follow through, reality lends itself to change and adapts. Favorable external conditions present themselves in an unbelievable way. A magical connection appears and reality conspires with the healer.

A very common case is the inversion of archetypes, which means a rather masculine mother and a father with feminine tendencies, which can cause some issues in the child. In this case, I have to put the archetypes back in their places to affect the unconscious. Here's how I achieve it.

The patient invites their parents over but the mother is dressed as a man and the father as a woman. They have to exchange clothes in front of their adult child and regain their identities this way.

Another problem comes up a lot: women with painful periods. It's the pain of unaccepted femininity. I ask them to use their menstrual blood as a tool of their creativity and pleasure by painting their self-portrait with it.

In the psychomagic act, the healer cannot place any limitations on healing. The more serious the problem, the more difficult the act.

In the case of women who don't have their periods, I prescribe imitation of the cycle for several months, at the end of which they put fake blood in their vagina to simulate a period and through this imitation, regulate their body.

Theater is real for the unconscious, therefore if we interpret a difficulty theatrically, it takes place in reality and we can act directly on this concretization.

Here's an example: a young woman whose family would meet for a meal every month and would call her a parrot every time she spoke. I asked her to show up at the next meal dressed as a parrot. This liberating act consisted of exteriorizing definitions to which we are subject, making them visible to their authors, and creating a real commotion in the family.

Another example: I advised a young woman, whose mother treated her like a little girl, to go see her dressed as a child, holding a briefcase. She was meant to undress in front of her mother and once completely naked, get an attractive dress and a big wig out of the suitcase to transform herself into a seductive woman.

Another law: to get the thing that was never given to us it is useful to experience it in a metaphoric way.

In my book *Metagenealogy* I explained labor's primordial role in birth. I used psychomagic to restore what was missing about the patient's development and emotional fulfillment. We have a fundamental right to be born to parents who love each other. Our conception has to be the fruit of a father and mother's orgasm. We have a right to be wanted and not feel we are a burden; the right to have a father attentive to our growth and a mother who is calm during her pregnancy. We should leave the womb not as a tumor, but as a gift. We have a right to be welcomed by a father and not a doctor, and a right to rest on our mother's chest without the umbilical cord cut prematurely so that we separate peacefully from our mother.

To manifest all these different messages I created a birth massage. This work is practiced on people who had problems at birth, such as being unwanted. If the mother holds this rejection during her entire pregnancy, she transmits it to the fetus. And the baby developing in these months in her belly grows feeling that once born, they will be rejected.

If the parents want a boy and it's a girl or vice versa, the child will symbolize the deception in face of their parents' desire. All these fears provoke premature births, C-sections, and breech births. In birth massage ritual, the metaphorical act is directed from the moment of conception to show the patient that he chose his father and mother. He declares at his two masseurs: "You are my father and you are my mother. You don't know each other but through my desire you will meet to conceive me and give birth to me because I chose you."

The first thing that the masseurs will do is to bring the person, completely naked, into a fetal state. Next, the individual is placed in between the legs of the substitute mother, on a wet cloth symbolizing the warmth of the mother's belly, with a silk rope that joins the mother's waist with her child, symbolizing the umbilical cord. The masseurs synchronize their movements to massage with four hands. They reproduce the entire process of conception and gestation until childbirth within a set time. The mother cuts the umbilical cord. Through this metaphoric birth we help the child grow and become the adult he was supposed to be, and we dress him in the new clothes he chose for himself before the massage.

Abortion is also of big importance in genealogical stories. A woman who lived through an abortion may sometimes keep a traumatizing memory of it, especially if it was experienced alone or in secret. How to heal from this trauma? The woman must find a partner she finds appealing. Even if her trauma causes her to hold anger toward men, by accepting the help of her partner, it will give her the opportunity to forgive at least one of them.

She has to imagine a fetus and choose a fruit that symbolizes it, such as a mango or an apple. She then has to keep it attached to her belly with a skin-colored bandage tied around her waist. Her partner has to cut the bandage gently with scissors and mime the extraction of the fetus as if there was a great difficulty getting it out of the mother's belly. It's at this precise moment that the woman has to express everything that she felt when she experienced this abortion. If she doesn't remember it, the memory will come up to the surface during the realization of this act, be it with screams or tears. We then put the fruit in a box like a little coffin that the mother builds with her full devotion. We close this box and choose a pleasant place in nature where we can bury it with a beautiful plant.

The actual interruption of pregnancy should happen under the best possible conditions. The man should be present and assume his responsibilities. This cannot be the case with a lonely, abandoned woman. Termination of pregnancy has to be experienced with a loving father, whether it's a man who made the woman pregnant or a friend who represents him. If possible, it's important to keep the fetus for a funeral.

If a metaphorical abortion takes place in the above conditions, the woman won't experience flashbacks. She will no longer experience the abortion as an embodied act of violence in loneliness tainted by shame or regret.

Let's say a woman with many uterine cysts wants to have a baby—without success. Generally, cysts in the reproductive system indicate the mother's problem with abortion. The woman collects feelings of anger against her mother and even unacknowledged hatred, which manifest in the form of cysts. The pregnancy will be charged with negativity because the aborted fetus somehow incorporates the cysts.

We will make a metaphorical abortion possible and pleasant. I recommend creating a baby figure out of marzipan. This baby should be formed in the shape of an arrow with arms attached to its body. The woman introduces it into her vagina and keeps it there as long as possible. This act is annoying but important to do. At this time she will be capable of accepting motherhood because she will have conquered her fear.

It remains a mystery but there seems to be a relationship between miscarriages and violent deaths such as accidents, suicides, or murders occurring in previous generations.

To some extent, a miscarriage symbolically recreates one or more brutal deaths. It's as if by subconscious magic, this death asserted its right to be recognized. Using this interpretation, it is necessary to spot the corresponding figure in the patient's family tree to this miscarriage: an uncle, brother, mother. . . . It could be a request of the unseen to find peace, requiring honoring the deceased, visiting their grave, cleaning it, leaving flowers, and praying.

With regard to stillborn children, we may view them as nature's draft, similar to an artist's sketch before realizing his final work. If it occurs not during the first but during the second pregnancy, we have to consider the mother's body as a murderer with an unconscious desire to eliminate the fetus. We then need to investigate if this could be a deep unconscious wish to get rid of a member of the family. In the case where the woman is the only child, she could be internalizing her mother's secret wish to eliminate one of her siblings through her organs.

I discovered a law when studying miscarriages. When a mother represses her desire for an abortion, this forbidden drive manifests in subconscious abortions, disguised as miscarriages. If among her ancestors, a mother, grandmother, or great-grandmother suffered multiple pregnancies, a direct subconscious genealogical transmission convinces the patient to obstruct her ovaries in order to respect the wish to stop giving birth, through miscarriages. Although the patient feels guilty of murder, she is not truly. In reality, she has been possessed physically by one or more women in her family tree. The death of a fetus may also mean guilt about incestuous desires. This happens fairly often in women with strong father fixations. The woman pays for the sin through self-punishment during pregnancy, getting rid of the baby that she subconsciously believes is her father's.

For some people the loss of money can be as tragic as the loss of a fetus. This is because both are connected to a problem with creativity. We don't all have the same money. It has to be understood: one hundred dollars in our pocket doesn't mean the same in someone else's pocket. Depending on the family tree, we may have a tainted, idealized, or despised view of money. If you're from a rich family living from one inheritance to another, your creativity will suffer because you don't know how to make your own money and you will have trouble earning it. If you don't create your own capital, you will always live off the creativity of your parents. It's not a *grown-up's* money; it's the money of a child who receives it like a toy.

For patients coming from poor families, I ask them to stick a gold coin to the soles of their shoes, so that they always walk on wealth.

Sometimes I suggest a money massage, where the person is massaged head to toe with banknotes in order to let the skin absorb their power.

As a result of their parents' financial issues some people feel like they didn't have a childhood. How to make up for this loss? I ask the patient what a significant amount of money they could spend would be. Once they gather this amount through their own efforts, I ask them to go to a casino and gamble that money. The instruction is strict and non-debatable: "Go and gamble until you lose everything. If you win, continue gambling until losing it all, no matter how long it takes you." In this way, the patient learns to gamble with pleasure, giving themselves permission to lose. It will serve as an act of reparation toward their childhood.

One of my patients started playing with two thousand dollars. The problem was, she won so much money that she lost the right to play. Several days later her family faced a problem and she had to give her son some money. The amount was exactly what she made in the casino.

The most extreme case I treated concerns a man on the verge of madness. He had witnessed an explosion take his parents' lives, an explosion caused by a bomb hidden in their car during the Algerian war. He hated his parents so much that this gave him great pleasure. Unconsciously, he suffered from massive guilt. How to overcome it? I asked him to estimate the amount of money he could invest in healing himself and to spend this money on jewelry. He then had to return to the site of the explosion and bury the jewelry. This fully cured his madness. I used his guilt by forcing him to put a high price on it so that he could free himself of it by paying that price. If we are aware we did someone wrong, a gift is necessary, for it represents making amends.

A very worried woman wearing valuable jewelry came to me for advice: "I have been scammed out of three thousand francs. This money came from my father and the scammer promised to multiply it. I put my trust in him. Now he's in jail. How do I get my money back?"

I told her: This money is in you and you have to learn how to earn three thousand francs. You have to recognize your own worth instead of judging yourself through your father's money. You haven't lost anything. This money was not yours and this man did you a favor by stealing it. You have to send him a letter along these lines: "I am deeply grateful, because by stripping me of what wasn't mine, you allowed me to become myself and develop a career to become financially independent. Thank you so much." With this parcel you send a beautiful doll as a gift. Through this act, you return to him your inner child and you open a business where you'll easily recover this amount.

Another patient: "I'm in big financial trouble—I make money but I am always in debt. My father is dead. . . . What shall I do?"

First, let's take a look at what the debt means. Getting into debt is another way to hold ourselves accountable. But in your case it's not you who owes something. It's you who are owed. Since money is phallic, debt symbolizes your father's money and indicates that it's your father who is indebted to you. You demand the attention you never had from him. You have to make a photocopy of all your debts, put them in a box, and go to your father's grave and leave it there, together with a funeral wreath made with leaves that you paint gold. You end your act by saying: "Now, let's talk! I will tell you everything I missed out on." Thereby, you begin to settle your debts.

"I don't have a place where I can paint the leaves. Couldn't I use beautiful yellow flowers instead?"

It wouldn't be the same thing!

A third law of psychomagic says that the unconscious has to learn to obey. In psychomagic, the first reaction is often what I call "the haggling phase." I prescribe a very precise act and the patient tries to do it their own way. When we enter a contract in psychomagic, it has to be respected in every detail without question. The prescribed act has to be done to the letter—otherwise it will not work! But sometimes I move against the current by giving advice so difficult or so close to impossible that the patient prefers to accept himself as he is. That's how I suggested an infallible treatment for hair growth to a man who couldn't accept his baldness: cover his scalp with a kilo of rat feces. The therapy resulted not in hair growth but in self-acceptance.

I treated a frigid woman who couldn't stand her lover touching her buttocks. She had been raped anally and she remained fixated on this trauma. I asked her to go to a sex shop and buy a phallus of a size resembling that of her rapist, and use it to penetrate her lover. This solved the problem. Her partner consented because it was obvious by being with a partner who took no pleasure in sex, he was expressing his resentment toward the woman, which suited his needs. During this act the woman would insult her partner, expressing all her built-up anger. Afterward the couple would go to the countryside and make love. When the woman felt her mounting desire, she would light a firework prepared carefully for the occasion before reaching orgasm. She had to see the ejaculation happen outside of herself. The mental introjection of this example allowed her to find resolution while reaching orgasm.

I could also suggest less complicated acts like advising a frigid woman to rub her whole body with a picture of an actress she believes personifies female seduction. This integration process ensures her skin absorbs the seductive essence of the actress.

I don't heal according to moral principles that operate in terms of fault or sin. Holiness is not therapeutic in the sense that if we are subjected to religious prejudice, we obscure the dark side of the psyche and deny the reality of the problem. If I feel that the patient harbors a desire to kill his father, it's not a question of suffocating that impulse but allowing him to act it out metaphorically. This means he will have to buy a rooster, cut its throat, cook it, and eat it with friends. His anger will disappear.

A woman told me how lonely she felt. Customarily this outer loneliness hides a secret childhood pact that involves an inner life as a couple with someone forbidden. For example: "Daddy, I will love you all my life, I will only be with you." The person respects this contract and imprisons themselves in illusory emotional belonging. Here is my psychomagic act: Take parchment paper and write at the top of the page "Contract with . . . ," indicating the name of the person with whom you feel linked. You add: "I promise that I will love only you my whole life." You sign with your name and a drop of your blood. Then roll it up and burn it in a place of your choosing, planting a plant in the ashes. You get up saying, "From this day on I will come once a day for a week to water this plant with heavily salted water so it doesn't grow."

If after this act the woman desires to finally take a lover, I suggest she spread honey on the lips of her vagina and go to a shooting club. Through its phallic shape and the sound of the gunshots, the gun becomes an organ of expression. By immersing herself in the world of men and the use of deadly weapons, she can confront her anger in order to free herself from it. In this place where the masculine rules, she will probably be approached by a man who will try to seduce her . . .

If children wetting the bed is the problem, I ask the parents to spend a night with the child after drinking a liter of water each before falling asleep, with the obligation for all to pee in the bed. This makes it a celebration and the problem disappears.

A man told me: "I have a very severe stomachache that arises after I eat or when I feel strong emotion. The first time it happened was when I was separated from my little boy after my painful divorce. The mother accused me of playing sexual games with him simply because we were walking naked around the apartment. I was cut off from my son for two years and I have never recovered from this pain."

I told him: "The burning sensation in the stomach is related to the anger you hold against the woman who separated you from your child, but it's only a projection of the childhood anger you have for your mother. Did she breastfeed you?"

"She did, but she never showed me any physical affection."

"Then she didn't really give you her breast, since there was no love in this relationship. Here is an act to recover the information in the source of your pain:

"You have to be breastfed with caresses and affection. Her milk was heavy to digest because the lack of love burned in your stomach and you're reproducing this burning sensation. You felt her maternal rejection through her milk. You must ask your mistress to put on fake breasts filled with sweetened condensed milk and nurse you while you make love with her."

When people come to you for advice, how do you identify the nature of the problem that will become the core of the act you prescribe? The patient believes their problem is personal, but what they really experience is a generational problem. I establish points of connection to all the twists and turns of the familial legend, with all its philosophy, morality, and religious concepts. The programming of the family tree affects the unconscious like an arrow: once launched, its course cannot be diverted. The unconscious carries it out like an order impossible to disobey. Generational neurosis is ultimately self-destructive, and psychomagic pushes the patient to achieve this through a metaphorical act that will satisfy the unconscious. If an individual feels the need to kill his parents, he must recognize it and take responsibility for what he feels in order to disarm his desire. Healing the tree is found in obtaining the means to metaphorically accomplish this self-destructive programming.

The Family Tree is a therapeutic tool that takes all the shapes of physical manifestations that have transpired across generations, using names, dates of births and deaths, illnesses, conflicts, betrayals, divorces, abuses, failures, suicides, financial problems, etc. It forms a series of patterns that the patient walks through like a labyrinth. Psychomagic is a transition by means of a metaphorical act that allows us to mold and transform reality.

In psychomagic, the patient becomes his own healer. I'm coming from a principle that it's anti-therapeutic to present someone with a solution. The person has to heal themselves and make sure they become their own magician, their own therapist. If someone else acts on their behalf, the healing power is annihilated, meaning there is a loss of identity coming from being penetrated by a substitute, which is pathological. It's our own identity that must save itself and that's why the patient has to become his own master. It's the difference between giving someone a recipe and serving a dish already made. Psychomagic issues a prescription made up of all the acts to be carried out, and the patient must do everything to follow it literally. It requires a wish to heal, and the research and interest to follow through. The person splits in two—the patient and the healer—and this is when healing begins. As soon as the person acquires the attitude needed to carry out the task, a part of them is already saved. This is the healer that shows up within.

I worked with a woman whose mother was murdered with an axe by a maid. I asked her to do extensive research on axes so that she could find their positive, mythological meaning. By means of this initiation, she could cleanse the tool of tragedy, exalt it, and subconsciously experience transformation. Sublimation feeds the transformation; the element of death becomes an element of life.

I was asked what I thought about verbal trauma in the family tree. Every word carries an innate threat if we don't consider its direct impact on the unconscious. I have an example of a therapist who, while addressing one of his patients, said: "Your index finger is too long. . . ." The next day, that person hurt their index finger while tinkering with a saw. He should never have said "too long," but simply changed one word. It would have been better if he said "very long." "Too long" is a criticism; "very long" is a statement.

I prescribed an act of psychomagic for a man who could never achieve orgasm. He was drowning in his mother's negativity. "You'll never do anything. . . . Who would want you? What a disaster!" He was supposed to write on a piece of paper each phrase that hurt him and stick them onto his naked body. Then, one of his friends would have to remove them one by one, as gently as possible.

What resistance occurs while carrying out the act? Neurosis, like any form of suffering, is an attachment, because it's an expression of an unfulfilled request for love. A false identity emerges through this fixation. To accept the healing process is to distance yourself from the request for love and the fake identity associated with it. At the beginning we can't envisage another way of being, and finding one's real identity creates anxiety. It's because of a lack of experiences that have nothing to do with words. Not having lived these experiences in childhood, we find ourselves completely unequipped to manage them. Psychomagic reestablishes the initial information and connects us to our essence. Sickness is nothing but a gap between our true essence and a false self-image. We live a kind of oppressive comedy where we're forced into behaviors, ideals, jobs, and loveless relationships that represent a repeated command from the family tree. "Don't be what you are, only what we want you to be, which means what you are not." Healing has to bring us back to the present. A person in a state of mental distress can be defined as someone living in the past or in the future—never in the present moment. By not being yourself, as if absent from your present, creating plans to accomplish impossible ends, you experience a pathological state of self-destruction. Patients don't show up to be healed but to find themselves. The questions we must ask are: "How do you feel? Do you like who you are? Do you really love what you love?" Patients must be totally immersed anew in what hurts them in order to move forward. The cup must be drunk to the dregs if we want to ascend. The metaphor is a tool we work with. An angry human being is like a child. His desire is like the trajectory of an arrow; once launched nothing can stop it. If he feels like cutting someone's head off, psychomagic must find the means for the arrow to reach its target with the use of a metaphor. This metaphor is as real and true as the reality itself. The conscious body therefore absorbs the value of the metaphor transmitted by the unconscious. If a son feels the need to free himself from the authority of his father (whom he admits he wants to kill), he will overcome the suffering by going through a metaphorical act of beheading the animals in a poultry factory.

In any event, we have to keep in mind that the people who come to me asking for help often fail to clarify what the source of their suffering is. The patient doesn't know what is actually causing their anxiety. This sometimes appears when I ask them to imagine that I am a magician who will make their wish come true. This is the precise moment when we can see that the person has no idea how to approach their problem; they get lost in words and cannot formulate their request. . . . It is sometimes necessary to grasp the metaphor that emerges from their language, to revisit expressions used by the patient personally. For example, one young woman complaining about the attitude she adopts when facing men used this expression: "I have no balls." The remedy therefore consists of providing her with the attributes she feels are missing. I advised her to make herself a penis from banknotes rolled up lengthwise, then put it in her underwear with two relaxation balls. She should take a walk down the street. What needs to be understood about the approach I suggest is that it allows reality to be altered, and virile strength supplied thanks to the imagination.

The simulation method is also a way to address the homosexual seeds that lie in us. Let's take the case of the woman who didn't mind being touched anywhere but her buttocks. This was a defense mechanism caused by her father's anal rape of her when she was younger (a rape she didn't acknowledge). Because her father's urge was homosexual, the only way his daughter could satisfy it was through anal penetration. In a way she repressed her purely feminine reactions in order to please her father. She became more masculine. She needed to release her repressed anger by adopting the role and sex of the father. I asked the woman to reenact, by her own account, the acts she was submitted to, because action creates reaction and thus transforms behavior.

The lack of emotional connection can be seen as a kind of mutilation. It's necessary to prepare for it. This can be seen in a woman whose husband had a heart condition. She didn't know how to prepare for the grief and expressed her suffering through dreams in which she would kill her husband. She could imagine his death and accept it but not actually experience it. She needed to prepare herself for his death. Following my advice, she put a picture of her husband together with his ID into a carton box serving as a coffin and buried the whole thing. Sometime later her husband did indeed pass away. This woman was ready to face the absence of her husband.

It seems that the more difficult the act of psychomagic is, the higher the chances are that it will work well.

To deal with a mother and son who were overly dependent on each other I advised the mother to go to the United States (experiencing the physical effort of travel and the financial effort of the ticket's price) and sequester herself with her son in a hotel room for twenty-two days. Opening up to the outside world must be gradual (open the curtains, receive information, feed him then wean him, and so on . . . .) The effort, expenses, and sacrifices required for this act are the fundamental aspects that led to its success. It's necessary to give in order to receive.

Belief is also necessary; we can only heal a person who wants to be healed. If one of your patients believes they are possessed by a person or the devil, an evil spirit, or a curse, and constantly fears they are losing their mind, you can try to free them through a breath ceremony, if the patient has confidence in your therapeutic ability.

Pull your lips and exhale deep penetrating breaths while imagining you are removing any intruder from the body of the possessed individual. Blow on the person, beginning at the top of the skull. Energetically breathe on the hair to eliminate any anxiety. Then stand in front of the possessed and continue exhaling on his neck, then in his ears, nostrils, and open mouth. Then, while asking him to close his eyes, blow straight in his face and on the nape of his neck. Grab his shoulders, still blowing, and repeat the phrases "Out!" and "Go away!" Press his shoulder to let him lift his left leg. Then move onto the right leg. Blow on the entire body this way, from the chest around to the back. Finish the act by breathing onto the soles of the patient's bare feet. Next, draw a circle on the ground around him with white chalk. Then, erase it with sponge and water, saying, "You are free! Absorb telluric forces! Let this energy rise to the top of your skull. Expand your being toward every corner of the world. Unite with the stars!"

This is how the entry ritual of psychomagic ends: the patient is freed from his obsessions. It's only now that the phase of healing can begin.

A woman with long red nails has a problem "making money with men." She tells me indirectly that men are supporting her and she wants an act of psychomagic so she can work without having to exploit her sexual attributes. I ask her to get a large seashell and fill it with soil, then plant ten seeds together with her cut nails in it. She should water it with holy water gathered from a church until the seeds germinate and plants begin to appear. By cutting her nails she performs an act. She understood that these ten nails are the symbols of her hands that don't work.

Michel could be fifty-eight years old or less. He is bald but wears a wig. I asked him to remove it and attend a class with his head exposed. He complied. He started complaining. "Everything is in crisis. I don't know what's going to happen to me. Many terrible things happened to me at the same time." He was worried to the point of tears. "Finally I separated from my wife. We will go live in different places. This separation is rather complex and painful. She may die, commit suicide, and I don't know how I'm going to feel. On top of that the economy is bad; I have to go to the bank and ask for a big loan. I don't know how I'm going to pay it back." I reply: "Be so kind as to repeat everything you just told me, one by one, in front of the group." (There are thirty-two of us.) "Leave the room and wait till we call you back." While he's gone, I discuss him with the group. We call him back. Michel begins: "I am putting a brave face on for my colleagues and patients. I don't know what's going to happen. I worry." We laugh out loud and applaud him. "I'm leaving my wife." We laugh, applaud, and shout, "Bravo! Bravo!" "The economy is not doing well, I don't know how I'm going to pay my debt." We explode in laughter, shouting, "Well done!" We applaud. Michel begins to laugh. He realized that he did exactly what he wanted to do and that his tragedy is in fact a celebration.

During one of my metagenealogy classes a man experienced a crisis and showed symptoms of anxiety, seizures, tensions, and so on. Nothing could calm him. His attack stopped immediately once, with a lot of work, he removed his wedding ring from his finger.

During a Marseille Tarot class I noticed that Daniel was wearing old, dirty socks. I picked up his right foot and caressed it. I took a new clean sock and put it on his foot. He began to cry. He had gained access to his anger thinking of his parents neglecting him as a child.

Often my son Brontis tells me about a bear I told him to bury when he came to live with me at the age of six. I gave him this bear when he was three years old, when his mother and I were separating. In my movie *El Topo* I tell him: "Today you turn seven. You are already a man. Bury your first toy and the portrait of your deceased mother." During the filming of this scene I made the mistake of leaving the bear and the portrait buried. When Brontis turned twenty-four, he confessed, "To appease my great suffering from losing my bear and the portrait of my mother, I imagine that ants came to live inside the bear, kept company by Bernadette." Trying to repair my mistake, I buried in our garden a plush bear and a picture of Brontis's mother, Bernadette. I dressed in a black leather suit (like in *El Topo*) and I told Brontis (naked, like in the movie): "At the age of seven you had the right to be a boy. Dig up your first toy and the portrait of your mother." I played the flute while he dug up the picture of his mother, this time in color, with the bear, this time soft and delicate. It began to rain. Like in *El Topo,* I led Brontis, who held onto my back while I imitated a horse's walk. Brontis, his face buried in the nape of my neck, cried like a grateful child.

Psychomagic in Action

A Lecture at Jussieu University in Paris, 1987

The setting of this lecture is a large auditorium with bleachers separated in the middle by a central aisle that goes to the bottom of the hall toward a very large table I am using as a stage.

Addressing the public, I say: If anyone asks I can perhaps give him some advice on the spot. I have never done this in public because it is necessary to focus on the individual's family tree, but let's give it a try. This way you can see psychomagic in action.

(A student asks the first question)

Q: Lately, every now and then I feel like I'm starving. Still I manage to be creative and study, but . . . my stomach, ugh. There is always a moment, a moment when I hurt too much from not eating.

AJ: Here is the advice for you, since you are scared of going without food. Look for a wet nurse who is nursing a child and pay her to nurse you for seven days. Live on this nurse's milk for seven days! Then your anxieties will end.

(Incredulous reactions in the hall)

Q: Why this act?

AJ: Because the fear of lacking food is the fear of lacking mother's milk.

He must overcome this. I see that he is quite thin. He has not been fed as he should have been. He has to overcome some resistance he has toward the maternal archetype and women. If he listens to me, he will be obliged to invest in an action, and pay. All this will cause things to happen. He is going to have to find a wet nurse and settle on a price. He is going to have to make some efforts to find her. This action will remove his anxiety. He will recover his trust of women and at the same time trust in his own creativity because he accepts his inner woman, his anima.

(A slightly mocking young woman)

Q: My boyfriend sent me a letter saying, "I never want to see you again unless you come see me with your tongue hanging down all the way to your belly button." What can I do? I still love him but I don't want to humiliate myself.

AJ: Make yourself a tongue from pink fabric. When you get to his place, put it in your mouth and knock on the door. When he opens the door he will see you with a tongue hanging down to your navel. If he laughs, he deserves you. If he slams the door in your face, be glad to break off your relationship with such a spiritually obtuse man.

(A very shy young woman asks her question in a very low voice while remaining seated)

Q: It's been several months since I've been trying to sell some things that I want to get rid of. . . .

AJ: Speak louder so everyone can hear you!

Q: I have . . .

AJ: Speak loudly! Stand up so everyone can see you!

Q: I put up ads. . . .

AJ: Stand up. Don't talk sitting down!

Q: I put up ads and I got a lot of calls but . . .

AJ: Louder! Look at the people!

(The young woman stands up)

Q: But people don't show up to the meetings and so I haven't managed to get rid of my things and yet . . .

AJ: What are these things?

Q: Furniture I own that I no longer want.

AJ: When someone asks you something, the unconscious never replies immediately, because the unconscious measures everything like a machine. Tell me your first name!

Q: Virginie.

AJ: *(Talking to the audience)* I have observed that Virginie cannot speak standing up but only sitting in her chair, therefore in possession of her furniture, and that she speaks to me as if I couldn't understand her. I have drawn some conclusions from this.

   (Speaking to Virginie again) You talk to a paternal archetype and you sit in your chair like a little girl. You want to sell your old furniture because you didn't have a home with a father. The desire to sell old furniture is the desire to get out of an infantile situation that holds you prisoner.

   In order to sell this furniture, you must decide to place a father in your life. If you do the sales through a father, I think that will work. The day when you want to sell your furniture, you have to dress like your father, creating him in your body as you imagine him to be. You will walk around this furniture as him. You live the presence of your father, you accept the man inside you. How old were you when you lost your father?

Q: Four years old.

AJ: He's therefore a mythical father, that's your problem. Once you have dressed up as your father, you will be ready to sell this furniture because you will have created him in yourself instead of creating him in the furniture, out of the desire to have a home with him. For until now, you have eliminated men from your life. Your father is eliminated, and also, if you allow me to say, your children's father. There is no father in your life because you are repeating your childhood model. So I am asking you to absorb a father and make him exist. That's when you will be able to sell this furniture and find peace in your heart.

(A young man at the back of the room, standing in the center aisle)

Q: Please . . . I would like to ask . . .

AJ: Ask.

Q: I have an enormous amount of energy, but I have a lot of trouble using it as I should.

AJ: What is your question?

Q: What can I do to channel this energy?

AJ: Go to the middle of the aisle and walk slowly toward me while concentrating on your heart!

(The young man begins to advance)

Concentrate hard! Advance! Advance! Come stick your heart against mine. Climb on this table! Good! What's your name?

Q: Bernard.

AJ: Bernard, embrace me tightly! Absorb my strength! Absorb! Stick your head against mine! Absorb!

(This exchange lasts several minutes)

Okay Bernard, continue clasping me closely. I will move forward and you will step backward . . . .

(I hold Bernard firmly by his belt. I stand up and, without letting him go, I walk him back while he remains clasping me tightly. I get down from the table while I speak to him again)

AJ: There, I represent your father's strength. I lead the walk. Have faith! Let yourself guide! Don't distrust me. Go back!

(I push Bernard forward, making him walk backward to the back of the room. Once we are there, and without separating, I speak to him again)

AJ: Now, trust yourself, advance and make me retreat. I accept that my son guides me. Make me descend. Make me adjust my rhythm to yours. . . . Bravo, you do it very well. Now raise me on the table.

(Once on the table, I separate from him)

There you go! You have learned how to drive someone. The son can take the father's place. What was your question?

Q: What can I do to channel my energy?

AJ: What we just did was my active reply: I saw in your physical posture, in the expression of your gaze, in the tone of your voice, that a profound relationship with your father was absent in your life. You didn't know how to use your virile energy because you never had a male model. In a few minutes, by using symbolic physical postures, and by playing the role of the father, I was able to make you feel that you were seen and understood; I transmitted sexual, emotional, and intellectual strength to you. I yielded my place to you. I allowed you to enter my being so that you would feel wanted, accepted, and I gave you the opportunity to transmit what you received. In other words, the possibility to be yourself a father, a creator. . . . Does that work for you?

Q: Thank you, thank you, thank you.

(The students applaud)

AJ: Does anyone else want to ask a question?

(Many hands are raised and several students ask their questions to which, for lack of time, I have to answer quickly)

Q: How can I mourn a romantic relationship?

AJ: A woman needs to be listened to. You drive five hundred kilometers talking about your romantic relationship to a friend who listens to you with the obligation not to say a word.

Q: My brother has attempted suicide, he doesn't want to talk to anyone, how can I help him?

AJ: Is your mother alive?

Q: No. She died when we were little.

AJ: Your brother is looking for a maternal archetype. As he needs a woman to listen to him you can help him by listening without giving opinions. Write "my opinions" on a [piece of] parchment paper and put a drop of your blood on it. Put this box in your left pocket and hold it through the time necessary for your brother to express what he feels, without you intervening one way or another. You commit to remaining silent.

Q: I know a man who moves me on all levels except sexually, because I don't orgasm with him. What do I have to do?

AJ: You have to steal your father's socks, underpants, pajamas, shirt. You ask your friend to dress in all these clothes. You have to drink a liter of water, sit on his lap, and urinate on him. Then your friend has to make love to you. That's how you will punish your father, by urinating on him and letting the orgasm flow.

Q: I'm a chocolate junkie. How to stop?

AJ: The next time you defecate, spread your excrement on slices of bread and bury them in a pot by planting a fragrant plant on them. Place the pot on your dining table.

Q: Every time I want something, I don't know if I'll be able to get it. How to solve this anxiety?

AJ: Do you have a sister?

Q: Yes, a twin sister. My mother never differentiated between us. Even to this day, she still calls us "girls." When we were children, she dressed us both in red.

AJ: If you're yourself, you want, but if you're your twin sister, you don't. She would like to have your life so you are guilty of having your life. Do you want your mother to differentiate you?

Q: I've been trying to ask her for years.

AJ: You dress yourself half in red and the other half as the woman you want to be. How would you visualize yourself if you went to a party?

Q: With a long blue dress.

AJ: You have to make yourself a half-red costume, like the one you wore when you were a child, and the other half, that of this new woman, in a long blue dress. Go visit your mother and tell her: "One half is my sister and the other half is me."

You will have prepared another garment in a bag. You undress in front of her and you give her the part of the red suit while saying: "If you want, you can give it to my sister. Her name is Red and my name is Blue."

Q: Why is life so hard for me?

AJ: The first thing we see of you is the cyst on your forehead. You have to make yourself a headband of very bright colors. You have to wear it publicly on your forehead. That's how you will have the certainty of being watched, because your unconscious desire is to attract the gaze of others, so go exist!

Q: I study psychology, and I would like to have the tools to communicate with my future patients.

AJ: Go to a joke shop, grab and buy the two biggest ears you can find there. Walk around the city all day with these ears. The best communication tool is concentration in listening.

Q: Why do I need to make others angry and how do I stop it?

AJ: It is a sexual language in relation to a sexuality that cannot be fulfilled. Your anger is the compensation for an unsatisfied desire. Make yourself business cards on which you will have written: "To communicate well, I need to anger the people I love. Thank you." Sign that business card and give it to the people you anger.

Q: I am a man constantly in doubt. How do I get rid of it?

AJ: Who taught you that to be a woman is to triumph and that to be a man is to fail?

Q: My father, because I have a sister and she is my father's favorite.

AJ: Here is an act to recover your self-confidence. Take a picture of your dad and have it laminated to waterproof it. Every time you go to the toilet, pee on your dad's picture. You have to do this act forty days in a row and each time you have to say "leave me alone!" while urinating. After forty days, you will feel powerful and you will be able to revolt.

Q: I would like to be able to recognize my creative femininity.

AJ: What art do you like?

Q: Making mandalas.

AJ: Make a mandala with your menstrual blood.

Q: I don't have a sight problem. But every time I look in the mirror, my eyes seem to fill with some kind of thick mist. Why, and how to improve this?

AJ: Not seeing your own image on the outside means not wanting to see oneself from the inside! You have to take a picture of your mother and stick it on the mirror in your bedroom. You have to set your alarm clock for three in the morning and fall asleep. As soon as it rings, immediately get up and rudely insult your mother's picture. Then go back to sleep and as soon as you wake up, call your mom and talk to her on the phone.

Q: I don't understand this act.

AJ: I will explain it to you: You wanted to be a man. Not seeing you is not realizing your impotence, your castration, and your sexual problem. Insulting your mother is insulting the woman inside you. To then telephone your mother is to recognize yourself as a woman, that is to say, to recover communication with yourself.

Q: My father is a famous man, how to be recognized by him?

AJ: Put your father in front of you and ask him to listen to you for an hour without saying anything. You will also have made three hundred photocopies of a photo of yourself. As you speak to him, you will put photos of yourself all over him: in his pockets, on his shoes, on his head. . . . Well, he's going to listen to you and he's going to see you!

Q: What should I do to be more structured and less worried to discuss money with the hospital institute?

AJ: The lack of structure symbolizes the lack of a father. You have to ask your boyfriend to cum on your back.

He spreads his cum all over your spine from neck to lower back and you let it dry. Put on a flannel garment and engage in your discussion in this institute. That's how you will have the structure of the father to be able to discuss business.

Q: I have homosexual desires. Should I let myself go or should I kill myself?

AJ: If your mother did not want to be pregnant, if she wanted to abort you, you will have a tendency to self-destruct, responding to her desire that you disappear. It is the maternal neurosis that you are undergoing. You have a feminine nature that you must let live. Did they want you to be a girl when you were born?

Q: Yes, my sister died before me. I had to replace her.

AJ: Buy a dead lamb from a butcher. A friend should rub it all over your body. Then you have to hold it very firmly in your arms and your friend has to violently try to tear it from your arms. Defend yourself with all your might. When she manages to take it away from you, wrap this lamb in a black bag and bury it. You end your act by planting a flowering plant. By doing so you will metaphorically bury your dead sister and you will feel free.

Q: My father was very hard on me. He kept criticizing me. I am obsessed with him and continue to obey him even though he is dead. How do I free myself from it?

AJ: What did he tell you?

Q: He called me "useless, ugly, stupid, an incapable woman like all other women. . . ."

AJ: Take two scrolls. On the first scroll, write down all the negative programming that your father gave you and on the second one, the exact opposite: "good for everything . . . beautiful . . . intelligent . . . capable of anything. . . ." Go to his grave and burn the negative parchment there. Collect the ashes and with them rub the positive parchment, saying, "I return all this to you!" Burn everything and dissolve the ashes in a bottle of wine which you pour on the grave.

Q: Me and my boyfriend just moved into his late grandmother's house . . . and I feel that the energy is not good. We don't feel at home.

AJ: Place incense in all the rooms of your house and burn them at the same time. Thus the house will be purified. Then, in the bedroom, using a compass, determine the cardinal points. Afterward, each prick a finger and put on the walls a drop of your blood: one in the north, one in the south, one in the west, and one in the east. At night, urinate into an empty pot. Then walk around the house and by each dipping a hand in your urine mark all the corners of the house with it. So, it will become yours.

(A university employee brings in a bulky package wrapped in gold paper. I address the students as I open the package)

AJ: I cannot give two hundred acts of psychomagic in one hour. I will end this course with a collective act. These notebooks contain a set of questions to develop consciousness, which each of you must answer in writing with the greatest possible sincerity, depth, and courage. When you're done, sleep for a week with the notebook under your pillow. At the end of this period, reread what you have written. If you realize that something has changed in a way you see in life, buy a beautiful plant, and, together with the notebook, plant it, preferably in a garden or in a pot. *(I distribute the notebooks. The students rush to read them, not realizing that I am leaving)*

What is my goal in life? What do I really want to be? What did I forbid myself? What or whom do I want to free myself from? Whom am I fooling? What do I accumulate? What do I hide? What do I keep in me, pure and intact? What are the experiences I want to have? Will I dare? Whom do I endlessly criticize? Who loves me and whom do I love? What relationship do I have with my mother? What relationship do I have with my father? Is it just what I have been taught or made to believe since I was little? Is there something that interests me more than money? If there was a God, what would he be like? Am I useful to others? Am I satisfied with my life? Do I take good care of my health or am I destroying myself? Can I teach others something? Can I heal or comfort someone? Do I live in a place that I like? Do I have a real partner? Am I happy? In what do

I feel dissatisfied? Am I achieving what I intended? What is the wisdom or doctrine that guides me? Do I truly believe in what I say that I believe? What do I admire in myself, what do I despise? Who are my allies? What should I expel from my life right now? What should I balance, harmonize? Am I giving myself what I deserve? Whom should I punish? What do I feel guilty about? What do I know the most? Even if it hurts me to do it, what should I sacrifice? Have I provoked my loneliness? Who can help me? What is it that I keep repeating? Do I let myself be overwhelmed by failure or do I take it as a change of direction? What is it that ties me to the past? What are my opportunities? Do I feel ignorant or stupid? Do I intend to change the world with my ideas? Do I feel selfish? Do I think I'm a coward? What is it that I must tame in myself? Whom do I hold a grudge against? Whom am I a victim of? What must I no longer put up with? What should I stop clinging to? What is the reason for my deep rage? If no one could punish me, whom would I kill? Who can protect me? Whom do I protect? What is my main injury? Did something make me lose faith? What sexual desire do I repress in myself? What temptation obsesses me? What should I use to achieve what I want? To whom have I sold myself? From what prejudices should I free myself? From what confinement was I able to escape? What are the energies that are being released in me? What is collapsing? Do I recognize someone as superior to me? Am I capable of admiring the values of others? Am I possessive, am I invasive? Am I afraid of madness? What vices dominate me? Do I share what I know and what I have? What is my impossible ideal? Can I accept success without destroying myself? Am I building something new and important? Do I trust others? Do I feel locked in an outdated world? With whom am I collaborating to do something that leads us to a higher fulfillment? Do I hang out with people who make my life happy or with people who lead me to destruction? Am I able to leave the past behind and start a new life? Do I accept the simple happiness of being alive? Do I accept becoming a humble channel of the desires of the cosmos?

Psychomagical Letters

Responses from My Tarot Readings at the Café Le Téméraire

Tarot readings do not present a reductive interpretation that tricks someone, like a fortune-telling, excusing them from the responsibility to act. Tarot readings view every spread as an individual puzzle of the patient's psychological structure. In the way the cards communicate lies a secret language of words that open, close, hide themselves, and reveal the untold. This becomes the reading's first step, and it will end with the suggestion of a psychomagical act directly emerging from the patient's subconscious depths.

Over many decades of intensive research in various parts of the world from Mexico to France, and finally to the Café Le Téméraire in Paris, I met thousands of people from all walks of life who came to consult with me in a state of distress. The unhappiness they reported was the result of traumautic episodes, existential questions, or painful situations. I would give them a tarot reading to identify their problem and then, in a trance state of total receptivity, I would suggest a psychomagic ritual for them to perform.

I sit in a café in front of a square piece of violet fabric, where twenty-two Major Arcana lie in a single pile. It's precisely 6:00 p.m. The first person sits down across from me. They are young, old, man, or woman, with a smile on their face or tears in their eyes. I notice, register, evaluate: the face, the hands, the body, the skin, shade, jewelry, clothes, way of breathing, mental, emotional, and sexual state. Peacefully born or not? Absence of a father? A dominant mother? An unloved child? Emotional emptiness? Narcissism or exuberant megalomania? Loneliness? And so on . . . I then ask: *What is your question?*

The person is there, accompanied by their family, their past, their lovers, fears, and hopes. *Should I sell my business? Why can't I make my own money? Why is my love life so disappointing? I would like to have a child but my partner doesn't. What to do? I never loved, I am a virgin and nothing makes me want to live. I am a widower but the memory of my wife is still present. What to do with my life at sixty? I want to be a painter but I'm running out of resources.* A life unfolds.

With every person, a novel, a story reveals and tells itself. Everyone brings their family tree with them. It appears in cards that were drawn: the ever-present family, ghosts that haunt us that, with work and the healing of the tree, should help us in life. I add up the numbers of the cards; I analyze, deduce.

My answer highlights the flaw, this emotional core at the source of the problem. I suggest an act of psychomagic as healing. I do this work for free. The only thing I asked them to do in return was to write me a letter testifying to the way I had identified their problem, the act I had advised them to perform, the way they had realized this action, and what experience it caused them to feel. I was able to develop my research by observing what kind of results were obtained in this way.

Over the years, I've received numerous letters from people who had come to consult me from all over the world.

The purpose of this second part of the book is to give the floor to some of the people who experienced psychomagic, showing their diversity as well as the wealth of human and psychological experience, thereby demonstrating how psychomagic is for everyone and can be practiced by any individual, no matter their social and cultural status, their religious beliefs, their age, and their education. Here is a selection of their letters.

⇢ LETTER 1 ⇠
....
From Ines

Dear Alejandro,

Here is my story: The first time you prescribed me an act, it was in the summer of 2009 in Formentera. I don't remember if I had asked a question or if it was a spread without a question but I remember the act very well: I had to present myself to my parents fully dressed as a boy, spend the day with them, then go to bed and the next day get dressed in my clothes, dig a hole, burn the men's clothes inside, plant a tree, and fill the hole. I was impressed and convinced: you told me that I was the eldest daughter of a couple who would have preferred to have a boy. A couple that was itself slightly reversed: a very masculine woman, a very feminine man.

Without being a tomboy, I felt deep inside the truth of this affirmation by realizing that my femininity had never been valued and that, to the contrary, my masculine side was always encouraged—which, among other things, led to my permanent self-devaluation.

I competed with men while adopting a haughty and condescending position with many women.

In the meantime, in 2009 I was twenty-one years old, still living with my parents. I said to myself that indeed the situation was suboptimal but not catastrophic. . . . So I did not perform the act at that time. But a problem we just ignore doesn't miraculously resolve itself. In the fall of 2014, I had reached such a frequency of urinary cystitis infections that I cracked. I had had them ever since I was fourteen and the beginning of my sex life, and I had the habit of being careful and taking care of the problem. I knew all the tips—stay hydrated, urinate often, drink cranberry juice, heather tablets, etc.—but nothing was ever enough and it kept getting worse and worse. I would get one for no good reason, a hot or cold snap, my period, a day out, three hours without drinking . . . I had it twice a month and I spent my time on antibiotics and I began to wonder if I wasn't poisoning myself instead of healing. It was so frequent that I realized it was not normal and I asked you for help, which you offered me in the form of an act of psychomagic: show up at my parents' home dressed as a man, then burn the outfit and plant a tree in the ashes. I was both embarrassed and flabbergasted. This was exactly the same act as the one given five years earlier—without you remembering it. An act that I had not accomplished but that needed to be done more than ever. This unresolved issue had taken the form of the disease related to my sexuality with boys, and that was problematic since my femininity was not accepted by my parents.

I understood the importance of performing the act this time and I felt ready to do so, especially as my situation had really changed since the last time: I no longer lived with my parents, so it was easier for me to distance myself. To be sure that I had the right outfit, you even gave me one of your beautiful black suits. We went through some details because I wanted to be sure to do everything well. I was both excited and anxious to finally get started. I prepared myself psychologically and physically. I decided on the date: I had to spend Christmas with my family at my parents'. I would go two days earlier to do the act. I bought a pretty tree, a small willow tree with fluffy catkins, to plant above the ashes. I warned my little brother who would also be present at the same time so that he wouldn't worry, without being too concerned about him because he had already done an act and understood my approach. When the day came, I was alone at home and prepared myself. I put on a white shirt (taken from my boyfriend at the time) and the black suit that you had given me. It was wide and had a very masculine cut. I gathered my very long hair in a bun, as tight and low as possible so that it disappeared under the collar of my shirt and my hair appeared short and tight in back. I made my eyebrows look longer and thicker and I drew myself a little mustache with a black pencil. The result, even without forcing it, was effective: in the mirror I felt like I saw my brother.

Normally, to go to my parents I would take the RER but this time I was weighed down by the tree, the Christmas gifts, and, above all, I did not at all want to meet people I knew or even to be scrutinized by strangers. So to calm myself, I ordered a taxi. Even so, the driver made a remark about my look and I ignored it. There was another thing that worried me at the time: I didn't have much money and the drive was long and

particularly congested. This is when a miracle happened: Recently I had
opened an online store where I was selling—and still do—my jewelry. It
didn't work very well at the time because it wasn't well known. And on
that day, December 23, 2014, at 3:00 p.m., I received an order for a fish
brooch at seventy-five euros. This turned out to be within two euros of
the price of the taxi ride. I took this sign as an additional encouragement: if you are on the right path, Heaven will help you. Once I arrived
at my parents', my father opened the door. I could see on his face he
was questioning the reason for my outfit. During the day he made a few
half-ironic, half-questioning remarks on the fashion I followed. I did not
answer. My mother, on the other hand, had absolutely no reaction. Not
one. Not a discreet raised eyebrow, no comment, no mouth open in surprise. My goal clearly was not to be questioned or even to get a reaction,
but I still found all of it crazy: I was wearing a man's suit way too large
for me. I had my hair slicked back, bushy eyebrows, and a mustache, and
she acted like nothing was amiss.

It didn't matter. I met my brother who gave me a look that let me
know he was on board by staying perfectly neutral. The rest of the afternoon happened as usual. We dined, the evening passed. When going to
sleep, I took off the suit, removed the makeup, and went to bed, my teenage bed, in what was my room for twenty years and which my mother
transformed into an office as soon as I left the house (while my brother's
room is almost intact even today, nearly ten years after his departure....)

The next morning I took a shower, got dressed in my clothes, and
went down to my parents' garden with the suit and the willow. I dug a
hole and put the suit inside, then I set it on fire and watched for a while
as flames consumed it. At some point my father came over looking puzzled. He wondered why I needed to burn a garment which seemed to
be in perfect condition: if I didn't want it anymore it was always possible to give it away. I told him that's the way it is. And that was it. He
stayed with me for a bit, perplexed, then walked away. The burning of
the suit took a while but I stayed until the end, careful to do well in
the smallest details and go fully through each step. Then I planted the

willow, wished it a good life, and went back home. Again, my mother didn't see or notice anything. But again, it didn't matter: I did what I came there to do. Then Christmas passed rather normally and we never spoke about this again.

It was December 23, 2014, and since that day the cystitis has subsided. Instantly. No more infections every fifteen days and no more antibiotics. At first, I was counting the days with a mixture of fear and excitement. Each passing month was a victory and I realized with happiness that I was healed, that you healed me! In six years, I had two more infections and both times it was directly as a result of my mother's violent intrusion into my intimacy: I am outside, I'm on the phone with her, she tells me something that makes me feel very bad, and as soon as I go home I'm sick. Having become aware of it, after the act that cured me, I could take more necessary distance to protect myself.

It was the most powerful act of psychomagic for me. Beyond the immediate effect and obvious benefits it had on my health by putting an end to my bi-monthly cystitis—which would have probably ended up degenerating into something much worse—it allowed me to become physically, intellectually, and emotionally aware of something essential: magic is real. I had always believed in magic but in the form of a fantasy, distant and abstract, like an echo of childhood. Suddenly, it was an accessible and benevolent magic directed by the mind. I become less afraid of the future and of what I was; my trust in the universe grew. More than ever before, I have faith in the future.

You gave me the keys to become the best version of myself. For that you have my eternal gratitude.

Ines

⇝ LETTER 2 ⇜

From Ruth

Alejandro,

I went to see you at Le Téméraire. I told you that I had a creative-sexual block, and I couldn't draw, which was my goal. I tried and tried, but after finishing my studies in fine arts and going through various circumstances (five years), I was unable to do what I supposedly wanted. You read my cards and you recommended three acts of psychomagic to me:

1. Draw a self-portrait with menstrual blood and wear it hanging for a week every time I went out on the street.
2. Paint a landscape not with brushes but with a false phallus, the largest that you find in the store. Give that picture to the director of a museum, accompanied by a sign saying: "This is a phallic painting."
3. Dress up in stars, invite my friends to a meeting, and tell them a story titled: stories of a phallus painter. Have the phallus on display and worship it.

Act 1. It was quite easy: the blood has a very good consistency for paint. I was a bit embarrassed to wear it at first, I had an impression everyone was looking at me, but I did it.

Act 2. This was a little more complicated. I would never see myself capable of taking the painting to the museum. I didn't even think it was possible to reach the director, and anyway I would not dare! It took me a while to decide and do it, as just thinking about it made me nervous.

I began by buying the phallus. I bought the biggest one I could afford.

It was difficult for me to paint with something so big, but in the end I did it. Since I was from León (Spain), you told me that I should take it to the director of the MUSAC, but I realized I didn't tell you that at that time I was living in Barcelona. I had to do it there. I hope I didn't interfere negatively by changing the place since in theory you have to do what you say to the letter. Thus, I found myself choosing a museum director in Barcelona. I looked at Google photos of several of them, and chose the one I found the most likable: the director of the MACBA.

I couldn't . . . I couldn't . . . the thought alone of walking into the museum with the picture on my back distressed me . . . so someone helped me. I explained the situation to a friend who lived with me, and she called the museum to ask if it was possible to see the director. She said that she was a student of fine arts and she wanted to interview him for a college project. It wasn't a problem . . . they gave her time the next week . . . a Tuesday at 5:00 p.m. Uh oh! Such nerves! So, the following Tuesday, I took the painting and went there with two friends. I wanted to do it as fast as possible . . . . When we arrived, the receptionist told us we had to wait for an hour because the director was in a meeting. How about we wait in the cafeteria? It started to hail . . . the falling stones broke a window . . . it was good because my nerves dissipated a little with all that. In the end, it was time. . . . We went upstairs with the picture, and we entered the director's office. He seemed rather friendly and quiet, he received us very well and asked us to sit down. Then I gave him the painting and told him it was a phallic painting. He wanted to know more, but I only said that it was a symbolic act, and that he could do whatever he wanted with it. To be honest, he didn't seem surprised, maybe he was bored that day, who knows. . . . Then he said . . . "Well, you're not going to do an interview or anything?" Just in case I had prepared some questions so I interviewed him a bit, took notes, and my friends and I listened to him with great interest! It was very curious, he was a very normal and approachable man, so we thanked him, we left the painting, and we left! I felt very free and happy . . .

Act 3. This part was pretty easy. I called several friends and we met at home, a normal afternoon with a couple of drinks. I told them I had to tell them the story of the phallus painter. I cut stars out of foil and I glued them on my clothes. I took the phallus and put it on a table, and after making several bows, I improvised more or less a story about life and wanderings of the phallus, who lived adventures, met other phalluses, and was very happy. After doing all this, I left to live in Berlin.

I think you have helped me because before, for five years, every time I started to draw, I did almost nothing—it was like a chore, an obligation. The associated sexual block, which I did not explain very clearly (perhaps next time), I think is going better, although I don't check it often.

Now I draw every day.

THANK YOU,

RUTH

⤖ LETTER 3 ⤔

From Roy

I came to see you at the Café Le Téméraire on January 2, 2006. I was entirely convinced you would be of help. To your question of what it was that happened, I replied that my greatest wish was to bow before the Essence, but there was something that distressed me. Thanks to your intuition and tarot interpretation you made me understand that the cause of that anguish came from my father, as when I was a child he projected his desires on me, forcing me to study piano against my wishes. I wanted to play drums like him. During our conversation I had the feeling of returning to my childhood, finally understanding with tears in my eyes the cause of my pain.

You advised me to buy a piano, put a picture of my father inside, and with the help of my wife and son break it on the street, in front of my house. Next I had to burn the photo and dilute the ashes in a glass of wine and drink it. I finally had to send three white keys to my father with the following message: "I return this because it is yours, I already have my own teeth." Once the act was completed, I would buy a drum kit to play in the company of my son.

I was confident that I could recover the piano of my childhood, which I had given to my yoga teacher years ago as a sign of gratitude for helping me get off drugs. Since he wasn't a yogi anymore, I asked his students who did not want to give the piano back to me. I was tempted to perform the act with any organ or keyboard or something that symbolized the piano since my budget did not allow me to buy one, but at your insistence in your books not to change anything about the act I ventured back to Paris on March 8, 2006, and as I intuited, you told me it must be a piano. Faced with my difficulty to buy one you advised me to find it, search the internet, anywhere, making sure someone would give it away. I took advantage of this second meeting to talk to you about a back pain on the right side that had been dragging for five years. You advised me to stick the photo of my father on a punching bag and hit it to release my anger. On March 13 I performed the act with the punching bag and I was exhausted from so many blows. Upon reaching my house, my six-year-old son Ananda made me an X-shaped drawing where you could read my name in one line and "La Muerte" in the other accompanied by thirteen drops of blood. In the center of the X there was the drawing of a skull. My entire being shuddered. Now all that was missing was the piano. I put messages on the internet, I searched and prayed to be able to buy it someday. Finally, I despaired. Eventually, the piano appeared in the most beautiful and unexpected way. A friend whom I had not seen for a long time who had been suffering with tremendous depression for several years decided to ask me to accompany her to Paris, hoping that you could help her. In one of our talks about your therapy, without me having specified anything about my own act, she asked me if your actions were difficult to carry out. I answered that in my case I needed to get a piano, which hadn't happened. The magic of life did its thing: she was offered a piano. She contacted the person who was giving it away and asked him to give it to me, and so it was.

On June 17, 2006, accompanied by my wife and son, I carried out the act of breaking the piano, witnessed by neighbors leaning from their balconies. When the back of the piano fell to the ground something fell with it. I felt a lot of peace. After burning the photo and drinking its ashes diluted in a good glass of wine, I sent the three white keys to my father together with the message that you gave me: "I give you this back because it is yours, I already have my own teeth."

Two days later I received a call from my father where he admitted his mistake.

It was the night of San Juan (mine and my father's saint) on the twenty-fourth, after your wonderful and magical conference in the Santa Susanna Magic Fair in Barcelona. Together with my son and some friends we contemplated the bonfire with the burning remains of the piano. The event concluded on August 11, 2006, the day I bought the drum kit. I enjoy playing it for my wife and son. Thank you with all my heart for your help. I have begun to see the magic of life and I hope to continue to keep my eyes open to notice the mystery. I know that I still have a lot of work to wake up and become fully aware of my being, but I also know that thanks to your love and help I was able to lighten the heavy load weighing me down. I can't find the words for my enormous gratitude, but I know that I can thank you by joining the great work that both you and others of the same lucidity carry out for the good of all beings and all life.

FROM A FRIEND FOREVER,

ROY

✦ LETTER 4 ✦

From Raquel

Hello Mr. Jodorowsky,

My name is Raquel. In March you read my cards in Le Téméraire. I asked them why I was alone and they revealed a problem with my femininity. Death—Wizard—Strength—Hanged Man.

It seemed as if I were like a boy (the Magician) since I was little, without knowing where I am from.

I asked you for help and you gave me an act to perform. I remind you because I know you see a lot of people. "Wander through the city where you grew up in Spain for four days, one hour a day, with menstrual blood on your face. Feel proud of being a woman walking among the people; even better if there are many men." I felt I should do it, but I was very afraid at the same time . . . of being mocked or ashamed, I don't know. Yesterday I came back from Spain to France; I'm going to rewrite the diary I wrote there, since you asked me to write you a letter at the end.

Villalhe, July 11, 2007.

I arrived last night. I spent four months looking for the best day to go depending on my period and my work; the time has come. My body was listening to me and that's why it was difficult to calculate everything with such anticipation. . . . Around 8:00 p.m. I was able to begin; in front of the bathroom mirror I began to put the blood on my face. At first it was consistent and hardly visible—maybe it would be enough? Or should it be more noticeable? I made more marks, resembling war paint, I thought. . . . I left at 8:15 p.m., it was sunny and I felt the blood dry and it pulled the skin a little. Every time I walked past someone I would glance to see if I was being stared at. . . .

I remember you told me: "You'll see how no one notices." I kept walking toward a square full of people. I was afraid, especially of running into someone I know who'd come to greet me with two kisses—not ideal! I walked main streets, I tried to think I should be proud of being a woman but I was still somewhat tense. I thought this hour would never end. I started walking down the path leading to my ex-boyfriend's house, first without realizing it. Then I thought, "why not?" I had many memories. That made me forget at times whether people looked at me or not. I started having more positive thoughts. Even if someone noticed some strokes on my face . . . so what? In the end I don't think a lot of people realized. I came back, the hour flew by, I washed my face, and I was glad to have overcome the first day.

Villalhe, July 12, 2007.

I get up early, take a shower, and start to reapply the blood on my face. Now there is more of it and it shows more. I go out and want to try to buy a juice in the supermarket to see what happens.

When I enter, I see my parents' neighbor; I get scared and I turn around so that she doesn't see me. I keep walking, I'm a bit nervous about what happened. I walk main streets; it makes me want to put my sunglasses on to get behind them and see if people look at me or not. . . . I think I'm doing worse than yesterday. The hour seems to last forever. I would like to go unnoticed. . . . I remember the purpose of this act: "Feeling proud to be a woman." I replay it in my head like a mantra and I feel better. I begin to feel one with the other women I see on the street. As if for the first time I realize that I am part of them and they are a part of me. I come back home. I feel confused, I feel bad and good at the same time. I think it's a tough exercise.

Villalhe, July 13, 2007 (Friday).

Today is market day and the square and nearby streets are full of people. Around 12:30 p.m. I repeat the act. I paint my face with my hands, I don't care, I like this ritual of connection with myself.

The fear starts again when I go out—I can't help it. Although to be honest it is nothing too visible. At some point you notice somewhat darker marks. . . . I go toward the square, full of stalls and people from everywhere. I'm wearing a miniskirt; in a way I prefer my body to be more noticeable than the blood on my face. The truth is that most of the people go about their business.

I turn off and go to a small store. I talk to the clerk but I don't get too close. I go out again. I go back to another clothing store to ask for a catalog. I'm scared and at the same time I want to see what happens. . . . nothing.

I go out and I repeat in my head that I feel good being a woman. I repeat it the entire way. I go back to the market. I'm calmer, I don't care. I go back home. I'm tired. Only one day left . . .

Villalhe, July 14, 2007 (Saturday).

Today I decided to take a trip to see my family. I wanted to get up early to walk for an hour before taking the car to go see my mother. But I got up late because yesterday my little brother broke his right elbow and I took him to the emergency room at night. Since I saw that I didn't have time, I decide to go to my parent's house as I am. I only place two darker strokes on the cheekbones, under my eyes. I enter my house; my father left one day before I arrived. Only my mother and one of my brothers are there. Surprisingly, they do not say anything about my face. I had made up a possible answer about makeup and fashion. It is also true that they were more worried about my brother's elbow and the stress from my father leaving. I get in the car with my mother; she doesn't say anything, and we don't look at each other much either. Within half an hour of driving I stop at a gas station and wash my face. . . . I'm supposed to be a woman. . . . We continue toward Galicia.

All this brings a positive change in my life. Thank you very much for trying to help me. I know very well what to do to find myself, to reclaim the faith and the mystery.

Thanks again for your time!

SINCERELY,

RAQUEL

✧ LETTER 5 ✦

From David

Dear Alejandro,

A year ago I showed up at the Café Le Téméraire to present a problem that tormented me. I was going through depression and I came to realize that practically all my life I hadn't loved myself—I profoundly hated myself. Through the analysis of my family tree and the tarot reading we saw that my maternal and paternal grandmothers had alcohol problems and that women dominated businesses and controlled men. My paternal grandmother despised herself and ended up losing her legs because of smoking and drinking. My father hates himself; he already has lost one leg and the other one is at risk. The conclusion was that I was what you call a "naked homosexual."

My psychomagical act was as follows: Dress up as a woman, a beautiful woman, and go to a gay club. Make a package with the clothes of that night and give it to my mother so that she stops looking for the woman in me. Buy arnica cream, massage my dad's legs, or what's left of them. Ask him to massage my legs because they also hurt. Bury what's left of the cream and plant a rosebush over it.

Before performing the act, I became aware of having always been surrounded by women, hoping unconsciously to be like them and rejecting the paternal model as something I didn't want to resemble. This corresponded well with the enormous influence of my mother's words, "You'll be good with girls," since my father was a chronic womanizer. The performance of the act was wonderful, amusing, and an explosion of self-esteem. The leg pain disappeared. Little by little my self-contempt decreased significantly, although not overnight. My self-acceptance began to improve.

Although I keep having certain problems expressing my sexuality, I accepted my sexual desire, which was not the case before. I no longer feel compelled to look like a woman and instead look more at certain men as a model. Even my voice and my gestures have become more masculine. The influence of my mother in my conscious acts has diminished, although that saying—"You'll be good with girls"—still weighs on me. Overall, there has been a great influx of self-esteem and strength that I see reflected in all aspects of my life.

Thank you very much,
David

LETTER 6

From Patricio

This is the act that you prescribed for me to do at midnight. I went to a secluded place, carrying a bucket with water and a clock. I had to do it naked so I took off my clothes and I knelt in front of the bucket. During the last seven minutes I counted every second and I focused on the question: "What do I want to do?" Time began to stretch. When the clock struck twelve o'clock I dipped my head into the bucket. It was a little narrow so I felt quite claustrophobic. I began to say: "If I don't discover what it is that I want, I'm going to die." I repeated it several times with more and more force, until I ran out of air. I was afraid that someone would find me, and that didn't allow me to concentrate. I took my head out of the bucket with the feeling of not having achieved my objective. Determined this time to resist for longer, I put my head back in the bucket, but this time just thinking, without speaking, because I was losing my breath screaming underwater, making bubbles. I tried to relax. As I was running out of oxygen, all sorts of speculations began to arise in my mind.

I thought maybe that was a symbol I had to interpret and that the "key" would guide me to a new vocation that I wasn't yet aware of: scuba diver, scientist researching sounds of aquatic mammals, an astronaut, who knows how many things; the thing was I ran out of air and I pulled my head out knowing that none of this was the answer. I decided to repeat the operation for the third and last time. I gathered air and submerged my head; I decided this time to drown if I did not find the answer. I faced silence inside me; I felt the blood run through my veins and I listened to the beat of my heart; I let myself go, I relaxed; I exhaled the oxygen slowly; I started to sink into a cold ocean, dark and silent, ready to swallow me; I felt a force pulling me, inviting me to disappear; I was afraid, very afraid; I felt filled with deafening emptiness. Suddenly I returned to myself and realized that I lost consciousness; I forgot the question. I pulled my head out of the water, took a deep breath . . . and the answer, perhaps because I was no longer asking, came to me.

What I want to do is live; to learn to live!

Since I was little I was assigned roles and responsibilities that did not belong to me. When I was seven years old, my father left home; my mother then put me in that role and never stopped reproaching me for not assuming it. When I turned eighteen I left my home willing to leave behind all my past, but I realized that everything is part of me; and so I started searching and I am still searching . . .

THANK YOU,
PATRICIO

✦ LETTER 7 ✦

From Virginie (thirty-five years old)

Dear Mr. Jodorowsky,

I am writing to you to bear witness to the beneficial and exceptional effect of a psychomagical act that you suggested to me at the Café Le Téméraire about a year ago. I have suffered with osteoarthritis from a very young age, unusual for a rather young person (I am thirty-five years old).

Last year I experienced a period of violent pain attacks. Having already explored the paths of a different diet (very little dairy), spa treatments, and many other things—which have improved my health, but not to a point of eliminating these very painful cyclical episodes—I said to myself, knowing your work well, that it would be good to share it with you during a consultation in Paris.

You connected this problem with unbalanced emotional needs related to my maternal grandmother.

This suggestion struck me as very relevant because there was indeed a problem of this nature in my family. You suggested I do something to rid my bones of the pain that I carried and that was actually most likely that of my grandmother. I performed this act.

I slept with a school skeleton, which I left in the cemetery with acacia honey near the tomb of my grandmother by expressing the need to "return her bones and her pain." Then I had to go to an African dance class to free the pelvis. Finally, I had to break contact with my mother, asking her to cut the string of a helium balloon from which her picture was hanging. I would like to bear witness to my sincere gratitude and my amazement because as soon as I finished the first part of this act (the skeleton) my seizures ceased instantly. It's quite breathtaking. Sometimes they would come back but only after arguments with my boyfriend, so linked to an emotional problem.

Even if osteoarthritis is likely still there it's because my case is very rare in the opinion of different therapists. I can testify that I have practically no violent pains anymore. And when I do, it's always linked to an emotional problem. You are simply a magician and a man of astonishing insight. Your perfect knowledge of what connects our conscious acts to the unconscious allows you to help the people who come to you, it's obvious!

THANK YOU FOR EVERYTHING!

VIRGINIE

→ LETTER 8 ←
....
From Frédéric

Thanks Alejandro,

We came to see you because my wife was eight months pregnant with our second child who was breeched. We had prepared for the birth with a midwife and consulted an ob-gyn practicing inversion (reversal of the child in the mother's womb). The inversion was scheduled for October 17, our last chance for a natural childbirth because it was almost impossible when the child was breeched according to doctors. They told us that if he didn't turn, we would have to consider a cesarean birth. I couldn't let my child and my wife go through this. The labor was planned for November 6. The deadline was approaching quickly!

The tarot consultation you gave was MAGIC! MIRACULOUS!

Here is what happened. We introduced ourselves to you: Ethan, my first son (four years old), my wife, and myself. You told us, addressing my wife and noticing that she was pregnant: "It's your second? What is the name of the first?"

"Ethan."

"And what will be the name of the second?"

"Nathan."

"No! You can't, you want to repeat Ethan. Change the name! Well, why are you coming to consult the tarot?"

"Precisely, the child presents himself in breech. Why? And what to do about this . . . ?"

And you responded:

"There are three possibilities for which he is turned. One: you don't want to relive childbirth. Two: you want a girl and it's a boy. Three: you are in crisis with him (the father). Here, take the tarot, shuffle . . . open, choose three cards."

She pulls out: Strength—Hermit—Hierophant.

After analyzing and interpreting the spread, the message was that my wife gave no place to the new child because of a deep crisis with me, the crisis against the father who betrayed her: she was in crisis because the second child was not a girl. (She is the second of her siblings, a boy then a girl.) Deep down she wanted me to give her a girl . . . to repeat the pattern. She was in crisis because in not doing so the Man, the Father, tricks her, betrays her . . . the child does not find its place.

In my story, this second child, who repeats the first, echoed my twin brothers, whose first names are Olivier-Pascal and Pascal-Olivier. In short, the tarot speaks! It sings through you to reach the essential, for real and deep communication.

What to do? Three cards: the Magician, Death, the Star. A fourth card on top of Death: the World. Then you say, "Okay, I understand what the tarot wants to say. Here's what you'll all do: Ethan will play the role of his brother; you place him head up on the naked body of his mother, in breech all while giving him chocolate sweets, and turn him on his stomach slowly, gently, delicately—until he's upside down and then you mime the birth, the passage between his mother's legs and you give him his new name." And, turning one last time to my wife, you say: "Search deep inside you for his first name." There you go, goodbye and thank you . . .

Coming out of the café, the shock, vibrating body . . . the end of the deep work begins. I waited for my wife to find the name deep within. For three days she searched and always ended up with names that are phonetically, symbolically similar to Ethan. And at the end of the third day, the name arises! Lucas! And we finally got to perform the act on the third day after consulting you. Ethan was happy to play the role of his brother, to help us . . . happy to play this act. He was naked, he was laughing. I placed him on her belly, and I started to give him chocolates (I had chosen chocolate eggs) and gently, calmly, with all the precautions, I started to turn him over. He laughed and ate his chocolates, one after another, and in the end I turned him over completely, mimed the birth, and we said: "Welcome to the world, Lucas!" We started this act at 2:59 p.m. We felt like it was a bit rushed and we decided to do it again. Ethan agreed, and we did it three times in total. He ate nine chocolate eggs with joy and with great pleasure. The act ended at

3:15 p.m. and lasted for fifteen minutes. Then they got dressed and we drank tea.

Epilogue: the Miracle!

We showed up on Wednesday the 17th, seven days after the tarot consultation, for the inversion in the presence of the midwife and obstetrician. He performed the procedure and to our great surprise it happened with ease, as if my wife's body was already prepared and Lucas turned over. Miracle! It took fifteen minutes, the same time as the act. Their bodies were soft, completely relaxed, my wife was totally confident and serene. How sweet! How beautiful! And what was our surprise when the doctor and midwife told us that they performed the procedure for free, we didn't have to pay anything! And it is with infinite joy that we are able to announce the birth of Lucas on October 28, 2007, at 1:05 a.m., a marvelous delivery by natural means and most importantly without an epidural. What a marvel, this birth. I will remember it all my life!

THANK YOU, THANK YOU, THANK YOU ALEJANDRO!

FRÉDÉRIC

→ LETTER 9 ←
. . . .
From Florence

Last week I came to see you at the Café with two problems. One involved my mother and the other one my dad. My mother suffers from psychosis and I struggle to accept it. My relationship with her oscillates between hatred and the will to save her. (I'm the only child, my parents are separated, and I lived alone with my mother for a long time: from six to sixteen years old.) My father lives in the West Indies; I lived there until the age of five, then when my parents divorced I came to France with my mother. Three times a year I took a plane to see my dad. I'm not close to him at all because he scares me. I have never understood where this fear came from. You told me that my father never saw me as a girl but as a woman/wife and while feeling this look on me I couldn't fulfill the Oedipus complex. I projected this fear of my father on men; I am unable to have a relationship with men because in their presence I feel threatened like a helpless child. I have to tell you that my father, although he never affected me physically, touched several of my friends and raped the daughter of his second wife when she was between twelve and sixteen. I learned it at sixteen but I was already afraid of him before that. As for the act, you told me to put on my mother's clothes, to enlarge a photo of her and make it into a mask, then go see the world with her eyes. Then you told me to call my father and talk to him as my mother would.

Thursday after seeing you at the Café I took my mother's picture pretending I needed to test my camera which did not seem to work very well. My mother was not well and was very reluctant to let me photograph her. I went to develop the photo. Her face looked tortured and full of pain; it was scary. I used the moment she was out to pick up clothes from her closet (I came back this year to live with her with the intention of helping her recuperate after five months of hospitalization and in order to prepare for my departure to Spain, where I will settle), but she came back unexpectedly and I could not hide her panties and her bra that I had in my hand. She questioned me and I answered evasively. I left, and when I came back to my bedroom there was a skirt and a t-shirt on my desk. She was glad I was wearing her clothes; she was encouraging me to do so. This morning I went to get the photo. The blow-up was very impressive. I asked a friend to accompany me. I arrived at her place in Marais in Paris, with all the paraphernalia. I got dressed: shoes too small, the skirt I couldn't zip up, the panties too tight, no bra because I didn't find any, a t-shirt, and the sweater. I started making the mask. I went to look at myself in the mirror and I was impressed. I was terrified at the idea of exposing myself to the eyes of others looking like that. But my friend encouraged me. We went down the street. I didn't put on the mask right away because I was scared, but after a few meters I put it on without thinking. I had the impression that my life would change, but no, people would pass us looking at me out of the corner of their eye. At first I hardly dared to look at them. Then I relaxed, I almost forgot I was wearing the mask, and I watched them watch me. I started chatting with my friend and we walked quietly to the Republic for about twenty minutes, maybe more, I'm not sure. On the way back, without warning, my friend went into a café to buy some cigarettes. I found myself all alone in the street with my mask and then the shock was very violent. At first I looked for a wall to blend into and hide from people's gazes. I kept the mask and I stood still waiting for my friend. Without her the gaze of people was not the same anymore; they could no longer look at her to make sure it was a gag or a joke. People were taken aback, almost shocked, and children were afraid of me. When my friend came out I told her I had to finish everything on my own, that it was very different. I let her go ahead and I began to walk alone. I was like a zombie, immersed in another reality. The way to her house was not very long but going through it was extremely violent for me. I went up to her house alone to call my father. I called him several times but I got his answering machine. I did not leave the message.

My friend joined me and we had something to eat. I kept the clothes on but I took off the mask. My friend left again and I put the mask back on to call my father. I tried to see him not as my father but as a man and to talk to him as such. I realized that when I talk to him I still seem like a little girl, who I am not anymore, in order to be rape-proof. I spoke with him firmly with confidence, in quite a direct way. The conversation was brief. I talked about my future plans: my holidays, my upcoming departure for Barcelona. I hung up, I got changed, and that was it.

The part of the act with the mask made me confront my dependence on the opinion of others and my lack of freedom. When I found myself walking alone, it was as if I was naked, exposed and vulnerable, while I was hidden behind another face, with clothes that were not mine. The part with my father was easy and natural for me even though it was the one that I worried about the most. It was something I had to do. I have doubts, I don't know if I've done justice to what you asked me to do. I believe that I cut a few corners. I get the impression of having taken a first step confronting my fears.

FLORENCE

⇢ LETTER 10 ⇠
....

From Marie

Alejandro,

Wednesday, January 18, I came to meet you at Café Le Téméraire with a question: "Why can't I lose weight, and is it a problem that my son Max, two years old, bears the first name of St. Maxime, day of the birth of my mother's first stillborn child?" You suggested two acts that I implemented. The first was to put three kilos of marzipan on my stomach for an hour at midnight, then shape a baby that I had to bury in a pot of earth in which I planted a shrub to give my mother.

I carried out this act consciously with concentration, like an official ceremony. I was apprehensive, but on the spot I performed the symbolic act serenely. I kept this house plant in my home watering it regularly to offer a beautiful plant to my mother. Ten days later, a putrid odor invaded the house, as if a body was decomposing in the dining room. My husband quickly spotted that the pot stank and took it out of the house to put it in a shed where it wouldn't freeze. But the plant withered away, it froze to death, and my act was not completed because I did not give it to my mother. On March 10, the day of her birthday, my mother invited us over. I decided to take the pot (the coffin) with me and give it to her explaining somehow our meeting in Paris and the symbolism behind the act. She saw the pot and said to me, "No, I don't want it, keep it!" Unable to tell her there was a dead child inside (made of marzipan) my husband said to me on the sly: "We have to leave it there, I don't want it either!" I found myself torn: was I ready to stop playing the role of mother's consoler in carrying her sorrow? Definitely YES, so in a hurry, I dug a hole in her garden, buried the contents of the pot inside, covered it quickly like a thief, and returned to my parents who were talking in the living room, like it wasn't a big deal. But I wasn't relaxed, I was afraid that my mother would find the "corpse" and understand what I had done. I was ashamed, as if I had betrayed my mother.

Back home, I called my mother to explain to her it was important that I leave "the baby" where it should have been from the start. My mother understood and we never spoke about it again.

The putrid odor had spread throughout the car that carried the pot. I have cleaned the car, disinfected it (with a disinfectant bomb used by hospitals when a cadaver leaves an odor), and bought a car air freshener to never again smell "that dead baby that was within me." Here is the end of the first act. I completed it with relief, because it was horrible to go through.

The second act was to change the names of my two boys to separate them from the story of the dead child. I have three children: Louise, eleven years old; Martin, eight years old; and Max, two years old. Thanks to you, Alejandro, I understood that Martin and Max stood for MAMA, so I explained to my two oldest our meeting and the symbolic meaning of changing their first names. To my great surprise they understood the meaning of the act very well. I had two matchbox-sized lead boxes made by a carpenter-roofer. I bought two pretty red and gold boxes that looked like small Japanese cabinets. I bought four medals: two silver ones on which were engraved "MAX—MARTIN" and two gold ones with new names, "ALEX—OLIVIER."

The choice of first names bears meaning to me: Martin chose Olivier; it's the symbol of peace and it is a beautiful way to make peace with history. For Max I chose Alex simply in connection to your first name. The Day of Saint Louise (March 15) I organized the name change ritual: each child put the silver medal in a lead box and took the golden one with their new name to put it in one of the pretty small boxes. They are displayed in the dining room. So I accomplished the end of act two and I said to myself: "Now I can lose weight!" On January 18, the day of our meeting, you said to me: "If you don't eat sugar anymore, you will lose fourteen kilos!" From that moment, I—who was "viscerally" drawn to sugar—developed a dislike of it. I quit sugar.

THANKS THANKS THANKS!

MARIE

⟿ LETTER 11 ⟸

....

Author unknown (thirty-three years old)

Dear Alejandro,

I came last week to Téméraire with the subject of sexual violence which took place ten years ago, of which I have never spoken except to a shrink, in a bubble. Since it upset me to have to say it in public, first I would like to thank you sincerely and deeply for the generosity and intelligence with which you welcomed this emotion. I think that this justice is only possible when one has suffered a lot, and I tell you this from the bottom of my heart: your human qualities and your extraordinary intuition marked me for life! Through the similarity of my father's name and the name of the one who abused me, and maybe also because I did not defend myself, you deduced that I felt guilty about it because of my strong desire for my father that I projected onto the other.

Here is the psychomagical act that you prescribed me: "Go and print a large picture of your father on a t-shirt and make a friend wear it. Looking at the picture tell him how much you love him, and how much you desire him. Then apologize, bury the t-shirt in the ground, and plant a plant over it. Then you'll feel much better. . . ."

To begin with, there were a few unexpected circumstances. There was a problem with a printer: the first t-shirt was green and made him look like a sick person! I was offered a second one . . . . My "paternal substitute" wore both t-shirts, so that I would bury both. After my confession, I decided to go to Bois de Boulogne with an olive tree (my father is Kabyle) under my arm. It cost me thirty-three euros. (I am thirty-three years old: the resurrection!) As it was difficult to find a wild corner, I forced myself a little to plant it in an isolated place, but the ground was hard and I got stung by nettles. Park guards arrived telling me I had no right to do that, that I had to go through the city council and all. . . . I didn't understand that they were in fact guides until they told me: "Can't you see how disgusting that is? This is the men's corner, they will piss on it, fuck on it, tear it apart. . . . You're doing nothing wrong, you are planting a tree! But you really chose the wrong place!" And so my subconscious was still guilty of sick love, disgusting, with rape, incest. . . . I left. I kept getting more and more lost and just as I was about to really get discouraged, I finally found a corner protected by a fence near a path, a perfect place, which was confirmed to me as if in a dream by an old gentleman of my father's age who looked at the olive tree and said it was beautiful. When he disappeared from my sight, I walked over to the fence, finding a small, protected corner that was clean, wild, charming, sunny, and spacious, where no one could see me, a perfect spot: the secret garden of my heart! The soil was incredibly easy to dig, I buried the t-shirt of sick love under the t-shirt of excessive love, and there was really a moment of grace. I'm sure I'll get better—anyway I feel liberated, free to love, and free to be loved.

THANK YOU!!!

✦ LETTER 12 ✦

From Noémie

Dear Alejandro,

Here's how the act of psychomagic that you "prescribed" for me unfolded. The act was to make love with a man in a cemetery. After I got the instructions, everything happened in a magical way! The Universe seems to have organized everything for me! That same night, a man invites me to spend the evening with him. The man does not look like those I have known in the past. He does not try to desperately seduce me, so I propose to him to carry out my psychomagical act with him. It doesn't surprise him, as he has also been affected by the particular energy of a tarot reading that upset him. . . . We go to a cemetery but everything is closed.

We give up, tired, but flirtation continues. I return to Grenoble where I live. A few days later, this young man calls me and offers to come see me for a few days since he is a few miles from my house. I accept a little anxiously. I see that he agrees to help me do my act of psychomagic. In the afternoon we go to a pretty cemetery in the countryside. But once seated in the grass he panics in fear of being seen by someone. The act becoming impossible without him, I suggest we leave. We try another cemetery further away, in the village where I lived my first months of life. We feel comfortable, and we kiss and hug with tenderness. Two teenage girls keep walking in front of us and disturb us. We go back. In the evening, I refuse to have sex. I find being touched repulsive. I'm worried: our moment of tenderness at the cemetery was not enough. I was comforted in his arms but not excited. . . . So I suggest we start again. My partner accepts, but only if we do it at night when no one can see us. But before we leave my partner tells me that he slept with a prostitute while traveling when young. And from there, everything seems to fall apart for me.

I have to find a man sexually honest, and he is not. . . . I'm beside myself: I cry, I'm inconsolable. It is this state of deep despair that makes me realize how important this act is for me. Lost, I can't calm down, and my partner is distraught. I randomly open the book *The Theater of Healing* and I read "faith or no faith, one has to be rather honest to follow the instructions to the letter. If you consult a doctor, and after the visit you don't bother to buy and take the prescription, how can you then judge the effectiveness of his treatment?" I can't believe my eyes, I needed to read this, it's magic and I have the impression of a greater force at work. . . . I am guided and supported. And how can I doubt at this point? I decide to trust, thinking of Jodorowsky. My partner is as motivated to help me and we decide to go, perked up. At the cemetery we climb over a wall, a little anxious and very excited at the same time. We walk hand in hand to the heart of the cemetery. We sit on a bench under a tree. Satisfied to have accomplished the first step we laugh like two teenagers, drinking and smoking a little. I reach my inner teenager (the one who was abused at the death of her father). Then we try to make an act of love despite the cold and the morbid world that surrounds us! Suddenly, time stops, everything seems unreal to me, like in a dream. I have a feeling that invisible beings work over us in a process of alchemy, which transcends me. I feel like I'm watching a scene unfolding from above. I feel I've known this man for a very long time, that we cross several lives. . . . In short, time no longer exists, it is suspended. Then, after an hour and a half, we come out of the dream and I suggest we go back. I have a feeling there's nothing more to do here! Back at my house, we feel triumphant and tired . . . like after climbing a summit that ends in a mountain hut.

The next day I wake up with my body heavy as lead. During the day I feel desire for my companion, and I am delighted by it; I feel like I'm healed already!! We begin to make love, but my companion stops—he couldn't go all the way and it hurt him. He's ashamed, he is not doing well. Nothing seems to soothe him. We try to find a way, to no avail. But the given act happens on the day it was prescribed. . . . Then the next day while saying goodbye, the act of love arises naturally and without blockage. We both seem liberated! He's got an impression of sleeping with a woman for the first time (he makes me a woman) and I sleep with an honest man for the first time!! Two days later I see blood between my thighs. . . . Frightened because it's not the date of my period, I conclude that I have lost my virginity! And, life being funny, I realize that this is not blood but chocolate that I dropped while eating my lunch! Another surprise the next day: I leave my house and an ex-boyfriend who left me three or four years earlier comes to drop off his contact details in my mailbox. He talks to me, excited . . . and while listening to him I wonder "but what could you possibly like about this man??!" I realize that this man whom I used to love, and who hurt and humiliated me, has no effect on me! I conclude that dishonest men don't excite me anymore!

It's a real miracle! It's impressive! I thank life for this gift that fell from the sky!

In conclusion, thank you for this radical and magical change that seems to have been liberating, insofar as I am in a relationship with Olivier (my partner in the act of psychomagic). And it seems all the more beautiful as our first names refer to the biblical story of Noah, to whom the dove brings an olive branch to announce the end of the deluge!!! In the story, would you be the dove?!

NOÉMIE

⇝ LETTER 13 ⇜

From Anne

It was the first time I went to Le Téméraire. I had heard of Jodorowsky earlier when I lived in Marseille. I was told that he was an exceptional man, who thanks to his talent as a tarologist and his psychomagical acts had helped lots of people from around the world. A few years later, I moved to Paris for my acting profession. I have always worked on myself (spirituality is something innate in everyone and so it was in my life). Since childhood, I felt different, "unwell" in my skin. I thought I was a boy. Odd, isn't it? I had a curious contact with people in general. With my family in particular, they called me "The Devil." My deceased grandmother (may God have her soul) called me *EL AHSSAN* which means "invincible and fiery horse" in Arabic. I was hyperactive, completely scattered. I had difficulty breathing, eating, going to the bathroom. I suffered from constipation for twenty-five years! Fear of "letting go," fear of falling into the toilet. On the emotional side, a real disaster. I fell only for men who had sexual difficulties, lack of or weak erections. Most were violent or chronically unhappy, didn't want to get involved with me, despised what I was (my origins, my physique at times too feminine, at times not natural enough). I was in psychoanalysis, thinking it would serve me well (it's a little long and expensive). I decide to go out of curiosity to Le Téméraire to meet "the guy." I see him coming to sit among this crowd awaiting him. A fabulous atmosphere where everyone feels like they're gambling for their life at the time of the draw. The first time I'm not drawn. I come back again and there I am drawn in seventh place. Curious, when you learn that I am the seventh of my siblings! I'm scared, I sit in front of him, I ask the following question:

"Why does it never work with men?"

He answers:

"Never never?"

And I say:

"Never!"

He asks me to shuffle the cards, he goes:

"I don't know, the cards will tell. . . ."

I put the cards down, I cut the deck. . . .

Three cards are drawn:

The Moon (Mother) to my left.

The Chariot (Young Man) in the middle.

The Sun (Father) on my right.

"In some families it's preferable to have a boy than a girl, that's the way it is, you're going to see a couple and do a 'birth massage.'"

I was completely blown away by what I had just heard. Indeed, I was not wanted as a child. When my mother married my father she was eleven and he was thirty. It was in Algeria. He was a great imam, medium, and healer. He said he would die at the age of the Prophet: sixty-two years. When my mother found out she was pregnant (with me) she hastened to drink vinegar to provoke a miscarriage. Apparently I hung on till the end. The day of my birth, in the clinic, I didn't scream, I couldn't breathe, they thought I was dead. Then, after a few taps on the buttocks, everything went back to normal.

Birth massage: I decided to do this ritual as quickly as possible. Three weeks later I had an appointment with two students of Alejandro's, a woman and a man. Birth massage is a ritual which allows, in the form of a role play, the reenactment of our conception, our birth on Earth: from desire, to sexual intercourse until gestation, to birth, and even the baby's bath. All this made with lots of love from the part of the "symbolic parents." This experiment lasted five hours. The weather was exceptionally nice that day. . . . I had the impression of being carried from the beginning of the ritual until the end. All this with great respect and modesty. This work activates the masculine and feminine energy so that within an individual can appear as a whole: complete and creative. At the end of this ritual, I left with new clothes (required for this work).

Results: I could breathe better, ten thousand times better. By symbolically leaving this virtual belly, I rediscovered the world, a wonderful world in which I have my place today. This work was a real switch: I changed, and everyone has changed in an extraordinary way; men notice me (unlike before), in my circle I am respected (while before it was not the case). The energy to create is there: I get up in the morning with the desire to live and to accomplish things. Sexually with my partner it's great and regular (whereas before it was once every five months). I have projects. . . .

This is just the beginning, I know the best is yet to come.

I give you my testimony. Have trust, keep working and live. There's no coincidence. Life is beautiful.

THANKS,
ANNE

✧ LETTER 14 ✦

From Virginia

Dear Magician Benefactor,

Coming to meet you at Le Téméraire, I asked you what steps to take, what cells to untie to incarnate myself in this life and with humanity. The psychomagical act of dressing up as a little girl and going with a man taller than me to Disneyland, a dad, was decisive. Life worked as if by magic, because without asking, I was given a day off, so I stayed in Paris carefree instead of going back to Marseille. This triggered the passage from a little girl into a woman. This gave me enormous confidence and helped me to no longer be afraid, to free myself from my fear of men. I finally realized that we can create our reality.

I feel liberated and I don't know how to thank you.

The night before I dreamed out loud, saying, "Everything is possible!" Thanks to this act I was able to understand an ambiguous romantic situation more clearly than before. It's daily work but everything is moving forward.

THANKS!
VIRGINIA

✦ LETTER 15 ✦

From Yvette

Sir,

The two men I loved left to build their lives elsewhere with other women. One had a child, while the other jointly purchased a house with his partner. They told me that they loved me and offered me a parallel relationship where I would remain in the shadow. My question was: What was I supposed to understand of these repeated situations? You asked me questions about my childhood. I told you that I had spent my first years with my grandparents and that I had witnessed their adversarial relationship and my grandfather's violence towards my grandmother.

On October 17, 2008, I visited the cemetery where my grandfather is buried to fulfill the "prescription" with the fear of being seen or heard, but I was sure that the cemetery would be deserted and I'd call my sister on my way out. So I took the RER with a bottle of water and a flogger that I had borrowed from my cousin (also a granddaughter!). Along the way, I drank water. I arrived in front of the church, surrounded by the cemetery on both sides. I went through the gate to the cemetery on the left side of the church to ensure that the cemetery was empty. I then went around the church to find myself in front of my grandfather's grave. I removed the flower pots and climbed on the tombstone and there I urinated. I came back down. I took out the flogger. I started striking the tombstone, I kept striking with all my strength. I had the impression that the sound of the blows echoed throughout the whole graveyard. I forgot where I was. I expressed my anger toward my grandfather, against him and his behaviors that had conditioned some of my behaviors as a child, teenager, and woman, and whose repercussions had weighed on my intimate relationships. I teared up. It was the first time I was able to address him directly, the first time I expressed my anger in front of him, when I accused him.

I put the flower pots back in place and walked slowly toward the door located to the right of the church to come out like an automaton.

The church was open. I lit a candle to Mary and sat in the place where I was baptized. I left the church without shame or guilt with the satisfaction of having done what I would have otherwise considered a sacrilege. I felt I was entitled to it. I sat on a low wall soaked in warm sunlight in front of the door of the graveyard. I closed my eyes and I heard the running water of the fountain. This soothing incessant streaming, this water was the hope of vitality rediscovered within me. I don't know how long I sat like that. Visitors arrived, others left. I took out my phone. I left a message for my sister telling her that I was in front of the cemetery and I got mad at grandpa. I started on the way back very slowly, as if in a daze. After getting the message, a few hours later, my sister asked me: "What is happening? You sounded 'from beyond the grave!'" I told her what happened. She was happy for me. Me too. I did it.

ALL THE BEST,

YVETTE

⇸ LETTER 16 ⇷

From Yan

Symptom: Loss of vision in left eye. Act of psychomagic: Slap my father back.

Being already in Argentina I went to see my father and once I had gathered the courage I apologized for what I was going to do and I slapped him; it was stronger than I intended, as if my unconscious did it with the force of all the years of repression.

Anyway, his reaction was totally unexpected, he hugged me and said, "I love you, I missed you so much," and silence fell in which we felt calm. He left to get a bottle of wine and invited me to drink with him. We talked for a long time like never before. I was able to express what I had felt since I was a boy and I freed myself of resentments I had toward him. I realized that although our parents project upon us and lock us in an image that does not correspond to us, we also do the same with them as long as we hold a grudge toward them, and this act profoundly changed the image I had of my father.

The next day my father gave me seven hundred dollars and for the first time in my life he said, "You can count on me no matter what." Thank you for this lesson that begins to have its effects on my life, changing what was my reality until now. For example, since I came back from Argentina I've been called nonstop about a job involving my music.

THANKS AGAIN...

YAN

⇥ LETTER 17 ⇤

From Alexander

Dear Alejandro:

I write to you as you write to a dear old friend, for that's what you are to me, a friend and a teacher. I'm finishing your book *Psychomagic*. In the end you say that whoever receives your psychomagic therapy should write you a letter about their experience, and that's exactly what I do in these pages.

Eleven years ago, when you presented your book *The Gospels to Heal* in Mexico, I was working as the head of information in a radio station's cultural newscast. I remember interviewing you at your hotel. I had not read any of your books and had only seen *Santa Sangre,* which embarrassed me. At the end of the interview, I told you I felt some kind of writer's block because it had been a while since I'd written anything. I didn't even draw.

As if seeing right through me, you asked if my father was alive. He passed away in 1992, I told you. *You must draw a picture of your father, write him a letter, and then burn both in the place where he is buried. . . .* We scattered his ashes in La Antigua, Veracruz. . . .

Your words stuck in my mind and my heart. My relationship with my father was always very important to me. Ten years have passed since the day you gave me my homework, and finally I complied.

In 2007 we celebrated eighty years of life of my mother and also fifteen years since my father's death. We decided to celebrate one and commemorate the other, making a family trip to Veracruz.

I knew that in addition to all that I had a pending task, an unavoidable appointment with myself.

Although the circumstances were radically different from 1997, I did what you entrusted me: I made a drawing of my father (inspired by one of the last photos I took of him, when he was already very ill, specifically on a trip to Antigua, looking at the river where not long after his ashes were scattered). I also wrote the letter to my father, where I told him, among many other things, that to lower him from his pedestal was very hard for me, but necessary. I also told him: "I am me, I don't want to repeat your story, because I have my own life claiming me. I burn you in this river to fulfill an old quest, but I also burn resentments, questions with no answers, history repeating itself. . . . I cried a lot when writing it because, first of all, it was a letter of love, farewell, but also a letter full of hope. I went to La Antigua with my mother, with my brothers, my son, my nieces and nephews, to the same restaurant where we met ten years ago to scatter his ashes. I walked away from everyone, I looked on the riverbank for a solitary space, I read the letter for my father and for me, and I burned the drawing. I returned to my family and my son. Throughout the trip, everyone told me: "You look so much like your dad . . . you're the most like him. . . ." While I told myself (and I keep saying): "I am me . . . I am me. . . ."

Thank you, Maestro Alejandro. With ten years delay, I pay my debt to you.

ALEXANDER

→ LETTER 18 ←
From Arthur

I waited for my father for a long time and my inner child continued to wait until recently. This childhood obsession began when his absences became longer and more arbitrary but I think the original impulse started right after I was born. After a difficult birth my mother wanted more than anything to go home. At the agreed time of departure, she was in the hospital lobby, overloaded with all her belongings, various gifts, and especially a big baby. The unexpected absence of her man, who was supposed to pick her up, transformed her habitual worry into insinuating anxiety: Did he have an accident? Did he run away? Has he forgotten me?

The unexpected arrival of my father, several hours late, calmed her nerves, but the various excuses and explanations could not offset my mother's intuition, and she later found out that he had spent the day with one of his mistresses.

I thought I was very close to my father when I was young. He was an artist full of fantasy, stories, and songs, closely connected with a child's imagination. However, because he was tormented by the past he was incapable of assuming a relatively balanced and conscious family life. The forceful violence pushing out from inside led him to have more and more affairs in a constant escape from everything that made him feel imprisoned. The deep love uniting my parents made these separations long and painful until my mother gradually pulled away, weary of these countless, never-ending departures and returns, and broken promises.

It was during this time that I began to wait. I was well prepared because, on the one hand, I loved my father very much, and on the other hand I was completely filled with my mother's anguish, so much so I made it mine. At the beginning my father would often show up on the spur of the moment, always with a gift or, returning from a trip, with something beautiful and fun. Sometimes he would announce his imminent arrival, on such and such a day, an evening, an hour, and would not come. But the most difficult thing, if he even showed up, was how late he would be. I would go through all sorts of emotions: moving from excitement and pride to worry, then a little later to resignation, disappointment, and indifference, always mixed with bitter anguish (morbid anguish which made me say to my mother at the age of seven during an absence longer than usual: "But maybe he is dead and no one knows!"). When he finally arrived I was already, as we say, stewed in my own juices. My emotional body was exhausted after these overheated feelings at the threshold of depression. I was no longer able to cope with my father's energy and while I was still happy to see him, I felt empty, unable to express my feelings.

Of course we were also able to connect and, when I was a teenager, he was often curious about the originality of my musical or poetic taste, thus encouraging me in my artistic pursuits. But the damage was done and I couldn't get rid of an underlying anguish related to the uncertainty of our encounter.

While telling this story to Alejandro another layer resurfaced juxtaposed with my childhood: a feminine, almost romantic dimension, that of an ever-worried and constantly disappointed woman hoping for the appearance of her moody and indifferent lover, unconsciously anticipating future abandonment. Me being me, all things considered, I identified with the feminine side of my family and felt this analysis reflected my deepest feelings.

After thinking a minute, Alejandro offered me a psychomagic act.

"Freud made a mistake," he told me. "You don't need to kill the father, (what use is a dead father!) but you can absorb him, make him yours, make him live in you. Symbolically, just once, become your father; be him and since like him you are a musician and a man of the stage, a public persona, be him in front of others, in a theater. Having incorporated him internally, you will no longer have to live the fantasy of waiting and you will no longer be the little boy confronted by an unattainable, peerless being. Dress up as him and sing one of his songs telling the public: I am him!"

My first reaction was to refuse, as if I had no right to touch something so sacred! But the more I toyed with this idea, the more it seemed both invigorating and liberating.

On the chosen day, I followed Alejandro's instructions to the letter. Before the end of the concert, on the first callback, I entered the stage alone, got a travel bag that I had hid behind an amp, and threw it on the piano. There was a loud noise, then silence, and I told the audience: "There is someone hidden in that bag." I explained that life is so close to a dream, tomorrow we will remember this evening just like this morning we remembered our dreams; however, in a dream we are free, we can do what we want, what we need, without limits.

In a comico-psycho-metaphysical way, I explained my relationship with my father, the wanderings, the expectations but also the love. While talking I undressed and ended up naked in front of the amazed audience. Here I am, naked in front of you, like on the day of my birth! (Curiously I felt very free and confident.) I then started unpacking my father's clothes that I had stolen from the bag. Here were the large overalls, studded belt, embroidered velvet jacket, and old sandals. It was quite a close portrait and everyone was laughing—me included. This was an act of psychomagic and I took on my father's identity. But when I started to sing one of his songs, silence fell, no more laughter, no more noise, as a kind of respect for the strangeness of the situation. I concentrated fully on my singing with a constant feeling of transgressing and crossing the line of something forbidden to me, something remaining in the desire of the small boy.

Once the song was over, I undressed and thanked the people for taking part in this dream. I then threw them the clothes as if I was returning the public part of our story (celebrity having hugely disproportionately amplified the imbalances of our relationship). Naked again, I called my musician friends to join me. This time I was fully myself. I felt deep inner joy and my friends were also overjoyed because they felt the energy of freedom running through us.

Alejandro had told me that the act would only truly be over when I wrote the report. Curiously I waited several months before doing it as if an old part of me refused to leave, afraid of destroying the illusory relationship (but a relationship nevertheless) based on this impossible wait.

Today I no longer wait for my father, I no longer need to exist in his eyes to fully exist, I don't need him to hear me to be able to express myself. I feel that there is always a certain charge of anger in my stomach, but instead of burying it and turning it against myself I can now feel it, express it, and even transform it to make it fertile, creative, so that it awakens me to the energy of life and pushes me toward the world and toward others. I also decided to forgive my parents, to free myself and them from the negative charge of the past and choose to see in them only life and all the love they gave me.

ARTHUR

→ LETTER 19 ←
. . . .
From Amania

Maestro,

Thank you again for your delicious, poetic act that I implemented literally. It was very effective on many levels. I came with the following question: although I am an artist full of creativity, I do not achieve the success and profits that my art deserves.

You gave me the following act: put four gold coins in my anus, hold them there for two days, then release everything, keeping the coins as well as the excrement, then bury them under a lush plant which I would take care of.

It happened as if by chance that the next day I had an appointment for colon hydrotherapy, so I put the coins in a freshly cleaned colon. I really felt like a "golden girl." It was great, not a problem to hold for two days, because that's how long it takes for food to redo the whole route.

My worry was rather whether it would be able to come out. Two days passed, it was the full moon that evening, in the afternoon I went to buy flowers and the florist offered me four blades of wheat (not bad), thank you sir, then the next afternoon I was able to complete the act.

A week later I left on a trip to Colombia and Costa Rica. I always had problems with constipation during my travels, but this has completely disappeared. Today, I am sending my portfolio to a large gallery in Brussels. My wish is that they recognize my work and let it shine. I hope my next mail to you will be an invitation to a gallery opening.

THANK YOU MAESTRO, PURA VIDA.

AMANIA

✢ LETTER 20 ✢
....

From Bertha

I came to see you for a reading concerning my relationship in crisis. We didn't know what to do; despite our work, our theories, nothing worked and we were unhappy and ready to split up. You asked me first if I was satisfied with our sex life. And there you hit the nail on the head, it being an ongoing problem since the birth of our daughter who was now four. I had trouble accepting it. You also told me that the problem was due to the fact that my husband saw me as his mother, and the problem came from him. For that to change I had to transform myself to allow him to see me with new eyes as his wife. You therefore gave me a psychomagic act: have him steal some of his mother's clothing for me to wear while we make love, and then sleep with it all night.

When you suggested this act to me, it was a terrible shock, it couldn't get worse than that and I needed a hell of a lot of courage. It was always a constraint for me (and for my husband) to go to his mother. She's nuts and I find her repulsive. Welcome to the show! She is three times my size and we are not really from the same era. . . . I could not find a better disguise.

When I told my husband about it, he was shocked and upset. We discussed it at length; the work had already begun, we grew very close between laughter and tears. It was very difficult for him because he was on the outs with his mother and seeing her greatly inhibited any desire to "go and steal her panties." His back was against the wall and he concluded that it had to be done as quickly as possible.

Three days later: mission accomplished!

During his absence it was like I was in a trance. I wondered if I would be able to put on this costume, I was very apprehensive; I wanted both to run away and make it happen as soon as possible to get it over with.

When evening came, we knew we had to do it that evening, the sooner the better . . . so I put on the famous costume and was very uncomfortable showing up in this outfit. . . . I quickly wrapped myself in the sheets and then we exploded with a crazy, contagious, demystifying laughter. We made love with a lot of pleasure, with much love and for me with this strange feeling of being in his mother's shoes and seeing him making love with his mother. We did it with such ease that the expectation and idea of doing it were much worse than the act itself. What I didn't anticipate was how hard it would be to spend the night in this costume. After making love and feeling so good, the idea of sleeping with this costume was unbearable. I only wanted to tear it off and snuggle in his arms, return to my identity. He was fine but for me the act wasn't over. . . . I began to cry and he looked at me with so much compassion, with eyes I hadn't seen in him for a long time. I cried with relief. I felt like a little girl in dress-up and he loved me so much.

You know this image is very strong, it was like a dream. The next morning I got up alone and went straight to the bathroom. And there, I experienced the happiness of removing this costume symbolizing his mother, to become a woman again. I was happy to be naked, to have a young body, and I felt beautiful. Removing this costume, I removed the role of mother, because if he saw me like this it was because I was assuming a motherly attitude toward him as well.

Alejandro, thank you from the bottom of my heart. As you told me, we cuddle like a "normal" couple day and night. While he sees me differently, that's even truer for me. This act brought us much closer . . . and also brought him much closer to his mother.

THANKS AGAIN,

BERTHA

✦ LETTER 21 ✦

From Charles

Good morning Alejandro,
I am writing you this letter to explain how things have gone after meeting you a year or so ago.

I had stomach issues since I was twenty-five years old. In recent months they became worse. I suffered nausea, my stomach hurt, and a feeling of anguish invaded my body. I felt very bad, it was chaotic, I did not understand anything and I had suicidal thoughts. In the winter I read your book *Psychomagic* and through a friend I learned where the café you met people was.

I showed up there one Wednesday in September.

When my time came, I sat in front of you and chose three cards. To be honest, at that moment I was having a panic attack. I don't even remember what cards I drew.

You asked me how I was born and I told you that it was a cesarean section. You asked if I had siblings and how they were born. I said I had four brothers, I was the second and they were also born by cesarean. You asked me about my father and I told you he died of cancer (my pains began when my father was sick—I found out before making the trip to Paris). You asked how I got along with him and I told you, "Well . . ." You told me: "Either bad or good! 'Well' in this case does not mean anything. How was your parents' sex life?"

I told you I never thought about it. "Well, think now," you replied.

You grabbed my hands and you said my father was a brute with my mother, that his death was a fair punishment for his behavior. Do you want to heal?

I answered yes. I was supposed to perform the following act of psychomagic in order to heal:

Buy a pétanque* ball, paint it black, dress as a woman, bandage the pétanque ball to my stomach, and stay locked in my house for three days in isolation. At the end of the third day a friend had to come pretending to be a doctor and mark me using lipstick as if I were to have a cesarean section. I had to cut the bandages with scissors and get the ball out; I should force it as if it was resisting. Once the act was finished, I had to take the women's clothes, bandages, and ball, then bury them and plant a tree over it.

The following day I was back home. I had been crying all day, I couldn't help it.

---

*Pétanque is a French-originated boules-type game, similar to bocce.

After the weekend I worked for two days and took three days off to perform the act. In those two days I went shopping for the pétanque ball, which was hard to find. I finally found it in a store in my village. I also bought lipstick and a bandage.

I painted the ball black. It was very heavy.

My girlfriend gave me a dress. She bought it secondhand but it was too big for her. She looked pregnant in it, but it fit me perfectly.

In Paris I asked you, since I lived with my girlfriend, if she would have to leave so I could be alone. You told me that if she didn't laugh and was respectful, she could stay. We live in a house in the countryside, an old farmhouse, with a ground floor and first floor. We decided that during the act we would not see each other. When she got home from work I would be upstairs and we wouldn't see each other until the act was complete.

Over the weekend I contacted my friend. I explained the matter to him and he readily agreed that on Friday afternoon he would be at my house to finish the act. He also told me that the only operation he had ever seen in his life was a cesarean section. The dance of reality?

I was nervous. On Tuesday I shaved, and at 7:45 I took a shower and dressed as a woman. I attached the ball to my stomach with bandages. I ate dinner and went upstairs. I woke up several times at night. The ball bothered me; I slept on my side.

In the morning my legs were cold, as I'm not used to dresses. I put on some sports tights that I bought on sale and they turned out to be for women—I didn't realize that when I bought them. I felt my stomach throbbing as if the ball was alive. This went on for three days. The following day the weather was wonderful and it was getting difficult to remain locked up. I slept quite a bit in the morning and evening during those three days. I could hear my girlfriend coming home from work at sunset.

During those days I looked at the pictures of my family and my brothers when we were little.

At some point I began to cry. I thought of my mother.

I have two dogs and they didn't get what was happening, and why they had to stay inside every day.

Friday afternoon I was nervous. At 7:55 "the doctor" arrived. I left the door open. He came up to the room where I was waiting. He puts on a white coat and gloves. I'm lying in bed with my legs open. He draws lines with the lipstick and begins to cut the bandages. I resist, and he extracts the ball. I cry. I take my clothes off, wrap them up, get dressed, pick up a hoe, and bury the dress and the ball in a nearby meadow and plant the tree. I go back to the house and shake hands with my friend.

I am a gardener so the end of the act seemed wonderful to me. I had a Himalayan oak and I liked it a lot. I didn't know where to plant it but I knew it was meant for something special. I decided to use it for the act.

Though I chose that tree for the psychomagical act I don't know why I picked a maple instead at the last minute and planted it with the clothes in a different spot. A few days after the act I still didn't feel well and I knew something was wrong. I began thinking and realized I'd made a change to my first choice. On Monday I took a hoe, removed the maple, removed the ball and clothes, then reburied them in the place I first chose. I then planted the oak, and *voilà*, the act was done right.

On Thursday I dream that I am inside my mother and a person in white tries to get me out. I resist, I kick, I wake up my girlfriend with a kick, waking up at the same time. We sleep. In the morning she doesn't remember anything but I remember my dream perfectly.

Have I been reborn?

I was feeling very low, and it took a lot to recover my energy. The recovery has been slow.

There is no doubt that I have changed, that I am a different person with different ideas. I no longer like to go out at night, I take care of myself, I have changed the way I eat. Moreover, my girlfriend and I have thought of having children, something we refused to do in the beginning.

My stomachache, that blockage that weighed me down, persecuted me, and didn't let me be myself, has disappeared.

THANKS ALEJANDRO FOR YOUR HELP. BIG HUG.

CHARLES

⇥ LETTER 22 ⇤

From Robert

I came with a friend who absolutely wanted to have her cards read by you. When the numbers were distributed, I was in the bathroom, and when I got back a number was waiting for me. I took it anxiously because I did not have any questions. Suddenly, enlightenment!

"Why do I have pain in my heart?" After looking at all three cards, you told me, "You haven't settled your problem with your mother," and you prescribed an act for me:

With a brush put acacia honey on her tomb and establish a relationship of forgiveness. Take a piece of paper and mark the word "PAIN" with your blood by pricking your finger and sticking this paper on the grave with the honey.

I hadn't visited my mother's grave since her death. I plucked up my courage and went to Briançon. My grandparents were waiting there for me. Two days later I offered to accompany them to my mother's tomb. My grandmother, surprised and moved, accepted with tears in her eyes. My almost-blind grandfather went to get a huge bouquet of flowers. "Here, it's for your mom!" and he started to cry. I took him in my arms and I cried with him, my grandmother too. It was an unforgettable moment for us.

Two days later, I went back alone with my honey pot, brush, paper, and a needle. I knelt in front of her. I spread the honey while experiencing instinctively a bond of peace with her. I pricked my right index finger and I was in a lot of pain but I realized at the same time that the pain I had in my heart was now at my fingertip. The blood began flowing and I wrote PAIN. Oddly, the blood stopped flowing at the last letter. I stuck the paper with honey and I saw my pain outside of me. I was overcome with peace and well-being. I smiled and I began cleaning her grave, sitting on it and caressing her, talking to her. When I left, I had finally regained my *joie de vivre* which hasn't left me since. I no longer feel this pain in the heart. I am well with my mother.

THANKS A LOT.

ROBERT

⇢ LETTER 23 ⇠

From Nelly

Alejandro,

I came to see you at Le Téméraire three months ago, to settle the question that blocks my life the most right now, and has for a long time: struggling to go all the way, to carry out my projects and my relationships until the end, my feeling like I'm always under construction . . .

I was picked to meet you. Throughout the consultation, which was short, you held my hand, so that I understood what you were telling me. I felt heard. We talked about my brothers, children that my parents had. Of the perfection that for me means death, to get to the end of a project is to die . . . the little brother who was born after me who died at birth. He was called Olivier. He became the one who was the perfect child. And this perfection is forbidden to me, for I live. You have given me a complicated act to do, which required some preparation:

I had to buy a bird, a dove to be precise, because my brother was called Olivier. I had to write his name and stick it to one of its legs. Then I was to go to the top of the Arc de Triomphe. There I was to release the bird. Then, up there, I was to get changed completely, with new clothes and a new hairstyle, and come down brand new and have a drink with a friend who would see that I had changed.

But first I had to bury a dead bird that I came across in a garden near my house. I had to bury it, also adding the name of my brother, and say a prayer to him.

This is how it happened: I bought new clothes. Then I went to the hairdresser, who cut my hair short.

On Sunday morning I do the act. It is about 1:00 p.m. when I get dressed. The bag with a change of clothes is ready. I get down and I go to the gardens of the Saint-Louis Hospital to bury the dead bird I found there. I feel weird, as if I'm outside of time. I have a feeling of doing something different from reality. The bird is still there, lying on his back, almost undamaged by death. I cover its little body with the soil that lies right next to it (coincidentally he is surrounded by clay lying there). I place the paper on which is written my brother's name. I get the impression that everything I do is essential, important, magical, fundamental; a basic sense that it's going to change me and rebuild everything differently . . .

Then I take the metro and head to the banks of the Seine to buy the dove. A question bothered my mind: Is the bird that grew up in a cage going to survive newly found freedom? The shop owners tell me everything will be fine. I am not convinced but I buy the dove, I hang the name of my brother inscribed on a paper on the bird's leg, and I take the metro again. It is raining now. It strengthens my concern for the dove's survival.

The Arc de Triomphe: a real adventure. I feel like I'm stepping into a mausoleum. The stone is cold and is full of tourists. The staircase is high and narrow. I feel lost in an unknown territory. I count the steps, then I stop: there are too many. It goes up, higher and higher. I have the impression of climbing toward my liberation as one ascends to the scaffold. The little death that gives great life . . . once up, I get lost. There are forbidden directions, corridors, still no outside terrace. I ask the seller at a souvenir shop for directions. It's at the other end, she tells me. More steps, the bird moves in its box. When I feel this little animal life shaking, I feel guilty for getting it out of his comfortable cage to throw it into the Great Metropolis, his fragile life in a world that is not his, which is neither nature nor heaven. I go around the terrace to find a quiet place. There are still a few scattered tourists, but it's raining harder. We are almost quiet, my bird and I. I find a corner of the roof that suits me. . . . I shiver at the thought of letting the bird go into the void. I look around: the first tree I see is nearer than two kilometers away. Will it get there alive? I grab the cardboard box and take the dove, symbolic of my brother who died at birth. . . . I hold the bird for a long time in the palm of my hand. I feel it flutter, live, breathe, move. His whole life is in my hands. I kiss him, I wish him to live and have a long journey, to convey to my brother that I love him, and then I release it into the sky. He flies away, twirls, is totally frightened, and then he turns to the monument and he comes to take refuge in one of the carved corners. I stay there for a few moments, then I go back out, light-headed. . . . I try to feel the transformation, but I can't feel anything yet. I stop on the top floor, heading toward the toilets or where I'm about to get changed. The place is beautiful and vast. There is a large mirror between the two sets of toilet doors (as if on purpose, since one was needed to observe the change). That done, I sit on the bench in front of the mirror to put on my new shoes. The heels are too high. The descent is vertiginous, perched on these high heels. At last, I exit. I try to catch how people look at me: nothing has really changed! It's still raining a lot. I head for the metro.

Once at the Blanche station, I bump into an actor friend, it's crazy! We chat for a while in the station. We are both soaked. I don't dare to offer to have a drink together as he seems in a hurry. We exchange our numbers. It seems I have changed. I talk to him about my radio show. He listens to me carefully. He's a bit overwhelmed, and he wants to send me some music. I have changed. He looks at me beautifully!

That's it, the act is over. I will come back.

See you soon, maybe pregnant.

THANKS,
NELLY

⇥ LETTER 24 ⇤

From Sergio

Dear Jodo:

During my trip to France I asked you for a psychomagic act because I have vitiligo, a disease that depigments the skin. When my mother and I went to live with her boyfriend and his son, coexistence was very hard and uncomfortable and the anguish led to parts of my skin losing pigmentation: I began turning part-albino.

I always carried a terrible hatred towards my mother's partner, long after they separated.

Many years later I met him on the street by chance. I first meant to hit him, compacting all my resentment in the force of a punch, but I ended up using that energy to give him a big hug, one I never got from him. I considered myself mentally cured of the disease, but the stains on my body were still there. You asked me about the disease, to which I replied that the spots could grow, and new ones could appear. You asked me what was serious about that, to which I replied if the disease took over it could turn me completely albino. You asked me what the problem was with that, and I didn't know how to answer.

The act you prescribed for me consisted of going out dressed only in shorts with my whole body painted white. I had to walk around, go get an ice cream or something, and at the end of the tour, my girlfriend had to take a picture of me naked which later I would hang in the living room of my house.

With a scant bathing suit, as white as the rest of my body, I went for a walk down the street in the neighborhood. A policeman, seeing me pass, touched his forehead with his index finger. Except the policeman, people took it very well: a drunk greeted me shouting and I answered him the same way, and some workers who were having lunch in the street celebrated my appearance, and I celebrated their lunch. Later, for the climax, I entered the pedestrian Florida Street, downtown, surrounded by a crowd of people who came and went running errands, and tourists.

I passed by a norteño* band playing in the Street. The guitarist yelled at me: "Me too, I want to be white." A man wanted to know if I was holding my bachelor party. Many pretended poorly to seem

---

*Norteño is a regional Mexican musical genre.

indifferent. When I got back home, my girlfriend took a picture of me completely naked, the one I will frame and hang in my living room.

Then I took a bath to get rid of the makeup with my girlfriend's help. I watched as the paint faded away and my own color came back. Now the stains don't look like expanding albino tumors, but as small white islands dominated by skin-colored surface that keeps them contained.

The act did me a lot of good. I'm much more in love, without fear of vitiligo because both my girlfriend and I accept it with compassion.

SERGIO

✈ LETTER 25 ✦

From Emmanuelle

Dear Alejandro,

I went to see you on March 15. I was passing through Paris. When I told you that I am Portuguese, you gave me a copy of your book in Portuguese: I loved your book and I am very happy to have a copy with a dedication. I had just passed by my publisher to buy my book, *Teenage Sexualities,* so to thank you for your gift, I gave you a copy of. My question was "how to trust myself in my professional life." You told me everything in a few sentences. The problem, in fact, was not a mystery to me: my mother is castrating and invasive, she prevents me from being a whole person. I had to buy a big rope, tie myself and my mother with it, then ask her to cut it. I had to keep half and give her the other half, letting her do what she wants with it. Then I had to put my part of the rope at the bottom of a pot and plant something in it. I did not know how to carry out my act: it seemed difficult because I didn't want to have to explain what I was doing, and there might be a problem with the rope size, because if it was too big, it would be difficult to cut. I ended up buying a random rope, telling myself that the important thing was to cut, symbolically. The rope that I bought was white and was five meters long. I didn't show anything to anyone, especially not my husband, who would have thought I was crazy. I was going to my parents' for the weekend. I believe it was during Easter. I still wasn't sure how to go about it but I knew I had to.

It was April 17. It was late and only my mother was still up, busy with household chores. She was waiting for the washing machine to finish so she could hang out the laundry. I told myself, "It's now or never." I had tried to cut the rope with secateurs earlier in the afternoon but in the end it worked better with simple scissors. I passed the rope around her and me and I asked her to cut it. She went with it without saying anything. Then she asked, "What is it for?" I replied, "Well, for example, to jump rope." My answer made no sense because due to her two different disabilities (feet and eyes) she cannot, among other things, jump. Nevertheless, she simply replied, "I can't because of my foot problem and my eye problem." She kept her part of the rope, without me having to ask. She carefully rolled it up and put it in the pocket of her blouse. The simplicity of the act impressed me. I don't know what she did with her rope. On my way home, I ran by several florists looking for a bulb to plant. I walked almost all morning looking for a bulb. Finally, I found a store selling them. It was close to the store where I bought the rope, by the way. The saleswoman was very friendly. I bought freesia bulbs. I like small, simple flowers. To be honest, I didn't remember if it should be a flowering plant, but I knew I had to grow a plant. I didn't plant it that day. I waited until I was able to buy potting soil. I was afraid it wouldn't grow so I used two of them. I planted two bulbs in a vase. Then I wondered if this impulse wasn't related to the fact that I have a twin sister. We are dizygotic and completely different. But we have always been close in one way or another. One of the plants sprouted first, one week before the next one did, which ended up catching up with the first one in the end. They did not flower, it was past their time, but they can still bloom next spring. I felt the first effects of my act the same week. My mother spent a week without calling me. I was very happy to feel the change. Since then, my relationship with her has been much more serene. Today, it was my first day of school since the first half of the last year, so since February. I believe that for the first time I went to class without having a lump in my belly, without being anxious and afraid. Today is October 20, 2006. I thank you very much and I send you kisses with friendship and gratitude.

EMMANUELLE

✦ LETTER 26 ✦

From Jules (thirty-eight years old)

Alejandro,

As agreed I am sending you my report of the psychomagical act that you gave me at the café. When I came to Le Téméraire I felt my number wouldn't be picked. I didn't believe it or didn't want to, and this was the case, but my neighbor gave me her number. She felt she had to give it to me.

In front of the cards I summed up my family situation for you: I hated my nervous father yelling at my grandmother. She was jealous of my mother, who threatened her with death by a madman whom she was taking care of as a social worker. Since I left my parents on a whim at eighteen, I live on financial support and stay more or less isolated from society, self-centered and in pieces, while I dream of being a famous actor. And I manage to be ignored by girls.

You told me: "Change one hundred euros into one-cent coins and on the Fontaine des Innocents, disguised as a policeman, give out a handful of pennies to passersby telling them, 'It's publicity for the police, we are good in the police.' Then you'll be stronger than your father who prevented your relationship with your mother. You will make your dream come true of being an actor, and you will protect your mother."

I was putting off performing this act and overthinking things. At the Fontaine des Innocents, there are a lot of guys from the suburbs, often in conflict with authority. Is my ad for the police not going to provoke, annoy them . . . ? And then there is a police station: I could be arrested for being disguised, or be taken for a bank robber? In short, all the endless questions of the overthinker.

I call a costume rental company in Paris but their prices are high and they want permission from the prefecture. Its competitor, on the other hand, is owned by Indians and their shop is called "Laughing Out Loud." With a name like that, they had a reasonable price and did not ask for permission. What's more, their costumes are real, because they are provided by the police.

Visiting Paris, while waiting for a train to Montparnasse (I live in Rennes), I decide to get a jump-start and change one hundred euros at the BNP in front of the train station. The cashier tells me, "You are my savior, it's been years that I've had this stash in my closet." I end up with twenty-four kilos of small coins in tear-able bags, it's heavy, it looks like it's going to break, and I drag myself to the platform, to the last carriage. (I just spent two months in China with plenty of luggage and I was always in the last carriage. Anyway . . .) Once at my place I keep overthinking. How could I manage to hand out ten thousand coins no one would want because of their insignificant value, and what's more, twenty-four kilos . . . ? The night before the act, I heard on the radio that Brussels plans to remove the one-cent coins, deemed embarrassing. You told me to put the money in a golden bag and take handfuls out of it. I find a suitcase with a golden lining brought back from my first trip to China. I unpack all the rolls into it, the ten thousand coins. The day before the act I go to my bank in the afternoon to change all these coins into ten cents, but they refuse. Same in Banque de France, so I come back to my bank and deposit the twenty-four kilos into my account. They cannot refuse. However, I have to roll them back up. In various banks I then change one hundred euros into coins of ten centimes, which seems to me more reassuring and plausible. The next morning, Wednesday, I rent the cop costume in Paris and go to the Fontaine des Innocents where Elvie (who offered me her number for a tarot draw) and her boyfriend are waiting for me. I give them a backpack with my clothes because I changed quickly as I approached the square. The streets are still quiet and I want to retreat, especially when I see my reflection with the police cap. I approach a woman, a group of Japanese people, without daring to speak to them, and I begin. I get rid of everything in less than an hour.

I was fast, I went to see everyone, and was not treated with hostility, especially not by those from abroad who were happy to receive the money and thought the police were cool. Some didn't want to take any-thing, especially women. Elvie and her boyfriend were waiting for me, watching me from the café terrace of Cœur Couronné. They told the waiter that I was celebrating my arrival and my transfer in the police, and I approved. After the act I found that the cop costume fit me well and I felt the desire to buy myself a suit jacket to get out of adoles-cence (even if I am thirty-eight years old). In the afternoon I went to Le Téméraire and you told me, with knowing anything of this desire: "Buy yourself a beautiful suit and wash yourself seven times, the whole body, then put on this suit and you are done with the past, you are new."

TEN THOUSAND THANKS,

JULES

⇥ LETTER 27 ⇤

From Nathalie

The Psychomagical Act:
One evening, I have to put a photo of my mother on a t-shirt. Thomas, my companion, must wear it the entire night. He must put condensed milk in a bottle and let me suck it while he rocks me in his arms. ("Be careful that his arms support your spine well and that you see your mom's picture.") Then I have to turn and he has to tell my back, "I love you, I love you . . ." while kissing the parts where it hurts, all the way down the spine.

I agreed with my companion on a date for the act of psychomagic that you prescribed on March 14, 2009. We had an appointment at 10:00 p.m. in our room. I bought a white long-sleeved t-shirt, condensed milk, and a bottle. I did not have any picture of my mother where she was all alone except for a photo ID from when she was twenty. I enlarged it and stuck it on the t-shirt. I must say the result was not bad at all! At 9:50 p.m., Thomas started preparing the bottle. Then he put on the t-shirt. We had trouble finding a satisfactory position that would both support my spine well and allow me to see my mother's face clearly at the same time.

We alternated throughout the night in different positions so that each of us, especially Thomas, could relax our legs and back a little. In any case, from the first glances of my mother, and the feelings of being held in my back, I felt good. It was a simple feeling of well-being with no thought, as the newborn must feel while feeding. I watched her for hours, sometimes with one eye open, and the other closed, eyes blinking to see if she was still present. I was like, "Mommy is here." Regularly rocking me gave the reassuring feeling that she took care of me. I felt safe. The bottle was nice, sweet, and warm. I had everything I needed! I liked the feeling in my mouth and in my digestive tract.

After the first two hours and because our extremities were numb we decided that Thomas would say, "I love you, I love you" to my back, because the advice was not clear to me anymore: should we change or wait for the end of the night? We gave it a try.

It was powerful for me, an acknowledgment. But at the same time, my intuition was telling me that we had to wait until the end of the act. . . .

The night continued with the rocking, looking at my mother, baby bottles, sleepiness, changes of positions . . . depending on where I was, I found her sad, calm, kind, loving.

At 5:00 a.m. Thomas was exhausted and aching all over. Since he had rocked me from 10:00 p.m. to 5:00 a.m., it had been seven hours, and given the difficulties of the required posture, we found this satisfying. So much so that I turned over and lay on the stomach. For a couple of minutes Thomas kissed my entire spine from top to bottom, saying, "I love you, I love you . . ." I felt good and relaxed. I don't have very precise memories, other than a lot of fatigue. Then we fell asleep. A few hours later I woke up because I needed to go to the bathroom and I had pain in my belly.

I got up and realized that my period had started (even though I thought they were finished . . .) It was extremely violent.

Then touching my lower back, I found that it was extraordinarily straight while most of the time I'm arched. As I lay back down, I felt energy circulating between my head and my tailbone down to my legs. A sentence came to me: "I accept the change. I change profoundly."

The more I told myself that, the more I felt vibrations inside.

I spent two strange days where I was in pain because my period was very strong, and at the same time I had a new feeling of freshness in the middle of my back.

Since then, I no longer have a backache. I don't have this feeling of oppression anymore on the sternum level despite the still-rounded shape in the middle of my back.

Thank you, it changed my life and my quality of presence. It's really unbelievable to me!

I am very grateful for the benefits and the support you have offered me. It's a very beautiful gift, very precious.

Sincerely,

Nathalie

✦ LETTER 28 ✦

From André

Sir,

A few months ago you gave me a homeopathic psychomagical act. Here are the results. It was a matter of taking two vessels and sticking a photo of my father on one and a photo of my mother on the other. In the paternal bottle I had to put a photocopy of the paternal picture and some brandy. In the maternal vial, I had to put some virgin olive oil and a copy of the maternal image.

Every morning I added ten drops of each of the two solutions to my tea or coffee.

At the same time, and in accordance with your prescription, I bought a pair of new dress shoes. Every day I would stick a gold leaf in the right one and a silver leaf in the left one (depending on the wear of the soles, of course).

The results of this psychomagic "prescription" are as follows. I must say that with the hindsight of these last months, I had kept a child-ish side, adopting the dress codes and communication of a teenager. Now I have the impression of having aged. I feel more mature, more responsible, and I dress like someone my age—at least not like an older teenager anymore. In connection with this, I have integrated a deeper realism in my behavior. I take responsibility for my choices to make life as gentle as possible. It's still not always completely perfect, but I have changed a lot. I have also incorporated a positive parental dimension without deluding myself—the good side of the tree; we are here also thanks to it!

Another significant change: I got into a relationship with a woman. This relationship is not at all easy, but as you said, the couple is also a series of crises. Not that I haven't had a relationship before, but this time I feel different. Finally, I launched several creative projects: the regular writing of poems where I learn not to judge myself, as well as work on a novel adaptation for the cinema, which is my current big project. Between the tarot and the singing that I started again, my time is well filled and I feel like a different man, like a lizard that left his old skin behind. I thank you for your help in these different projects. I remain eternally indebted to you and thank heaven for allowing us to have easy access to such a wealth of knowledge and of wisdom.

THANK YOU WITH ALL MY HEART.

ANDRÉ

✢ LETTER 29 ✢

From Julie

My act of psychomagic:
December 23, 2004, 1:00 p.m., Bagneux Cemetery, Paris suburb.

When I went to bed the night before, I spread marzipan on my chest. It became one with me, and I slept with it as best I could, which was rather badly in fact. Upon waking I needed a moment to collect myself; everything was stuck together (as in my life's beginning . . .). I made a marzipan baby with a face, eyes, mouth, and the sketch of a nose. I was into it because my feelings were intense. I wrapped it in aluminum and made sure to acquire some more soil.

The cemetery was extremely quiet that day, just before Christmas, a gray day with the threat of rain. I removed the rather large planter which adorns the tomb of my parents, then dug a place to bury the marzipan baby, my sister unknown to me until the age of eleven. Then I added some fresh soil and put back the ornamental shrubs.

In a soft voice I pronounce these words: "I give you back your dead child, it's yours, I no longer carry it." What I experience in my body is a feeling of loneliness, abandonment, a great internal void, an uninhabited space. Death, half-death, at this moment all I have left is me. I have to meet myself; my intuition tells me that I won't have to visit this grave anymore (these are the words—"no longer obliged to"—that I hear). As a young teenager I would often walk in this cemetery without knowing that my parents would be buried there one day.

Around me every tree, every tomb has changed proportions: everything has become smaller, human-size; the place seems bare to me, simple and calm, no longer charged with the same emotions. The colors are slightly different, brighter. I wake up from a bad dream.

Seven days later I find that I have suddenly developed eczema on the right elbow. I only previously had it twice in my life: the first time when my mother weaned me and the second time after a breakup. This eczema disappeared on its own within a month without any treatment.

The beauty and simplicity of the act that you suggested to me deeply moved me; I also believe that it bears a more potent dimension of which I only caught a glimpse for now: to part ways but with love.

Performing this act made me essentially experience a shift of perspective.

I'm sure that the immediate, sensitive, very present understanding you expressed about my personal story allowed me to receive this tarot reading at a deep level.

THANK YOU,
JULIE

⇥ LETTER 30 ⇤
....

From Emmanuelle (thirty-five years old)

Mr. Jodorowsky,

When I came to Le Téméraire in April, my question was: "Why can't I make a living? I am often unemployed, I am never satisfied at work." The draw revealed that I was still a child. You told me: "The child does not earn money, it receives it."

My parents remained children in the same way. I know my grandparents would always help my parents financially. As a result, the act consisted of leaving a fifty-euro banknote with honey on my grandparents' grave, telling them that this money belonged to them, thanking them, but telling them now I wanted to make my own.

I went to Nîmes and Bordeaux. I had been unemployed for several months. I took advantage of this time to take stock without actively looking for a new job. Two weeks ago I was about to return from vacation with the intention to seriously explore job offers and update my CV.

The day before my return to Paris a cousin called me to offer me a job in her company—an interesting and well-paid position for an international brand. I immediately responded to the offer, I had an interview with the director, and I was hired.

I didn't even have time to look for a job. It arrived on a silver platter. . . .

The same day I received my tax notice. This is the first time that I paid taxes—not very much, but for me it's symbolic. I'm almost thirty-six years old. . . .

Thank you for your presence and your attention.

ALL THE BEST,

EMMANUELLE

↦ LETTER 31 ↤
....

From Marisol

Last year I participated in a workshop led by Alejandro Jodorowsky in the literary café and I was fortunate to be chosen from the audience for an analysis of my family tree. From that, Alejandro designed an act for me that I did a couple of months later . . . it had to do with my father who disappeared seven months after I was born and never returned to my life.

The experience was impressive and touching.

The design of the act was seemingly simple: I had to travel to the city where my father is buried, wash his tomb, and write the word "LOVE" on it with honey.

To fulfill it I began to research how could I get to Caleta Olivia in Argentina, where he died and was buried. . . . I found out that My father had been thrown into a mass grave, that he died an alcoholic, alone and poor. In the face of difficulty, I modified the act. . . . My intuition told me that what mattered was the act itself. My father could just as well be represented by any grave, anywhere. I decided to go to a general cemetery and look for a tomb which at least coincided with his date of birth. One Saturday morning, I prepared my tools: two large plastic bottles, one with water and a little bit of detergent, the other one with just water; a broom; and a jar with honey and flowers.

I arrived at the cemetery and entered carrying all my implements. Every step of the way my heart beat harder and faster. I didn't think about anything, just felt a deep sorrow that made me cry like a girl lost among that crowd of the dead. As I was approaching the idea of the date of birth faded and another appeared. . . . It would be my father who would guide my steps toward him. I walked and walked, I took narrow paths accompanied by my tears and my sorrow, my pain, my emotion; suddenly under a tree about fifty meters in front of me, I spotted a gray cement tombstone with the grave made of the same material . . . that's it, I thought. I moved closer and was surprised by two details: The appearance of the grave gave the feeling that with any luck this gentleman would be accompanied by the date of his burial. It was altogether abandoned and completely uncared for despite being a costly structure. . . . The second detail was that on the tombstone was only a name "Francisco delle Piano," no date of birth or death, nor a RIP . . . nothing at all. I did my task in the midst of crying and an internal conversation with my father came up spontaneously. . . . Why did you leave me? Did you ever think of me? Would you have liked to meet me? Never before in my life did these questions come to me, at least on a conscious level. The grave was gleaming, the questions were cleared with water that washed away the remaining soil as a sign of abandonment along with my pain. I left the flowers, wrote "LOVE," and also wrote my father's name with honey on the tombstone. A feeling of total peace came over me. I returned home and slept until the next day. I had the impression of having been tired all my life until this day. . . .

I know that my whole emotional structure changed that day. I have become more gentle, peaceful, serene, more sure of myself. If I ever think of my father, what I see is that tomb.

What I feel is that now I know much more who I am.

I need Alejandro to know this in order to continue to heal.

ONCE AGAIN, THANK YOU VERY MUCH.

MARISOL

⇥ LETTER 32 ⇤

From Fernando (thirty-seven years old)

Dear Alejandro:

Last January the 5th, I visited Paris with the intention of having a consultation with you in the café which you attend every Wednesday. My purpose was to find a remedy for my illness, a cure.

Since puberty (I am now thirty-seven years old) I've suffered from a skin disease called seborrheic dermatitis, in my case quite intense. I tried many therapies without visible results. I needed something pivotal, because my desperation was tremendous; I was on the brink of the abyss. I couldn't stand the tremendous itching anymore, the redness of my face, the scabs that form on my face and head. Since I learned about psychomagic I thought it could help me. I got a consultation with you Wednesday, January 5. They gave me number 5. In the tarot appeared the Hermit, Justice, and Judgment. We talked about my parents. My father died of cancer eighteen years ago and my mother is an absolutely sardonic woman (sometimes called "the sergeant"). You told me that my mother, after having castrated my father, began doing the same to me. On the other hand I don't have a virile paternal role model.

You told me that what I have is rage toward my mother and lack of virility, and that you could give me a psychomagic act that could heal me. I listened, absolutely absorbed, absolutely open to experience. My partner María José accompanied me to my right. The act that you prescribed me is as follows:

The first thing I have to do is to tell my mother that I went to see you, explain who you are, how you work, and that she has to help to heal me; I have to ask her for collaboration in everything I have to accomplish.

Then I have to tie her to a chair with a cotton rope—"the kind used in the cinema," you said—to not hurt her hands and feet. After tying her up I should have a fit of rage in front of her without a warning; I must scream and kick. I have to carry golden chocolate coins in my jacket pocket and throw them at her. I should wear one more coin in a bag tied at the height of my sex—I have to take it out, remove the gold paper, and put it in her mouth to eat it. Then I must untie her and kiss and hug her. Finally enters my companion María José with three dozen red roses to offer them to my mother.

Once it's done I must drive to my father's grave and during the journey I have to drink three beers without stopping to pee. Upon arrival, I must pee on my father's grave and immediately leave him three dozen white roses as a symbol of purity.

From the moment I decided to travel to Paris I sensed that what was really needed was an act of psychomagic, and lo and behold, I have done it. As soon as I returned from Paris I fell sick; flu like never before had come over me. The key word seemed to be rage. I felt anger toward everyone and all very skin deep. On the other hand that time in bed helped me understand that the psychomagical act was inevitable. I remained very hopeful.

My mother lives in a small town twenty-eight kilometers from Salamanca. On the day I visited I told her the first thing that you told me: I told her about my trip to Paris, about you, and roughly what psychomagic consists of. I also told her that I needed to do something with her and I asked her to help me. At no moment she refused; what's more, she seemed open, yes, maybe a little scared in the face of uncertainty of what was coming. "Oh Mother! What is he going to ask me to do?!" she said, but at no point did she refuse. This was a few days in advance; I was already preparing the ground. I decided to do the rest on the January 28 and 29—the 28th for my mother, the 29th for my dad.

First I bought the gold coins. I thought about buying three dozen too but it didn't seem enough so I ended up buying fifty. I also bought the rope. I hesitated at first about where to get it, but then I had no difficulty deciding. I bought twenty-five meters just in case. I ordered the roses, the red and the white ones. Interestingly, at that moment it started to snow and got very cold.

It seemed like a great omen to wrap it up that weekend. The roses were sold in packs of twenty, so I bought two packages of red and two of white. I would have four of each left. On the appointed day I prepared myself mentally. We went to perform the act in my mother's house, in one of her rooms at six in the evening. I did everything to the letter. I dressed in a maroon jacket and prepared the coins for the jacket and for the little bag. Before going to my mother's house María José and I stopped by the florist's to pick up the roses. We decided María José would buy them, because that part of the act was hers. As there were forty of them, we put aside four to keep a bouquet of three dozen. I was nervous at that time.

My mother allowed herself to be tied up; she was totally submissive, like a little lamb—really astonishing. I took quite a few minutes to tie her up; I wanted to be sure. Even then she kept giving me orders, she wouldn't stop! "Pass the rope through here, pass it over there." The hardest thing for me was to start screaming, to show a fit of rage, but I forced a coarse scream; then everything went by itself. I screamed, I hit the sofa and the wall, I hurt my hand. I threw the scarf and a jacket against the floor. I kicked hard. I lost track of time; I don't know how long it lasted.

At some point I looked at my mother, she was scared. She had a gesture of disapproval, of not wanting to look. I also threw a pair of scissors and the glass cleaner. She did not say anything.

Then I started throwing the gold coins at her that I carried in the pocket of my jacket; one stayed on her head, some on her lap, others on the ground. Then I gave her the one I wore near my sex to eat. She didn't say anything. I untied her, hugged her, and kissed her. She said several times: "May God heal you!" She was still sitting on the chair. Then María José entered with the three dozen roses and handed them to her. She asked why we had to bother with so many roses. I asked her how she felt, especially if she was scared during my fit of rage. She did not acknowledge it but I knew she was. Despite that she had collaborated in everything; she even went so far as to say: "You could have punched me."

And so that part of the act ended; I thank her. She seemed to be in a more relaxed mood now, softer, and she was nicer to us. I ended up very tired and with a sore throat from screaming.

That rage so ingrained in me that comes out so often in certain situations did not disappear. That night I could feel it again, at home, in everyday things. It was still there, on the surface. Sometimes I imagine that it transforms into roses, into the roses of my face, just like it transformed into real roses during the act. It transforms into red roses with their thorns.

The whole act lasted half an hour. During that half hour time stopped, like it did in Paris. The temporal dimension seems to have distorted; it was like an unimaginable dream. I felt that a gap had been created, a fracture in reality so that something else could emerge, so that the possibility of the unthinkable could manifest.

The next day, the 29th, I performed the final part of the act.

My father is buried in Bilbao, four hundred kilometers from Salamanca, which means a three-to-four-hour drive. Days before I spoke on the phone with the cemetery undertaker to get the location of the tomb and the opening hours of the cemetery. It had been a long time since I went to visit it; I had only been a couple of times. My father is buried in a niche, that is, on a wall, with the number 425 if I remember correctly. I decided to perform the act at noon, when the undertaker was absent and probably an hour with few visitors. So I left Salamanca together with María José and with the white roses that I bought just before leaving. I also carried Five Star Mahou beers.

I love to drive so there was no problem. I tried to drink the beers slowly as I wasn't accustomed to drinking.

We left Salamanca at ten in the morning and the trip lasted three and a half hours. During the journey and between beers I ate some bread to make it more bearable. I finished the last beer just as we arrived at the small town, called San Miguel, where the cemetery is (curiously San Miguel is also another brand of beer). Little by little I was noticing the effect of the alcohol at the same time as my bladder was filling up progressively. As I drove, the scenery began to change; it was snowing. Everything turned white; alcohol, beers, and snow on the road, a strange mixture, like a surreal, wonderful dream. I arrived at San Miguel just in time with a bursting bladder. I got out of the car immediately and searched for the niche of my father. I found it quickly. Luckily he was in the wall but on the lowest row. My father's place is covered by a dark-gray marble tombstone with his name, the date of his death, and a picture of Christ. I urinated there, spraying all over the stone. It was a long clean pee; I don't know how long it lasted. I pulled out my penis well to show off my manhood, to show it to my dad.

There was no one there; I only saw a woman with her daughter heading to the exit as I went up to my dad's grave. While urinating, from time to time I glanced out of the corner of my eye in case someone appeared; only a few dogs barked outside the cemetery grounds, near where I was. By the time I finished the dogs seemed to shut up. It was a liberating piss. The urine mixed with the water that was in the soil due to recent rains.

When I finished I went back to the car for the roses and placed all three dozen in three vases, two plastic ones that I brought and one glass one that I found empty. Dogs started barking again. After I was silent for a while, remembering my father and wishing him all the best. It was cold and no one was there. I went back to the car and caught up with María José.

Like I said before, I had four red and four white roses left. I gave one of the red ones to María José and the rest I gave to three young girls who were chatting next to the gate of my house. They were very surprised but appreciated the gesture. I left the white ones on my grandmother's grave, in the same cemetery where my dad is buried. My grandmother was called Gabriela. I looked for her grave and stuck the roses into the earth, next to her cross, two on one side and two to the other.

We stayed one night in Bilbao, the city where I was born. From our hotel we went downtown taking a street called Zabalbide, which I think means "open road." In the hotel room there were two pictures with two tulips, one yellow for day and another white for night, as if yin and yang—complete, balanced. In front of our bed there was another larger painting with sunflowers.

And there the act ends. Some things have changed.

My skin improved a lot during the weeks after the act. For nearly two months I have felt almost, almost, almost on the brink of healing. I feel full, open, and trusting, a feeling that keeps growing. My skin has practically cleared up.

My mother seems to respect me more; it's like she somehow understood that healing was also up to her. Despite this it still takes a lot for me to love her. There's something like a repulsion ingrained in me; to touch her and give her a kiss is difficult for me.

Is the act I performed a seed planted inside me, unaware that one day it will bear fruit, or is there something else I can do? In any case, thank you very much for magic and for the opportunity.

HUGS,

FERNANDO

→ LETTER 33 ←

From Rosalie (forty-three years old)

Goal of the act: I come from a family of finally divorced parents who kept on arguing and maintaining a heavy and unbreathable atmosphere for my brother and me. My mother, a lover wronged, kept getting rejected by my father and expressed her suffering in every form of somatization. I became her mother very quickly, seeing myself obliged to care for her, to listen to her confessions, to cook when she slept in, or care for her migraines. . . . Her work kept her away from home until very late at night and in the morning I had to shake her awake (she adjusted her biorhythm with sleeping pills and amphetamines). My father had moods and could sometimes be violent. However, spending fewer hours out than my mother, he was the one who took care of us most and in the absence of my mother, he was much nicer.

It was when she was there that he became irritable and we had to walk on eggshells. When I became a teenager he used me against her by stimulating my oedipal feeling in an exaggerated way. I became his tool of revenge. Of course, both in their "parental spirit" felt the duty to prepare me for my future love life. It looked roughly like this:

My mother: "Above all, don't act like me, let them desire you, play hard to get. Be cold, distant, never say what you think, and if you're in love, don't show it."

My father: "At least you are not like your mother; I could get along with a woman like you. Do not get married, have lovers, have fun. . . ."

As children, we had to ask for forgiveness for existing, as their life revolved around problems with their relationship and they were literally obsessed with each other. We were even forbidden to cry. They counted to three—on three, it was the slap. At three years old, I already "controlled" my emotions; you had to behave, to not disturb.

As an adult, despite years of self-work, I still couldn't find a workable way between these two extremes. The weakness and the vulnerability that I felt every time I approached my femininity made me jump straight into the opposite pole, my father's model. So I wanted to perform a psychomagical act that would balance the masculine and the feminine inside me and give me back the childhood they stole from me.

The act: I would arrange a meeting with my parents in a neutral place. I would explain to them what my life with them meant for me as a child and then as an adult. I would give them each a pot of water in which I would have poured a few tears, saying: "Here are the tears of a child that I had to cry as an adult."

I would dress up as a little girl and I would go with them hand in hand to spend an afternoon (so that they would symbolically give me back the childhood that they stole from me by forcing me to be their mother). We would go to Waterloo, to the Lion's Mound, at whose feet I would ask them to get married inside of me.

I would climb alone to the top where I would release a dove over the battlefield (thus ending the war between the sexes, Napoleon representing this anti-feminine force). I would then put on normal clothes and go and bury with them this little girl after urinating on it. There I would plant a beautiful tree that I would ask them to water with my tears.

Procedure of the act: I flew to Brussels, rented a car, and settled in a hotel. Immediately, I started looking for everything I needed to perform the act. It took me a day and a half. It was not at all easy to find the dove. I also went to Waterloo as a scout because I didn't know the place at all (while I was plugged into the conception of my act, I saw myself releasing a dove on the Lion's Mound; I went there once with my grandparents when I was little). Then I called my parents. Not easy to locate them either, even harder to agree on a day and time (let's not forget that they are divorced and were not especially pleased to see each other again), but the concern that my sudden arrival caused played in my favor. We made an appointment for two days later. Of course everyone tried to lure me home but I would see them together or not at all. This wait to me seemed endless. I wanted to relax but it was impossible, I was very anxious (were they going to agree to carry out this act which would seem crazy to them?), and I fell sick: fever, sore throat, a day in bed.

As expected, my father arrived way in advance and tried to pry information from me before my mother arrived. I explained to him that I wanted to talk to both of them. Throughout the act, I would often have to stop my father who wanted to do something alone with me under the pretext of my mother's health.

I invite them to the room I rented and there calmly explain to each of them all that I have to reproach them for, what my life as a child was, and all the problems I still have now because of this experience. They listen to me carefully, trying to justify themselves from time to time to which I answer that it is about my experience. I see that for my mother it is much more difficult to accept. At some point my father gets up in tears, begging me for forgiveness. He also wishes my brother could one day do the same and break free of everything he did to him. I give them each a pot of my tears and immediately they begin to cry. I then dress up as a little girl and say that I want to spend the afternoon with them in these regalia so that they can give me back the childhood they stole from me. They collaborate perfectly. During the few hours of our walk, I play the difficult, capricious child and ask them to do things like play with me, sing. . . . In a store, I ask them to buy me a pendant in the shape of an eagle. Then we go to the Lion's Mound and there it's a very moving moment. I sit in the middle of them both, take their hands, and solemnly request:

"Jeanine, do you take Jackie to be your husband inside of me?"

"I do."

"Jackie, do you take Jeanine to be your wife inside of me?"

"I do."

I kiss them both, take my dove, and begin the long climb to the top of the lion, asking them to watch. Once on top, I take the dove and caress it a little before letting go. Surprise! The little dove does not want to fly away. It's a shock and straight away I understand that she expresses all the reluctance of my unconscious. So I start talking to the dove and I explain to her that from now on she is free, that at the beginning everything may seem surprising and difficult to her, but everything will work out well. I reassure her but nothing works. I therefore decide to leave, telling her that the ball is now in her court. I go back down, go to change, and we go to a nearby wood to bury the clothes. (I would have liked to bury them on the battlefield but my mother can no longer walk that far.) My father digs the hole with me because the ground is very, very hard. I urinate on the clothes, plant a very beautiful tree, and ask my parents to water it with my tears, which they seem to do with pleasure. Afterward I drive them back to the station.

They would like to spend the evening together but I refuse (I only wanted to see them within the framework of the act). I spent the evening with my brother and told him what I had just done with our parents. He was very moved. It's worth knowing that my brother and I saw each other maybe five times in eighteen years. That evening we talked like never before. It was extraordinary, miraculous! Going back to Spain I felt sad, and I still felt this ever-present bitter taste of a thought that anything positive only happens in my life through the masculine (my father, as on numerous occasions in my life, had shown himself much more cooperative and allowed himself to be moved).

On the plane, I spot a young black woman whom I met several times in Brussels. At the exit, she asks me to take a picture of her and also wants to take a picture of me. She has a rather carefree and casual look. I ask her if she lives in Madrid; she replies that she is passing through to Libreville, where she lives. She adds, "I will show your picture to all my friends." I saw in it a wink; the magic was working in my unconscious. A woman completely opposite to what I am was in the process of breaking free. Since then I have often thought about what Alejandro teaches about forgiveness—that is, that you have to forgive but you also have to know how to ask for forgiveness for leaving this "emotional collective."

I took two months to really understand what that meant, two months during which I still felt bad, held back by, I believe, an immense feeling of guilt.

One day while driving, while I was listening to the radio and singing a song—"Por ti volaré"—and while feeling sad to see how I was still aggressive with my mother, I suddenly reviewed a scene from my childhood where, from the top of the stairs, I threw myself with confidence into the arms of my mother, who was downstairs. I understood that this act was not suicidal, which is what I always thought. I felt that I invested heavily in my mother, with a quest that no human being can fill: that of replacing my soul. I still resented her for not having been able to complete this impossible mission. I hated her because I loved her with an insane love like no other. I cried for hours and hours and the more I shed tears, the clearer everything became. I was finally able to write to her and explain that the frustration caused by our relationship had been the most powerful force in my spiritual search.

I asked her for forgiveness for having often caused her suffering and for leaving to finally find my home. I also wrote to my father and told him that the explosive duo that they made had propelled me into the group of humans who have no other choice but to look for new means for men and women to get along. I thanked them for being my greatest weakness and my greatest strength. I had never been so far and so close. I no longer felt any aggression. I was free. Since then, my relationship with them has been sweeter, I can finally resemble them without fear of being swallowed. I love and begin to take advantage of my good heritage.

THANK YOU ALEJANDRO.
ROSALIE

⤝ LETTER 34 ⤟
....

From Silvio (forty-six years old)

The goal is to act against my phobias. There are all sorts of social situations in which I often feel that I am out of control, and it's almost always related to the presence of someone who has power, an authority, someone I don't know and who is beyond my influence. As a result I have panic attacks, tremors, sweats, tachycardia, and at this rate, in the future, tumors. In my childhood memories there is a disastrous character whose memory alone awakens in me all kinds of fears, resentments, hatred, and desires for revenge. This is Don Ramón, the teacher I had as a child in my village between the ages of six and nine. He was cruel, a fascist out of vocation and devotion. I remember him hitting viciously and without apparent reason. He hated our town and I remember that he always praised the children from the other villages who came to school. Instead, as children of our village, we were the object of his rage and his outbursts. He also was a staunch enemy of my father who at that time was the mayor of the village. His authority was bloodcurdling. He must have had a habit of playing with the keys he always carried in his smock's pocket because even today the unexpected jingle of keys startles me. One fine day he followed a more attractive destiny for himself and left town. Oh! All poor little homeless orphans.

Probably doing an act with Don Ramón could free me from this tyrannical vision that I have toward authority and allow me to live life with less terror. The act therefore consists of the following:

For a few days live and exaggerate my fears and tremors to their maximum. Build a cabin with cardboard in my room and expect the world to fall on my head. Immersed in this state go to see Don Ramón.

Since Don Ramón is dead, go to his grave. When entering the graveyard start jingling my keys so he can hear me from hell and begin to tremble at what is going to fall on him.

Violently reproach him for everything he put me through in my childhood and the following dire consequences in my life. Soil his grave with my excrement and also reproach him for making me hate my village and abhor my father, and because of that for my living uprooted like a wanderer. Then clean everything and plant a plant at the foot of the tomb.

The next step of the act is to go to my town and ask an old local man to hug and welcome me since I am a son of the town who left one day not to return.

The first thing I did was find the "address" of Don Ramón. It's been forty years since our endearing friendship. I picked up several scattered clues and at the first phone call I found his whereabouts. I spent a week exaggerating my fears. I built a hut out of cardboard in my room and between slots I watched the door and the window for some aberrant Polyphemus to appear. I walked around the house with a box on my head so as not to be seen and to not see. At first it seemed forced but little by little by little I got into the game. Although I was put off by the presence of anyone who passed by my side I began to perform the act. I warned my relatives not to worry if I seemed weird. One thing I felt was fear of my mother, fear that persisted during the days of the act.

In the whirlwind of fear and hate I took a train to Barcelona without saying a word to anyone. The journey took forever. Near Valencia, a storm brought down the overhead lines and after several hours of blockade, "Luz" buses were arranged for Barcelona. My program was somewhat disrupted and I had to stay in a run-down hotel. I didn't want to go out. I was afraid of meeting all the members of my extended family who live there and all the people I have met in my life. I was afraid that they would see me in this altered state. In my delusions I saw posters of my face stuck on the buildings. I went out to get a few chores done, hiding behind a newspaper, terrified.

The following morning, clear and determined, I rented a car and went to a Barcelona cemetery. When I arrived I parked the car and started looking for the "address," jingling my keys. As I approached the tension was rising. When I determined the location, my heart almost sank: the tombstone in the niche did not hold the name of Don Ramón. It was a momentary panic because as I came closer, there it was, his name written on the side of the tombstone. There were several people buried in there, including his wife and a girl of a very young age. I apologized to them for what was going to happen, because it had nothing to do with them. I focused on the central engraving of the tombstone representing the bleeding head of Christ covered with a huge crown of thorns.

The image took on the features of the old teacher and so I turned to it.

What happened is hard for me to describe because at times I was carried away by emotions. In other moments I had to detach myself because there were people wandering around. A long burial was taking place a few meters away and people were in tears.

I think I said all I had to say. All I could recriminate him with. During this long meeting many childhood memories came back and were exposed and clarified. Along with my tears and my muffled screams came insults, amongst which, mostly in French: *salopard.** Later I took a ladder to get there to reach his level and smeared the tombstone with my droppings. I think I was saying, "Here! Take that! . . ." Pretty much in front of his niche there was miraculously a fountain with a tap.

I brought cloths and cleaning products with my stuff and cleaned everything neatly. Then with my hands and a stick I dug a hole in a flower bed at the bottom of the niche. There I planted a flowering plant that I bought the day before and watered it copiously with the fountain water.

Then I did something unexpected. I went to the car and drove it up to the foot of the grave. I opened the doors and picked the music. It was the "Pavane of Fauré" performed on the guitar. This music filled the placid air that enveloped this place and I felt it go through the atmosphere to infinity. Mentally I removed the crown of thorns from Don Ramón's head, to free him and myself from this cruel relationship that united our lives. I felt as the calm and the light settled in this corner of the mountain in Barcelona.

I then got in the car and headed to the town where I was born and lived in my childhood, Maldà, a town of three hundred inhabitants in the middle of Catalonia. I parked the car in the town center. Not a soul on the streets. I walked around. I walked past the church, past the old school that was demolished, past the town hall, the old castle . . . and there I saw the first man, the man who had been prepared for me to

---

*Bastard.

carry out this act. I recognized him right away and my heart skipped a beat with joy. My father worked as a laborer for him for a long time. He was accompanied by a young man.

I approached him, introduced myself as a son of the town that I left in childhood and which I had not visited in many years. I asked him to hug me, to welcome me as a son of the people. He accepted and hugged me tightly. I returned the hug. When we let go he started crying with emotion. I was not expecting this. It was a very intense moment. On the spot he invited me to his house. He lives in a beautiful house, maybe the biggest in town. There I was introduced to his family and showed around the house. To my surprise he told me that many years ago Don Ramón and his family lived in a wing of the house as tenants. He told me about the death of Don Ramón and his wife, that he went to his funeral, that they were close. He told me that my father when he was mayor built a new school with housing for Don Ramón, but that Don Ramón did not like it at all and did not want to move from where we are now. It seems that he was forced to move. I figured this was the cause of the arguments between my father and the teacher. I was very surprised. I had just set Don Ramón free one hundred kilometers from here, and now I was being shown his splendid old house. I spent a couple of hours at this house and I said goodbye at sundown. I found myself again in front of Maldà castle which stands on an immense plain at a time drenched in the setting sun. Standing there looking at the horizon I knew that a page of my life had definitely been turned. I left town and took a winding road that several kilometers further joins the Mediterranean Highway.

At midnight I took a small break in a road hotel, near Valencia. In the lobby a large glass cylinder rotating slowly on its axis caught my attention. Inside was a huge stuffed lion in a jump-attack position with its claws spread out and its jaws open. At his feet a poster with his story: *My name is Simba, I was one of the biggest lions in Africa, etc. . . .* I had something to drink and left. The image of this lion stuck with me.

THANKS.

→ LETTER 35 ←
....
From Sarah (thirty-three years old)

The act is supposed to help me lose the negative femininity related to maternity. . . . I have a strong association of illness with pregnancy. All things lunar are related to mood swings, depression, bad temper, etc. In the future, all this could harm the baby we want to have and it would provoke my partner's rejection of him.

For one whole day I will carry a cushion on my belly; inside there will be a lobster and a fruit (a mango or a melon). It will be attached with a flesh-colored bandage. On my body I will place images of pregnant women who are crying, sick, sad, etc. . . . I'll write a letter explaining why I don't want to have children. I will express the sufferings to which I am exposed: *Children are killed in wars, they make you sick, you don't stop suffering for the rest of your life. They just bring misfortunes, etc.* . . . I'll place that letter on my body as well. During this time I will be ill. I will rage, I will cry, I will keep repeating I don't want to suffer, I don't want have children, that I don't want to be a mother, etc. . . .

At the end of the day I will go to the forest and will cut the bandage off. I'll take off the cushion and everything it carries. I will shout that I do not want to suffer anymore. I will bury it all. I'll walk away crying. For the next day I will cry for the death of my son. At the end of that day I will go back to the forest. I'll dig up everything and I will burn it, taking the ashes home. I will tell my boyfriend that I love him, that I want to have a son, and ask for him to give me his seed. He'll pass me a red candy from his mouth to mine.

Then, from clay and some of the ashes, I will fashion a baby. Later I'll put it in a pink bag with rose petals. I'll place it on my belly and I will carry it for three days.

My boyfriend and I then will go to Alhambra. Dressed in colors and with a rose in hand, in each room we visit we will dance a waltz. We'll tell the people we're going to be parents, and we dance because it is a joy. I'll throw some of the ashes into the river. I'll put the rest in colorful balloons, filled with helium to let them get to heaven.

After three days, I will put the baby with the bag in a very pretty vase. The vase will have a lid.

When I'm pregnant, I'll bring the clay baby to the Virgin. I will thank her for entrusting me with childhood and adolescence of this soul.

Here is the realization of the act: On Wednesday morning at about 7:45 I get ready. I put on the cushion with lobster and mango and get dressed in black clothes, a t-shirt, and wool sweater.

I have collected drawings and photographs of pregnant women, crying, vomiting, with allergies, with scars on their bellies. They are of all races. I quickly enter my negativity. I put them on my body, underneath the clothing. I begin to write the letter. Uninhibited, without limits, I express the worst of myself. It is a horrible macabre letter. In the beginning all my egoism comes out. I write that I am going to suffer because I am going to feel horrible being pregnant. It's like having a son means my life is over, in a very narcissistic way. Then I write all kinds of deaths that occur to me for children and the suffering that this causes me: death in war, murder, suicide, disease, hunger, abortions, etc. . . . Over and over again I write that children make you suffer.

Little by little I take a turn and see myself writing backward things, that is, things that hurt me directly; they kill me, they abandon me. When I can't anymore, I stop. I have a headache. I place the letter in my underwear.

I leave the room and I replay more or less what I've just written. I start to clean. I won't stop complaining about how hard life is for me. That I don't deserve it. I make myself a martyr. I feel a dynamic I know very well from my old relationships. I enhance that feeling by cleaning clumsily. I go from one place to another complaining nonstop. After a few hours I'm exhausted. I go back to the room. I am completely depressed. I throw myself on the bed. I start to cry. The headache gets worse. I feel aggression and I squeeze my belly. The lobster begins to thaw and creak. The mango drops and looks like the head of a child. I have to get up to throw up. I spend the day like this.

Around six in the evening I leave the house. I get to the forest. I cut the bandage and scream that I don't want to suffer anymore. I take off everything and bury it.

Upon returning, I start to say that my son has died. I'm shedding tears, but I have a contradictory feeling of being liberated. The lobster started to smell and wet my clothes. I walk all the way like this. I have the impression I'm crazy. I get a suicidal feeling. I think it is normal, but I don't feed it. I get home, I take a shower, I keep crying, but without tears.

The next day when I wake up I continue crying. I get on my knees. I cry and repeat endlessly: "My son has died." My crying is still dry, it worries me. I have visions of myself. I look like a Jewish woman who has been taken from her children. An Arab woman whose son died in the war. An Ethiopian woman whose son died of hunger. I'm exhausted.

It's 5:00 p.m. I'm going to the forest. I dig up everything. I'm looking for a place close to some barbecues. I brought a bottle of alcohol so that it burns quickly. I spray it all. The clothes burn well. But the lobster and the mango do not! The fire goes out, I add leaves and twigs but it does not burn. I throw everything flammable I have in the bag. But nothing! I come up with the idea of taking rags from the motorcycle, soaking them in gasoline, and setting them on fire. It just turns everything black.

I take off a t-shirt, I do it again. Impossible. The mango is still in one piece. I wonder why it doesn't burn. I can't find a logical answer. I'm going to town. I buy newspapers and alcohol.

When I come back it's night and I collect everything. It's been three hours. I think that I'm going to fail.

I go to the office where I work, empty the wood stove, and go back to try it. When I get home, which is next to the office, I lie down because I feel very bad. All these negative thoughts.

I feel like quitting. I'm in a sorry state. I start to rave just like during a fever. Time goes by, I don't know how long. I return to the office and collect the ashes.

The next day, I'm going to buy a pink bag and pink roses. The roses are intense. I like them!

I want to feel good. I'm putting on colorful clothes and makeup. After two days, it's a pleasure. I prepare the bedroom where I sleep with my boyfriend. I light incense, put on calm music, I call him. When he comes, I tell him that I love him and that I want to have a child. I ask him to give me his seed.

We hug and I feel a lot of emotions. Then he gives me two red candies from his mouth and he tells me: "Twins!" He laughs. We hug again. Then he leaves. Everything goes through my head.

I wonder what to do. A baby, two babies? I don't want to feel bad in this special moment. I concentrate and work the clay. I mix a bit of ashes and I start to enjoy the work.

The baby is done. I have put a lot of care and love into doing it, and it looks lovely. When I put it in the bag with the petals, it is really magical and I start to cry again, but this time not with sadness. I put it on my belly and tie it up with a colored scarf.

In the afternoon, my boyfriend and I go to the Alhambra. We are nervous. It's a splendid afternoon. First we go visit Generalife. In every room we dance the waltz as planned.

We say that we are going to be parents and that it's a joy. People congratulate us. We take several laps in the same room and we move on to another. Each time we enjoy it more and I let myself go.

On Saturday I throw the ashes into the Guadalquivir. On Sunday I fill the balloons with helium and I send them to the sky with the other part of the ashes.

During the days I spend with the baby on my belly, my mind and body are focused on it. I try to feel good, but there are very strong waves of paranoia. Paranoia above all that I have done something wrong. I understand that my unconscious is trying to come out. I'm going to buy the vase on Thursday. It is really beautiful. Blue with plated-copper embellishments. I put the baby inside with the bag and tell it goodbye.

Now I hope to get pregnant soon. I return to see Mr. Alejandro. To achieve what I want I must leave my hatred toward men, which prevents me from having a good relationship. The problem comes from my parents, as their wish was to have a boy. Also from myself: to please them I wanted to be the boy they didn't have. I am the youngest of five girls. For this reason I have not incarnated in my body as a woman, and a part of the act was dedicated to this.

I have to go to my father's grave dressed as a boy. I will also put a banana and two eggs inside my underpants. When I'm in front of him I'll tell him: "Here's what you wanted me to be." I'll take out the eggs and then I will crack them on his grave, together with the banana. Then I'll take off my clothes and I will put on a colorful dress and high heels. I will burn the boys' clothes. I'll clean up the remains of egg and banana and I'll put the ashes in a pretty plant that I will leave there. I'll save a symbolic part of the ashes to drink in a glass of wine for later.

Then I will go to eat with my mother. I'll bring the food. I will go dressed in my colorful clothes. I'll bring deer meat that represents my flesh; wine, my blood; grapes, transformation and also my essence of a woman. We will have to prepare dinner together and then eat it. I'll drink the ashes in the wine.

About 3:00 p.m. I am at the graveyard. It takes me a long time to find my father's grave. I am given the old location where he had been buried. I finally have to call my mother.

Here I make a mistake. I was supposed to dress as a boy. I did not do it because I thought maybe I'd have to go to ask for directions at the cemetery reception and I didn't want to get dressed until I was sure I was in front of the grave. I realize the mistake and get dressed. I do what was planned. When I am in front I tell him: "Here you have what you wanted me to be!" I crack the eggs and the banana. I am afraid of breaking the crystal of the niche, because I do not control my strength. I feel a very strong energy that surrounds me. I take off my clothes and put on the dress with high heels. I burn everything and clean the glass. I put the ashes in a very beautiful plant with pink petals.

I wait until 9:15 p.m. to go to my mother's home. When my mother sees me she tells me that I look very pretty. I am wearing an off-the-shoulder dress in shades of red, high heels, and a bit of makeup. We cook together. During dinner I have to hide my glass of wine, because the ashes have formed little floating balls.

Besides, my mother controls the amount of wine I drink. Every time that she goes to the kitchen I have to take big sips to finish my cup and fill it again, without her realizing.

Starting to eat, she asks me if I am going to announce that I am pregnant. She thinks that's why I am there and that I went to the cemetery for this reason. She tells me that having children is the best thing that can happen in your life, but that from this moment you won't stop suffering. . . . I ask about me and my sisters. She tells me about her pregnancies and when we were little. How she took the news when she got pregnant and about our births. This conversation is illuminating and I feel moved. At the end of dinner she gives me pajamas. A small rabbit, a small puppy, and a kitten are glued on them. Totally childish. A rose near the top, when you separate it from the stem, turns into red panties. She also gives me some normal panties.

I go home the next day. When I arrive in Granada, those gifts she gave me are so symbolic I think I have to do something. It all represents what she has passed on to me. I sleep in my pajamas, the rose and the panties, for four days. Then I burn them. I put a symbolic part of the ashes in a glass of milk and I drink it. I put the rest around an olive tree that I plant. After this act I feel more strength and energy, eager to face maternity.

✦ LETTER 36 ✦

From Catherine (forty-nine years old)

I have done the following act to cure my obesity, the origin of which is a great intellectual complex. My grandmothers were illiterate; my mother knows how to read and write with difficulty. The intellectual complex pushes me to pour a lot of hate toward people who surround me, in the form of envy, vulgarity, and bad character, among much else.

After one of these violent demonstrations, I feel bad.

The psychomagic act is as follows: I need to cancel my bank account with Caja Madrid (Madrid being the city where I was born). Then I will make myself a fat suit and sew the money around it. (My mother weighed about ninety kilos at my age.)

Dressed like this I will visit the places where I spent my childhood and buy nine kilos of meat that I will give to my mother. I will eat a part of it with her. I will leave the fat suit in the room I lived in when I was with my parents. I will tell my mother when saying goodbye that the meat belongs to her.

Then I will go to the University City of Madrid, choose a career, and buy books to study for twenty-four hours straight.

After forging a degree, I will go back to the University City to receive it from the hands of an accomplice, with the academic robe on.

Then I will buy a uniform of a flight attendant of Iberia, and dressed this way I will buy gifts for my friends, with the money that I had sewn to my body. Finally I will return home with the diploma, the stewardess uniform, and the gifts that I will give to my friends.

Here is how the act was realized:

Canceling the bank account was not difficult; it was harder not to spend the money. Suddenly I wanted to buy everything. Trying on the suit and large underwear brought up many memories. Sometimes I felt sad and other times very sensitive with the people to whom I was closest. I visited the most significant places of Vallecas (the neighborhood of Madrid I am from). Every time I saw my reflection in shop windows it scared me; throughout the day my face was marked with hatred and fear. The house where I was born still exists; it had been renovated. The stone patio staircase had been covered with a kind of reddish asphalt. When I recognized the iron railing, it brought up images of childhood games on these stairs. I tried to visit the house where I was born. Now a fishmonger lives there with his wife and son. The current owner, a fat lady with glasses, slammed the door in my face. Although I understood it was logical that she wouldn't let me in, her violent slamming of the door made me cry.

I told a young woman, a neighbor of the building, that I was born there. Seeing me cry she answered me very gently: "Your mum passed away, didn't she?" I took that phrase as a good omen.

Walking past the bakery Bella Luz, a lady kept staring at me. I went in to remember the cakes I used to buy there as a child. I left quickly; it had become a cafeteria and there were too many people inside.

I went by subway to the Rastro de Madrid, the neighborhood with Humilladero Street, and I drank in the heaviest atmosphere in the city. The building that used to be a butcher's still exists. Now it is an electrical supply store, which seemed like a good omen too.

I bought nine kilos of meat in a market on the same street. Tired and suffocating in the heat I sat down on a bench. The lady who was sitting on the next bench had a limp. My intellectual limp, I told myself. From time to time the lady would get up for short, slow walks. I thanked God for not finding myself in her physical state and said goodbye to this neighborhood that brings me such heavy memories.

The next day I brought the meat to my mother and ate a little with her. Another part we ate with my sister, my nieces (my sister's daughters), and my daughter. At night I felt bad. Maybe I shouldn't have eaten this meat with the generation that follows me. I felt responsible for my daughter's obesity, for her sad look and her big honey-colored eyes buried in a huge mass of meat.

The next day I said goodbye to my mother, telling her that the meat that was in the fridge belonged to her. She thanked me.

Then I took a taxi to the University City. I did not specify the place to the taxi driver. I had never been there. For me it was a place for students and I was from Vallecas. The taxi left me in front of the Faculty of Information Sciences. I understood that there I would get inspiration for a career to choose. I asked for a rectorate catalog and I returned to the Faculty of Information Sciences, where I quietly turned the pages of the brochure until I saw Hispanic Philology and I felt: that's the one. To my mind came my niece-goddaughter, Laura, the youngest of the four of my older brother's children. She is the only one of the siblings who completed university studies; she is doing a doctorate in Hispanic Philology. I realized that there is a parallel between my older brother's family structure and what ours was thirty years ago: a female, then two boys, and the last one—Laura, like me—unwanted. My brother Manolo was the only one who encouraged me to study in my childhood. I thought maybe he did that also with his youngest daughter.

In my last year of high school, I preferred the letters to the sciences. Without hesitation, I went to the Faculty of Philology where I bought the books. I studied for twenty-four hours straight. It was hard to stay awake at night. The liters of isotonic drinks that I drank upset my stomach and I was afraid I'd get sick.

The next night I slept like a baby. I woke up with an incredible energy and at times I felt like a real college girl. I bought the clothes to wear to receive the diploma that I made for myself. Calmly and happily I walked for an hour through the University City of Madrid. In front of the Faculty of Philology I dressed in my robes and blue cap. I had prepared my camera to ask someone to take a picture of me when receiving the diploma, but it did not have batteries. I put it back understanding that I should keep this act to myself. I didn't want to choose the person who had to give me the diploma. I entered the building and waited for someone to come in. I asked two people to give me the title with this sentence: "I am doing a psychomagic act—would you be so kind as to put this diploma into the hood please?" Scared, they didn't even look at me, so I changed the sentence to a simpler one: "Would you be so kind to put this here?" I pointed to the object and the place. A handsome gentleman put my diploma in the hood without saying anything. I thanked him and left. To get my flight attendant uniform, I went to the airport, where I asked where they make them. Despite my efforts I couldn't get them to sell it to me. Iberia Airlines gives its employees vouchers to collect the uniforms in the store. I went there and said that I needed a uniform for my daughter. They told me it would be very difficult, that if they gave it to me they risked their job. Previous euphoria turned into pessimism at the idea of not being able to finish my act. Nevertheless a lady who was listening to my story gave me the telephone number of a person responsible for the uniforms in the Iberia warehouses.

I preferred to talk to this person directly; it was easier to turn me down on the phone. I got lost in the industrial estate of the airport. Suddenly a truck stood before my eyes with huge capital letters: "SIMON." There was no smaller print to specify the activity of the company that owns the truck. My husband's name is Simon, so I understood that it was a message from you, that you wanted to tell me not to despair.

When I found myself in front of the woman who could help me, I noticed my mouth was very dry. I told her the same story about my daughter, looking into her eyes and with more force than previously. In fact I was talking about my inner girl, about my materialism (obesity), about my teenage complexes, about my need to get the uniform. I touched this woman's heart to the point that without a word, she indicated to follow her. We crossed a courtyard and entered some old warehouses where I picked my size. The control number 14 was attached to the bag containing the suit, a good number for me.

Accessories were not in stock. I asked the woman how much it was. She replied that the only thing she wanted was for me to give her an update on how things were going.

With the uniform in hand I felt able to get accessories with ease. The friendliness and kindness of the Iberia hostesses helped me a lot. They gave me gloves, handkerchief, and a flight bag without any difficulty. I thought that if my life had taken such a different path, my neurosis would have been different, too, and my character would have been better and less hateful.

I went to buy the bag, the only thing missing; I was attracted to the name of a perfume ("L'Heure Bleue") and I bought it to use it all the next day, when I turned forty-nine.

Over-the-top and overflowing with joy I went out to the street dressed in this uniform. I spent the whole day buying gifts for my friends. In El Corte Inglés, a young man confused me with a saleswoman. I answered him that I was not from there and he apologized, telling me that he did not realize that I was a stewardess. Although I knew I was performing a psychomagic act, the fact that I was called a stewardess got me intoxicated for a few moments. The day I was supposed to go home, I went to El Corte Inglés in the morning to spend the rest of the money on the last gifts. I saw my sister but she didn't see me. I would have hugged her but I didn't want to have to explain or confuse her with my stewardess uniform. I wondered the moment I saw her: "Am I getting closer to a friendship with her, having performed this act?"

As planned I returned home with the diploma, uniform, gifts, and a feeling of having lived magical moments. I have stopped hating everyone. I have started to lose weight.

⤗ LETTER 37 ⬳

From Eugenie (forty years old)

Born into a poor family of illiterate parents, daughter of a single mother, prostitute, dancer, and singer, I never got to know my real father. As a child, my father model was that of a drunk grandfather who despised and ignored me, and that of the men who were with my mother (contemptuous and vulgar). To protect me from all this lack of love and the subhuman environment in which I grew up, I lived in a bubble outside reality. Rejecting my origins, I became a complete maniac about cleanliness and hygiene so as not to turn out like my mother.

I wanted to be pure and immaculate. My mother is someone with a lot of vital energy. Scared of resembling her, I have rejected displaying that vital energy and everything that is happy, instead staying sad and disconnected. To release that energy, I did a kind of psychomagic act two years ago. For three days I imitated my mother: singing, dancing, and seducing men (in fact all my vitality is expressed in dance; I love to dance and I dance well). Despite being thirty-nine years old I was still a little girl looking for a father who would give me all the love I never received, filling all the emptiness I have as a woman, asking everyone to take care of me. I have failed in my marriage and was also a failure as a mother. My daughter was becoming a copy of me and of my mother. She complained all the time and at her young age she had an unhealthy relationship with sex. She was expressing the prostitute within, which I always found scary in me.

To help me get through this block and release my daughter from this baggage I had to perform the following act of psychomagic:

For thirty-nine days (representing my age) I will dress as a little girl, all in white, including wearing a little girl's underwear. I will carry white latex gloves and a mask over my mouth (to represent my obsession with hygiene and not wanting to contaminate myself). I will wear my hair pulled up tight. I'll wear a lot of perfume and face powder (to represent a saint). I will glue a few coins to the palms of both hands to indicate my laziness. At the same time I will beg men with this phrase: "Dad, fill me up," and "Daddy, give me femininity." After thirty-nine days I will send a letter to my father on which I will write as his address: "Mr. Absent Father. City of Myself. Universal Awareness." I will sign it in my blood. I will put it in a mailbox in my hometown dressed as a little girl. The next day (which will coincide with my birthday, on which I will be forty years old) I will dress normally.

I'll go bury all that I wore during the act, minus a piece of fabric from the skirt which I will save for the end of the act. Once buried I will pee on top and then I'll leave a flower. I will leave this place never to return. I will make myself a skirt incorporating the piece of cloth that was saved.

Here is how the act developed: When I started dressing as a little girl I began having memories from my childhood. When doing my hair I saw my mother combing my hair very tightly, making a very high ponytail and putting on a lot of perfume. When I saw myself dressed for the act I felt like a monster. I got into the character of a little girl, sad, shrunken, and always in a bad mood, isolated and closed toward others, with a lost look. I realized that that was my usual behavior with others.

I realized that all my obsessions with cleanliness and being "white and immaculate" were because I felt very dirty inside. There were days when I felt so dirty that my whole body itched, I didn't feel good in it, and I couldn't bear to live in it. I felt disgusted with myself, so much so that one day, before sleeping, I felt my body full of dirty and greasy water. I was full of this water up to the neck. I realized that so much eagerness to control and hide what I really am and where I come from prevented this water from being taken out and cleaned.

Where I felt the most resistance was in begging. Pride and shame took hold of me. In a way I did not want to face my reality and I was about to sabotage the act. To give myself strength to carry out the act I thought of my daughter. I had to go beyond my selfishness. Since for me it hasn't done a great deal in life at least I would do it for her.

Every time I begged the men, calling them Papa, and they rejected me I felt humiliated, despised, a worthless thing, a failure. The more I was rejected the more hatred I felt toward them and toward my dad. I was facing what I had been avoiding all my life: having been abandoned and rejected by my father. I felt that the breastplate I had built myself to protect myself from pain has been kicked in. Sometimes I felt bad, but other times I felt that my hateful part was happy: it was a way to get revenge on their slights. I began to see that I was the one who caused this humiliation and this rejection, behaving like a girl begging for affection. I felt the lack of love very strongly from a father and I had moments of great anger. I cried like a little girl. The last days were unbearable. I was afraid I'd go crazy, I wouldn't endure. I despaired to see that I was only a little girl and I was afraid to stay like this all my life. I felt very empty as a woman, as a human being. I saw my daughter as a rival and I felt bad for all the mistakes I made as a mother. I was very tired, I couldn't take it anymore!

One day after begging and having been rejected I had a strong suicidal urge. Thank God this madness lasted a tenth of a second and sanity returned. I felt sick of myself. I looked like an animal in heat every time I waited for a man to beg. I felt like a whore who humiliates herself and sells herself to men. On the other hand I was tired of asking and receiving nothing. I realized that all my life I had been asking men for the impossible.

The day before my birthday I went to my hometown to send a letter to my dad. In it I wrote with a little girl's handwriting, telling him everything I suffered from his absence and his abandonment and all the damage he had done to me. I insulted him. It'd been a long time since I'd been there and I didn't remember where the mailboxes were. But once there I had no difficulty finding them.

I didn't feel alone; I felt the presence of a force that protected and guided me. I got to the center of town (meaning for me the center of my neurosis) and I put the letter in a mailbox that was next to a bar where there were only men. Perfect! I was surprised seeing how much the town has changed. There were new shops, new bars, and many houses under construction. I looked at the people and I recognized no one. Now there was a new generation. I saw my mother's family's house and it gave me the impression of something old, dead. Besides, there were two new establishments in front of it. I saw what was once a funeral home was now a store. I took this as a good sign. I left town quietly. I felt enveloped in a cloud of magic. I had just made a trip to my childhood to settle a debt with my father. I had the feeling of something new.

When I got home I had a good shower.

The next day I went to bury all that I wore during the act. The bag I put it in was heavy. It felt like I was really carrying a dead little girl. It weighed a lot, it had been a great burden in my life, and it had begun to smell bad. While burying her, my heart was beating fast. Every time I placed a garment in the hole my hand stretched out to retrieve it. I felt attraction, something diabolical. I felt that I was resisting burying her. I gathered strength and began to bury it as fast as possible. Between sobs I told her to leave me alone. I felt all the damage this little girl had done in my life and in the lives of others. I peed on it and left flowers. I had an upset stomach and a strong desire to vomit. I left this place with a strange feeling; I felt very tired.

After the act I met the men whom I begged, asking them to fill me up, and sadness overwhelmed me—I felt bad. I felt that I had hurt them, humiliated them. Now I saw them differently. The day of my birthday I felt loved and respected by those around me.

⇥ LETTER 38 ⇤

From Iris (twenty-two years old)

The purpose of my act was to free me from an enormous weight that I felt in my solar plexus, a knot of spite and resentment that polluted all my relationships, but which came from the role I played in my family as the eldest, strictly raised child. To get some love I tried to be perfect. It only gave me a horrible feeling of abuse; I was used.

The act was therefore going to allow me in the first phase to devote myself fully to this role that I have always desperately wanted to play: that of the more-than-perfect girl, that of a virgin in the service of her parents (I am also Virgo with Virgo rising!). A vision came to me. I saw myself white and sad, washing, for example, humbly the feet of my parents. I would do this for three days, holding a metal object closely on which I would focus my rage, my chest bandaged. I would ask my parents to each take a photo of me when introducing myself to them for the first time, and I would keep the pictures. After the three days, I would be operated on for this disease. However, just before the operation, I would give each of my parents back their picture of me as a virgin and tell them to keep it for twenty-two days (because I'm twenty-two years old) before burning it. My father would then scatter the ashes at the feet of a young olive tree that I had planted and mix them with the earth by working it, and my mother would scatter them where she would find irises (this is my first name). As for me, the day after my operation I would go and burn my "saint regalia" and throw the ashes in a wheat field.

I started by collecting the necessary material. I even tried on the disguise and makeup so that from the beginning of the act it would be MY clothes and so that I especially would have no question to ask myself on this subject, since from then on it would no longer be a disguise, nor makeup, but my natural self, my *personality*. . . . To tell the truth, this made me nervous, and I was shaking and had cold sweats. On the other hand, the morning of the first day I was calmer. I got ready slowly, watching myself in the mirror while I gradually whitened my face. I was already under the yoke of immense sadness. I felt heavy sorrow, serious, a weeping virgin, full of "moral" obligations like those of my maternal grandmother. I put talcum powder on my body and my hair, too. I loved all that whiteness, that smooth, soft whiteness. When I bandaged my chest, to make me flatter, everything seemed to slide over me. I didn't belong to this world anymore; I was elsewhere, away from everything like I always was when I was little—consciousness separated from my body, which scrutinizes the smallest detail so that nothing escapes my control and maybe displeases me. I placed the metal piece tightly against me where I usually felt my physical rage. I had squeezed this part a long time in my hands earlier, charging it with all this hate. Then came the clothes and the crown. What a picture! I gave myself some time to get centered before I left my room. When I started down the stairs that would lead me to other people, my family, my friends, to the confrontation of looks—that was when it became very hard. Me who wanted to be so perfect, I almost bailed since I knew very well that people wouldn't really find it *perfect!* In other words, I was always ready to be a virgin, but fabricated externally in one way or another, depending on what people expected of me.

I was completely dependent on others' looks in my quest for approval and recognition. The descent from this staircase—however small—put me in front of the obvious: my life and ability only existed dependent on this gaze. After this fear of the first meetings, I began laughing inside. I decided to introduce myself in advance so as not to scare people. To see my parents I again got ready in my room, with candles to be even more spiritual. Then I made my sister call them while I waited, facing away. When I was sure they were behind me I turned around. My mother almost immediately broke down in tears. But I felt solid. I explained that I embodied what I always wanted to be for them, a virgin at their humble service, and I asked them to let me serve them for three days. My father couldn't help himself, straight away he wanted to make it about him, correcting me: "What we wanted you to become . . ." Then we took the photos, which I kept without explaining any further. When my parents left and I held both photos that I was going to give them back three days later, I felt much better. I had passed the first step and I was passionate about the act. But I was still shaking with fear and excitement.

The cold sweats started again with the first meal I served them. I had to try to control my gestures. I was even afraid I'd end up spilling something, I was so clumsy. I needed to insist more because my parents, embarrassed, didn't dare to ask me for things. With time they let me go more and I could often anticipate their wishes or desires like I did as a kid when I wanted to prepare everything, organize little surprises, etc. But the second day, if I was still shaking, it was no longer anguish, but rage—I would have thrown the plate in their faces!

The third day was easier. I was in a better mood, I felt freer to do the little things I had planned, and I was full of imagination to invent others. In fact, in this straightjacket of false impeccability, I was almost incapable of performing acts or saying what I had to say: the things, my ideas, my projects, turned in my head, and I tossed them and turned them again, studied them, reformulated them endlessly, but it never came out. It was terrible. I had little sentences to say, for example, that I couldn't let go of until the last day. Likewise, facing the moment to wash their feet seemed an insurmountable obstacle. But once I was there, with my soap, my towel, my bowl full of hot and fragrant water, when I told my mother what I was going to do to her and when I took her shoes off, it was fine, and the rest happened more naturally. I had the opportunity during footbaths to explain separately to each of my parents how they contributed to my neurosis. My mother again broke down in tears. I felt the situation was dangerous with her; I saw the emotional blackmail and the risk of me falling back into the guilt that could spoil my act. It was complicated because, on the one hand, I had to explain to her what I owed her and, on the other hand, as a virgin I was at her service and a bit like a mother to her. But above all I had to not pity her. I believed that I had faith and I received help necessary to remain firm inside myself. With my father, washing his feet was not easy simply because being ticklish he didn't take it well. But his agreement and his understanding surprised and helped me. Finally I had to put in more hours as a virgin because in the midst of wanting to be perfect and above all not to disturb, I did not remember that I wanted to be operated on at the right time . . . my bad! So I gathered courage to carry on and serve my parents some more with a smile.

The moment of the operation finally arrived. I was again extremely anxious. I didn't know how it was going to happen. Then my surgeon, a woman, asked me what I wanted and I explained to her how I felt while crying. I couldn't take it anymore. I returned the photos to my parents and clearly explained to each what they should do. I hoped I could trust them. Then I got undressed and lay down. My surgeon told me to scream my rage as she cut the bandage, then tore this ball of aggressiveness off me. Twice I screamed terribly, loudly and for a long time. They were cries that came from the depths of me and they wouldn't stop coming out. Then I was in pain, but it was already like a stitched-up wound and I did not feel the ball anymore. I was crying softly, of relief, of gratitude. It took me a long time to recover. I was exhausted. The next day, when I went to burn my clothes and my wreath to scatter the ashes in the wheat field, I did not feel alone. . . . My state of exhaustion lasted several weeks. I preferred not to analyze it intellectually or precociously to feel I had changed. In fact, I still felt convalescent.

Today I feel much less depressed than before and I am more attached to life. The act gave me confidence and I feel that I can have a life of my own, that I can develop my personality. I also manage to make myself useful without projecting being used. Lately I haven't felt as if I'm "the object to be placed in accordance with the requirements of the moment." Curiously, I stated with joy a short time ago, when

I danced at the end of my act, after the operation, it was actually the realization of a visualization: in the latter I had seen myself dressed in black (and no longer white!) and dancing, very cheerful, free in my head and in my body. . . .

⇢ LETTER 39 ⇠

From Eloise (sixteen years old)

My overflowing eros, my constant need to please and seduce, prevents me from thriving in many areas. I sell myself to men. I only think of seducing, flirting . . . I even went so far as to cause the breakup between my sister and her companion. It horrified me because I adore my sister. When I'm in this "Lolita" aspect, I have no control at all. There are no limits anymore.

In hindsight I realize it makes me suffer a lot. This problem is related to the relationship I had with my parents and what I inherited from them. During my childhood my relationship with my father was unhealthy. He projected a lot of libido on me. My mother, in her youth, was also like me—a little "Lolita" who was only looking to seduce.

My act breaks down into two parts. First I make two photocopies of a photo of me as a child, of whom I have bad memories. I put each of them in a big ball of black wool and give them to my parents separately, saying: "I return what belongs to you." I keep the original on me throughout the act.

In the second part I deal with freeing myself from what is really mine, from what I created: myself. For three days I must dress like a whore. We say that clothes are the extension of the self. Every day is a lifetime and therefore every day my outfit is different. In the evening, very late at night, I take the clothes of the day, wash them, and go to sleep right after. So every day is a life, the evening a death, and the morning a rebirth. I free myself from all these layers of accumulated dirt, of this filthy relationship with the man that has weighed on me for a long time. The last evening, after having washed the last clothes, I make a mask of clay all over my body to extract everything still left.

The next day I throw all the clothes in the fire along with the original of the photo that I gave to my parents. Next I offer the warmth of this fire to the people closest to me.

The three days seemed to last forever.

Throughout the entire act I had a lot of emotions and feelings, sometimes very contradictory: shame, attachment to this persona, horror, sadness of being the way I am, exasperation, contempt I thought I saw in the eyes of people, and many more still undefined.

I also felt that this character deep inside represented amazing but poorly used energy, a ball of raw, still-wild energy. But it was there inside me and I knew that I could use it positively one day, and it would give me a lot of strength. It gave me hope. The first night when I went out in the dark, to hang my clothes, I started to feel scared. I felt a presence . . . and I wanted to quickly let go of the clothes that I held in my hand because for me it was clear that if I kept them any longer something was going to happen to me. On my way I saw toads, a cut-tailed salamander, and many black insects. The day after I was no more comfortable but I was much weaker and I saw nothing in particular. The last evening, when I freed myself from my last pair clothes, I had a feeling of incredible faith. Félicie, my friend's dog, accompanied me everywhere. The events of the first evening seemed important to me because they showed the diabolical side of this part of me.

After the act I felt a great sadness followed by a feeling of release.

Now I realize that I have another extreme side that is hard, cold, and very critical of men. An untouchable saint. I have no middle ground and I'm going through hell in relationships with men because I am torn between these two characters who are the only role models in my family. Both the whore and the saint. I feel very bad and I make myself suffer.

It was the psychomagical act that allowed me to understand this and I am very grateful. Now I am determined to engage with pleasure in other acts of psychomagic to evolve in self-discovery.

Today, six months later, this act has had many more consequences in my life.

⇾ LETTER 40 ⇽
....

From Samuel (twenty-seven years old)

I asked for an act to stop seeing only the negative side of life and to give my life value. Despite being good at a large number of activities in various fields, I am unable to appreciate my work and even less my personality. The core of this heavy pessimism is linked to my relationship with my mother. I discovered that for her I was nothing but trash. I had to be able to embrace the reality of this "child-trash" once and for all, otherwise I would find myself doomed to go through life as undead, a sad puppet, envious of everything others have more of in my eyes.

The act is to live this "trash man" to the fullest so I can then give it back to my mother. So, for three days, I shall live in a room transformed into a dump: there I will accumulate garbage cans and miscellaneous waste. I will build and keep a life-size doll representing a child with me in this landfill. The fourth day, when I feel the time is right, I will undress and leave everything I wore in this room during the act. I'll go clean myself up and change. I will then take my mother to this dump and tell her: "I give you back all your trash. I am not trash." I'll leave with no future worries about this room.

When the act was explained to me, at first I felt despair roll through me like muffled waves at confronting this reality. However, the preparation of the act put me on a completely different wavelength. The desire to go all the way to the limit of this knot that has always been deep inside grew and compelled me to act. I have suffered enough pain for something that does not belong to me. The desire to get free of it inspired a lot of ideas about living this act to the fullest. I'm ready, sitting on a bench, surrounded by trash cans, on which the doll is slumped. The excitement of preparation gradually falls, replaced by a cold and smelly silence, broken only from time to time by the screeching of the plastic. The atmosphere is grim and sad. It's like the end of a journey here. It is impossible to fall any lower. It's abandonment, resignation without hope of recovery. We are no longer quite human, in a place like this. I have nothing left to do but perceive this emptiness, this absence of exit.

I take my meal alone, in my dump. I meet people on my way to pick up food. I'm ashamed, I feel contemptible. I would like to shout at all of them not to look at me. This experience of the view of others will evolve—as a consequence, becoming more and more dirty myself, I stop giving a shit. I even rejoice somehow in no longer needing to worry about my appearance.

The first night passes and I sleep despite the stench. I'm getting used to it, actually. . . . In the morning, however, it is horrible for me wake up in the middle of the rubbish. On the other hand, I feel an urge to push this child-trash experience deeper. The meals that I still have in my dump will become in this sense a terrain of intense experiences: I discover with disgust that I can be worse than an animal. I no longer eat, I guzzle in the middle of the filth, I lose all human dignity, and this dump becomes my refuge, the lair where I'm hiding. In the afternoon I sculpt in clay and I wonder with distress if I will ever become human again. I smell this filth so embedded in me—how will it be possible to clean this? I'm crying for being with this for so many years, and always feeling the void, the absence of life. From my hands emerges the face of a man-fish, mouth open, swallowing the air with a distressed and stupid look.

I look at the doll. I understand little by little how this child-trash makes me live all wrong: he's ready to do anything to compensate for his feeling of nonexistence. How often it was he who expressed himself in my words, my attitudes, my tantrums, was frantically seeking to avoid facing this unbearable experience to be nothing but remains, detritus, a filthy thing that we throw away as soon as possible?

This is the third day. I have no more restraint vis-à-vis the "trash man"; it has become my way of life. But when I spend a little time in the presence of friends I feel terribly isolated. I sink into some kind of perverse pleasure, watching them do things together and live. Hate grows inside; I would like to scream at them that they are probably as horrible as me inside. But I then understand my complicity with my mother in this chronic pessimism that binds me. If I wish, I can counter this trash man who isolates himself so as not to suffer—I can go toward life, movement, people—but I choose to follow his tendency and I'm sinking into destructive isolation because I believe I'm only this child-trash. I eventually discover it is in fact only a part of me!

The day continues, many memories come to light; I see again the situations where this child-trash prevented me from acting, from living experiences, from living altogether.

On the last evening, however, again I feel terribly distant from others. Doubts turn my stomach inside out, I feel like tomorrow I won't manage to finish my act, that I will remain the trash man. This is a terrible feeling and I don't want to be confronted by it any longer, especially not in the murky solitude of my dump. I think like crazy of death, of suicide, the only truly definitive escape. To die, rather than live this emptiness in me. I cannot stand it anymore.

The next morning I find it hard to decide to finish my act. I fear I won't do it at the right time, I'm afraid to confront my mother. Finally I start, following some signs and because I remember what I want: to get out of there, to go toward life.

In the shower I gradually become human. The scents of gel and shampoo seem divine to me, I shiver with pleasure feeling and seeing myself clean. Quickly I find my mother and ask her to accompany me, a little nervous but without aggressiveness—simply, it's time. Once at the landfill I say the magic phrase and leave calmly without waiting for her reaction. Returning, I receive a warm hug from a friend, and it's like a welcome to humanity. I feel disoriented like I'm walking a tightrope, but I don't want to analyze anything yet. I enjoy contact with a group of friends, and everything seems more colorful and alive.

With hindsight, I see that this act enabled me to clearly identify this trash man and understand what he awakens in me. It's no longer a vague feeling sending me into a downward spiral, it is a part of myself with which I have communed. Through this act I gained the right not to be its toy anymore, as if I had extended interior territory.

This act is like a starting point from which I can consciously undertake the edification of the man I want to be and not the man my mother saw in me. My experiences now serve me not to obtain recognition to fill the emptiness but to enrich an inner domain that grows gradually.

⇾ LETTER 41 ⇽
....
From Meryl (thirty-three years old)

I asked for this act to free myself from very heavy issues related to my mother. Like her, I'm so cold and insensitive that I have no concept of reality. For a few years my mother suffered from multiple sclerosis and she is in danger of ending her life completely paralyzed in a wheelchair. I'm very afraid about ending up like her and giving this burden to my daughter.

The act is as follows:

Spend ten days in a wheelchair with arm splints. A friend will be completely in charge of me (dress me, wash me, feed me . . .). On the last day cover my body in white candle wax then massage a large block of ice until it melts. Mix the water thus obtained with earth and use it to clean myself.

Then use this mixture of soil, water, and wax to fill a doll that I will return to my mother.

The first days were very hard physically. I had never felt such pain for so long. The highlight was the evening of the third day. I had an uncontrollable fit of rage: I suddenly tore off my splints but as if I also wanted to get rid of my arms. Then I burst into tears, refusing to let my friend take care of me.

It didn't last long—ten minutes according to her—but afterward I felt very guilty and I was wondering if I'd messed it all up, losing it, or if I could continue. I decided to carry on by adding an hour on the last day to make up for the wasted time and not allowing myself to "cheat."

Despite this, the physical problems were less painful than feeling monstrous, like a slimy and repulsive being who no one dared to look at and whose presence was intolerable. I wanted to hide because I had the impression that after having seen me like this no one would stand my presence. I especially felt very bad with regard to my husband and I thought that this act risked ending our relationship. Being like this and not being able to move made my mind crazier and more negative than usual. Either I repeated, "You are like that, there is nothing left to do, you are just that. . . ." or I tried to cut myself off from reality and enter a state of apathy where nothing mattered. It was demonic.

One evening I fainted during a meal where the conversation turned to surgical operations and blood. Later I thought that this certainly showed that I still did not accept my blood, my lineage. Shortly after I received family photos that my mother promised me a long time ago. There were lots of photos from my childhood and two photos of my mother: in the first she was with her four brothers, all of them taller than her by at least a head, and she wrote on the picture: "Why are they all so big?" On the second she is at communion and wrote: "Don't I look like an innocent lamb?" To me she seemed diabolical!

Seeing these photos I felt how bound we are by hatred and how the image that we want to give of ourselves opposes reality. Toward the friend who took care of me, I first felt a terrible maternal need. I saw myself like a beggar perpetually demanding attention; but little by little aggressiveness appeared because I felt humiliated and despicable.

Yet despite moments of tension I always felt emotionally supported and my friend helped me not to sink into depression. The last day of the act, the one where I finally left my chair, I was anxious and I felt physically weak, but I was very determined internally. First I made a fire in the bedroom and melted some white wax to cover my body. At first it burned me and then would partially peel off. I felt like I had blisters all over my body, a lot of wax was falling, and I needed time to cover myself completely. Then I started massaging my ice block. I froze six liters of water and it took me almost six hours of intensive massage to get it to melt! The first four hours I warmed my hands against my body but then I gradually brought them closer to the fire to warm them more and accelerate the transformation. Through the act of massaging I entered a different state; I had no mind, no more notion of time, I wanted to melt my ice at all costs and I started talking to the fire to help me. I wanted to become fire to melt my heart of ice. When the last piece of ice broke in my hands I was shocked, and while continuing to massage small pieces I picked up one and threw it in the embers saying, "Burn me!" It immediately evaporated, leaving a black trace in the red of the embers. I felt like a witch and thought maybe I'd gone too far.

After that I mixed part of the water with earth and clay and used it to clean myself. I had trouble removing the wax, especially from my hair where I had to cut some locks. Then I rinsed myself with the remaining water and let the muddy mixture of earth/wax/water dry so I could use it to fill my doll. I showered, dressed, and went to the kitchen where I met my friend. She explained to me that my daughter (four years old) said that I got rid of a body that was too small and a mother too big. That moved me a lot. The next day I melted the wax that I had not used, to remove it from the pan, and I caused a huge fireball that flashed at me twice and burned the canvas awning above me. It scared me a lot. I thought it was my hatred that caused this: it was a destructive act that ruined everything. But in the evening, lighting the fire, I saw myself again throwing my ice and asking the fire to burn me and I understood how I provoked the fire. I didn't know what to think anymore—I was totally disoriented. It took me several days to make my doll and fit everything into it. I made it all white to represent my desire for perfection and because that reminded me of my mother in her communion dress. I sent it to my mother stating that this was the result of a psychomagical act.

After the act I had some water left that I used to wash myself. I filtered it, cleaned it, and added orange blossom, honey, and rose petals. I used it to bathe my daughter. After this bath I massaged her, then we drank apple juice in champagne flutes.

She asked me a lot of questions about my act. I explained to her what I was doing and why. She was very moved that I did something with her, for her. She thanked me warmly.

I was also very moved.

→ LETTER 42 ←

From Charlotte (thirty-eight years old)

This act is intended to deliver me from my rage at being born a woman, and for also giving birth to a woman. I also have to free my daughter Isadora from the same pain I passed on to her.

The deed consists of the following parts:

Kill a goat, skin it, cook it, and serve it to Nicolas and Isadora (my husband and daughter). Go visit my mother, Clotilde, who still lives on my childhood farm, and after a long conversation ask her to participate in this magical act. Explain to her how much I suffered from being a girl, bringing back the memories, especially those related to Grandma, my paternal grandmother who lived with us and who embodied a pinnacle of hatred of the feminine. Show her how very badly I experienced motherhood because of all this. Then explain to her that what she did with me I reproduce with Isadora; the very strong symbiosis between us comes from the fact that she wanted to make me her accomplice in the misfortune of being a woman. In this dynamic we were born and live to suffer.

I will also recreate what I lived through at the time of my mother's remarriage, namely the mother selling her daughter to the father believing that if he finds her kind, lovable, cute . . . if the girl seduces the father, a little of this "love" will rebound on the mother who will be forgiven for having given birth to a girl this way.

I will tell her about a memory that has indelibly marked me and that I had erased until recently: I was about four and my mother and I went to the hospital to visit my biological father, Roger, who was suffering from brain cancer of which he would soon die. My mother put me on his bed so that I could give him a kiss. He pushed me away like he was repelling an unwanted animal, accompanying his gesture with a violent interjection in patois. My mother consoled me, asking me to forgive him because he was very sick. . . . A few minutes later, while I remained sulking in a corner, Roger asked about the cows, worried about their health, demanded that Jean-François, my elder brother, prepare a new pasture. . . .

Following this recounting I have to cover myself with cow dung and wander around the farm for three hours, after which I will ask my mother to wash me like when I was little, in front of the fireplace, in a basin. I will then put on a very beautiful dress—new and feminine—and I will burn the filthy clothes.

I must visit Roger's grave with cow dung, telling him, "What I was to you, less than a cow patty, I give back to you." Then I must visit Grandma's grave to express all my rage toward her, let everything out, even urinating and defecating on her grave. Clean up, and plant a rosebush. Accompanied by my mother, go to the cemetery where my maternal grandmother, Cécile, is buried. Get out of the car, both of us with a ball and chain attached to the ankle bearing the following inscription: "My misfortune is to be a woman." Then put four steaks on this grave, one for Cécile, one for Clotilde, one for me, and one for Isadora, saying, "I give you back what you transmitted to us, that we are only pieces of meat." Clotilde removes her ball and then mine.

Go to the big neighboring city together to pamper ourselves for a few hours in a spa or such. Go out for dinner in one of the most chic restaurants. During the evening, while chatting with my mother, learn what she would have liked to study. Back home, make a diploma for her desired studies and send it to her.

I did the first part of the act on the farm where I live. Taking advantage of a lull in the rain, I took the young goat that I was going to sacrifice and I went into nature, far away. I barely had the goat in my arms when a violent emotion took hold of me. How could I commit such an act if it cried like a child, weighed as much as a baby, and radiated living heat? Crying and shouting, I thought of the purpose of this act: to free myself from my death compulsions for being a woman, which I extend to my daughter. All while screaming, crying, and stumbling on the soggy floor I suddenly realized that the goat could escape at any time and that everything would be a failure. This is what gave me the strength to take the knife. Seeing life leaving by this blood I was shedding made me feel like a criminal. The blood, the blood of the heritage that we carry, the blood of menstruation which marks well my belonging to the feminine—although depression and anorexia have always tried to distance me from it—the blood that as a mother I finally spilled to give life, the blood that today nourishes the baby that I carry, this blood, all these bloods, I got rid of them for death.

My whole being was torn and still is when I remember those times. Where to find the strength to carry on? The butchering was even worse because I saw quite clearly it was a female that was sacrificed. I was monstrous, as are all those who through the centuries killed baby girls at birth. The heat emanating from the body, which seemed to still be throbbing under the heavy rain falling from the sky, only increased my horror. The complexity of everything that constitutes the anatomy of this animal made me feel deep respect for Life. How could I in seconds destroy such a great wonder?

Back at the farm an armor numbed me while I cut and cured the meat—then waves of intense emotions overwhelmed me again. The day after, Nicolas and Isadora found the dish I prepared delicious. Personally I found it difficult to not gag!

The day after our arrival at my parents' home, as soon as the sun rose, I found myself looking for cow manure in the thick fog that covered the surrounding meadows.

Unusually, there was not a single cow in sight! Finally I found some dung, although it wasn't very fresh. Then I asked my mother to have a quiet conversation, just the two of us. We went into the kitchen of the old house nearby, the place where we lived when I was a child. There, while preparing the meal, we talked. Clotilde immediately feared that I was seriously ill. When I reassured her, she relaxed. I had warned her though that we were probably going to cry a lot and that it would do us good. She replied that she would not cry because for her the worst thing was what she went through with Roger, the disease that led to his death. From that moment, I sensed in her a sort of barrier that didn't allow her to listen to me fully, taking care of trifles instead. She worried that I would make an exhaustive list of things she had done wrong, debt-settling style. Her attitude was attentive. Once seated near the fire at my side, she spoke very little and did not interrupt, allowing me to delve deeper into my memories. The memories she tried to evoke were meant to soften my point. I told her that we weren't there to be *nice,* we had played that for too long. She finally cried when I brought up the memory at the hospital, but the next day she reminded me of when Roger was waiting for me with his arms wide open. . . . What struck me was that she didn't want to hear how differently she treated my brothers during their childhood instead of caring about me.

Typical! This triggered a lot of aggressive feelings over the next two days. Concerning motherhood, she reminded me how happy she was the day I told her I was going to be a mother, because what I had said until then about motherhood made her very sad. From the beginning of adolescence I told her that I would never, ever have children. Later I would talk about "knocked-up" colleagues with contempt.

Concerning the misfortune of being born a woman, she told me that her mother said to anyone who would listen that if she could she would have called her youngest "Sintufarion," which in patois means "we could have done without you." Our conversation made her realize it was because of being born a woman, something that had left its mark on her whole life. Indeed, in this sharecropper family with a status resembling serfs of the Middle Ages, what mattered were the arms of men to work and not mouths to feed. We also talked about our shared vision of man, of all the negativity we projected on him as we put him on a pedestal and hated him at the same time. The last word made her jump at first but in the course of my explanations I believe she finally understood. In talking about my past relationships with men it was easy to show that my vision of a couple was disastrous. But my relationship with Nicolas showed that something harmonious was possible if the two of us were trying to understand what was happening in our unconscious. We talked about my mother's relationship with her second husband who became my dad. I told her that she had chosen to sacrifice her life as a couple because of this hatred toward men, while Granny openly hated this newcomer who somehow came to replace her own late husband, who died very young, or her two sons who successively passed away around the age of thirty-five. I reminded her how I was also fully complicit in this, treating my own father in the worst way. Clotilde looked like she had discovered a new vision of things. She told me that Jean-François had explained to her that according to him Granny had lost her sons to become the protagonist herself. My interpretation was harder: our common hatred for men went so far as to eliminate them. Castration was so strong in our minds that it didn't bother to express itself symbolically. My mother listened with great interest. When I told her that Granny was also a part of us, she who always saw herself as the nice one recognized that there was some wickedness in each of us. She seemed to meditate on it for a moment.

I also told her how much I was concerned about Isadora, who refuses to sleep, something that could be explained by the fear of death since I transmit to her that she's not worth anything because she's a girl. I also told her about the rage Isadora expresses openly, unlike me who internalizes, causing depression. We talked about the hardest times of my life. Clotilde subsequently agreed to do whatever she could to help us heal.

The three hours I stayed in the farm covered in cow dung seemed like an eternity to me. I moved from moments of despair, rage, and anger to infinite sadness. The places where I was wandering were practically abandoned for twenty years, but the worst is that this abandonment added to my mother's tendency to hoard all sorts of things, and so the entire space started to look like a dump. In fits of rage I began to burn a pile of old things in an open fire behind the farm, especially those that belonged to Roger or Grandma. Freezing cold, while I was sitting on a pile of dry manure, as if lifeless, a fly we call *verminière*— shit fly—came to rest on me. . . . I couldn't help but think that I was on the right path. I threw up several times because of the stench and emotions stirred by this act. When it was time to meet my mother I had to wait a few minutes . . . again her indifference, I thought. When she arrived she was almost bubbly, carefree, she seemed not to want to see that I was covered in shit. Her coldness and superficiality hurt a lot. While she was washing me I cried. I found the situation symbolically terribly strong and my mother seemed indifferent to that. I thought of Isadora, that I would like to be able to wash her of everything I burdened her with, with more heart that my mother put in it.

Afterward I put on my flowery dress in dusky pink tones, and I felt potentially able to heal. I had trouble finding it in the time between when the act was defined and arriving at my parents. I needed a dress and I could only find ensembles! I wanted color and lightness and I only found clean lines and black that made me look like the family widows!

The fire pit, in which I had burned all that my rage had thrown there, now welcomed the dirty clothes that I wore. I chose for this occasion Grandma's or Roger's clothes that I had no trouble finding among my mother's relics.

The next morning I went to buy the rosebush I had to plant on Granny's grave. At the nursery a large sign greeted me: "Today is Grandmother's Day, give her a rosebush!" I thought that it really was going to be my grandmother's celebration! I took that as a wink from above.

Roger and his mother, Grandma, are buried in the same family vault in a countryside cemetery along a busy road, on a hill. It was windy and exposed to rain that day. First observation: it would be difficult to hide myself from the eyes of the neighborhood, and I would have to rely on luck. While giving Roger back the cow dung, I was taken by strong and contradictory emotions. In fact it felt like when I was a little girl, where before this vault every Sunday for years I read Roger's name and said, "Our Father who art in heaven . . ." thinking of him and moping, as my mother and Granny urged me to do in this cult of the dead. Absolutely criminal for a child. At the same time another part of me was rebelling as never before and it was with this rage that I threw the manure on the vault. I already felt empty, exhausted, and yet the part about Grandma was still to start. I thought back to what I had been through with her, about her wickedness, about what she transmitted to me as a negative image of life, and then I kicked the vault. My rage did not rise to the extent that I expected so I thought that my actions really had to be absolutely remarkable. So I spat, urinated, defecated on the edges of the vault. Finding it wasn't enough because I couldn't get on top of the vault, it being too high and wet scum from the rain making it too dangerous to climb in my state, I took a stick and smeared copiously on the engraving of Grandma's name, Angèle . . . speaking of an angel! Finally satisfied with what I'd done, again without energy, I began cleaning. Alas! The faucet that I found in the cemetery didn't work, and on top of that it stopped raining! Here I was going around the cemetery looking for a ditch filled with clean water. Nothing. I went back to the faucet, thinking that since it was winter the faucet could have been protected from freezing, and I discovered a concrete slab that seemed to confirm my intuition. Here I was, armed with a piece of wood to pry, lifting, sliding, moving this heavy slab that reminded me of a tombstone. With great effort I finally managed to reach a second tap protected by fiberglass. It worked, I had water. There too I felt the symbolic load of this search for water, emotions, and life. As soon as I started cleaning a car stopped and someone entered the cemetery. What I did was quite visible, especially on the engraving . . . it couldn't be the little birds that did that. . . . Quickly, I cleaned first the engraving, with difficulty because a sponge at the end of a stick does not do wonders, and I just had time to crouch near the rosebush waiting to be planted when footsteps approached. I then heard: "Ooh! But it's LauRRRette"—the typical rolled "RRR" of the region—"Ooh! But you haven't changed, I recognized you . . . you're getting down to one hell of a job to clean up all that." It was Ginette, a cousin's cousin; everyone knows each other in the area. A reputation of a nice-girl-who-plants-a-rosebush-on-her-grandmother's-grave-on-Grandmother's-Day-when-she-lives-so-far will go around the block!

I finished the act in the rain; it helped the cleaning and the rose-bush will grow better! Two days later my mother and I went to her mother's grave. We tied the ball and chain to our ankles and I asked my mother that during the journey she concentrate on what we carried: "My misfortune is to be a woman." She cooperated and shared with me her thoughts about her mother and her sisters. As an absolutely striking fact, by analyzing the lives of her sisters, it seemed to us that Juliette, the eldest, died at the age of twenty-two because she literally killed herself working in the fields like a man. Yvette, on the other hand, preferred to remain at a mental age of ten so her mother would be obliged to take care of her when she only had eyes for her son. I learned that Yvette had tried several times to die by refusing all food.

Clotilde chose to enter the cemetery by the lower door because it is on a steep slope and we would no longer feel the weight of the can-nonball that we were dragging. The rest of the act went as planned in a climate of gravity and concentration. In the end my mother asked me if I thought it was possible to throw these balls in the river and I thought that was a great idea. She then explained to me that she thought of that because in the prayer that she said to cure neuralgia (a secret of a healer transmitted to her by her father on his deathbed) she asked for the pain to go under the stones of streams and seas.

The afternoon and evening we spent in town was very pleasant. We talked a lot and for once this was not her usual incessant grind of words; she also tried to get me to talk, showing more interest and even showing me admiration. The spa with oriental decor was a real cocoon. One of the treatments particularly moved me. I was wrapped in a large electric blanket after a big tonic seaweed bath, surrounded with a soft light and delicate perfumes. It made me cry from well-being in the great warm arms of life.

The restaurant where we dined was really great. Delicious dinner.

This act made me aware that I have to free my daughter because I live her life as I lived the arrival of my brother Jérémy to my family. That is to say, I believe that she is considered better than me, that she takes up all the space, that no one loves me anymore because they only love her . . . as the birth of Jérémy made me feel. He was a boy and so was considered better than me. This discomfort concretely manifested itself through my daughter complaining all the time and becoming unlikable—reflecting my desire for her to be pushed away and for me to remain the nice one who is accepted.

I have to get Isadora out of this place and clean it up as soon as possible because I'm pregnant with a second child, and in the current state for me to have children means to lose my own existence. I have been immersed in a deep malaise which has been expressed by an inner character: a woman full of hate.

I realize it is easy to rant about everything. I understand the connection between the need to feel alive and rage expressing itself. Everything merges in my emotions because I live the despair of Isadora who feels obliged to complain, to say no continuously to feeling alive. Whenever I ask if I exist I become upset because the question concerns both my own existence flouted within my family but also the existence of my daughter and the baby that I carry; everything collides.

That first day exhausted me emotionally. I barely slept, so little that I had the impression that the leg that dragged the ball and chain hurt. The next day I started to experience the act as a game. I was still unpleasant but more inventive in my way of taking space. What was hard was to meet the puzzled and deep look of Isadora. I was avoiding her but felt like I heard her crying continuously.

Gradually the tears that accompanied my questions about life have been transformed because some people have passed on to me the absolute reality of my existence with strength and enthusiasm. I came out of this exchange fulfilled. Giving and receiving at this time meant the same thing; love must be something like that. That same night I received a letter from my mother apologizing for the insensitivity. When

I lit two candles while thinking hard about Isadora and the baby, the baby started to move in my belly, as indeed it does as I write this. This is magical.

THANKS,

CHARLOTTE

⤏ LETTER 43 ⤎

From Chris (sixty years old)

At the end of December 2002, I had a dream harshly scolding me, urging me to feel, to embody emotions, and to communicate: "Tell your brother André that you love him, tell your son that you love him."

I've known for a long time that I literally live in my head. What psychomagic act could make a breach in this fortified dungeon? None I guess, but I will do it anyway because I know from experience I am ignorant of many things.

My mind is full of scenarios that turn like carousels: I like this a lot and only come out when the outside world requires it. These scenarios are technical and scientific in content, always fascinating. It's about problem-solving in my head; the suspense can last for weeks. I have learned to control it well, with one exception: I regularly become obsessed with everything connected to the world of flight. The little mental computer keeps redesigning my glider, which will one day allow me to explore the world of birds, the magic of the third dimension.

The goal is to free myself from this obsession to finally be able to live in my body rather than in my head. To break contact with the ground, I will nest in a tree from sunrise until sunset. I will make myself a helmet that isolates me to the maximum, making me blind and deaf. It will envelop my head completely and have the shape of my glider, with feather-covered wings. At nightfall, I will throw this helmet from the top of a dam so that the river carries away its debris.

Beforehand, I will remove three feathers that I will keep to write and remind myself that my name is Chris. I will attach my pilot's log to a balloon bouquet and let it fly away.

After much research (my tendency is to complicate everything in order to delay taking action), I simply picked a tree that I called Merlin—possibly disruptive noises will disappear in the incessant babble from the nearby stream. A big rope stretched between two branches provided the seat. The helmet was a sturdy wooden crate stuffed with foam into which my head sunk completely. Two large wooden wings covered with feathers gave it the appearance of a turn-of-the-century glider.

Sunrise found me perched in the tree. Then the inevitable small inconveniences appeared: the north wind blowing up the stream forced me to spend the day in a fetal position to keep from freezing; I had to cling to the branch because if I fell the heavy construction that imprisoned my head would certainly break my neck; I thought I would spend all those hours in a total absence of sensation. I was shivering with cold, I was thirsty, I had cramps, the blood beat in my ears, my head resounded with the sound of my breathing, and above all I had a disastrous impression of having prepared all this like a dumbass.

I resisted the urge to take off my helmet, even when I sensed that an intrigued vulture had just perched on my tree. I lost all notion of time, an eternity went by, the cold became sharper, and then I freed my head—the sun had just set. I was not going down immediately because the twilight, the noises, and scents that flooded me suddenly made me dizzy. It was wonderful and I took advantage of it until nightfall. Then I awkwardly resumed contact with the ground and focused on the next step because I didn't want to deepen the impression of a failed attempt. Fortunately, while going to get the car, I met friends gathered around a bottle of wine, obviously a good omen. . . .

I left at night with my helmet-glider from which I took three beautiful feathers. When I dropped it from the top of the dam, its fall was impressively realistic. I saw the silhouette of my glider in the chiaroscuro falling toward its death on a huge block of concrete. It was really the Monarch* crashing down there, with a sickening sound of an egg cracking, and then it was engulfed by waves.

But what happened was quite unbelievable: this heavy wooden construction hit the flat stone with full force, the noise was full and dull, both dry and definitive, but not one plank shattered, and only a few feathers stuck out. The engine remained planted on its snub nose, an improbable image of a stubborn thing that does not want to die.

I remained briefly paralyzed in disbelief, then fled the scene, not allowing myself to think, focused solely on driving.

What happened next fell into oblivion, and I can't manage to reflect on what happened. The turkey feather pen writes well, thank you.

Then came the end of the act: at the edge of the steep slope overlooking the Valley of the Garganta Fría,† I filled twenty-six helium balloons (the binding of my flight log was heavy . . .) while thinking back to the times and the circumstances of these carefully recorded flights. When I dropped the notebook hanging from its balloons, it actually flew away! I instinctively jumped forward to catch it and almost rolled down the slope. I watched the log merge with the cloud and didn't feel at all relieved; on the contrary, I had the feeling of an irretrievable loss, as if I had voluntarily amputated something.

The next few weeks are without dreams; I feel repugnance deep inside me. I am happy to live in the moment, obstinately. I feel it will take time, I feel like a convalescent. This obsession with flight has been my escape route for fifty years. My mind feels loss. . . . It would like to believe that nothing has happened. At that time, a twin-engine would pass daily above the farm with the insistent hum of an insect; for me it is worse than a boil, until the day when I don't even look up anymore, and it's getting better. Day after day, manual labor keeps my feet on the ground and I start enjoying life fully in the present, without

---

*Monarch could be interpreted as the name of the patient's father, or as a critical image of himself, of his egocentrism.
†A place in Andalusia.

the necessity of an escape-refuge into the mind. I increasingly have the impression of living in colors, then I start to dream again.

I imagine that there will be setbacks but I know that this obsession has lost a lot of its attractive energy; I now know that those hours spent recreating myself in a mental fiction subtracted from my life experience. I try not to forget that I didn't give up a child's dream, but a convenient chimera rooted in childhood, at the age when physical inferiority began to hurt and pushed me to cast off my moorings with the real world.

End of one life, beginning of another.

⇻ LETTER 44 ⇺
....
From Emily (forty-six years old)

Objective: overcome my legacy fashioned from hatred, fear, envy, lack of will, and lack of aspiration.

Design of the act: Choose a tree that is not very healthy, and choose my branch. Put fresh soil in a jar. Stay awake all night by the tree, with the new earth beside me, and take stock of my life. The purpose is to examine what in me is well attached to this tree.

Cut the branch in the morning, at sunrise. Burn the branch and mix its ashes with the fresh soil. For a while I must pay close attention to my new soil, to water it and watch over it every day. Finally, when the time comes, buy a sweet orange tree and plant it in this new ground.

First I chose the tree. I found a very dry strawberry tree. I chose a solitary branch; other branches were all intertwined.

I pitched a tent near the tree to shelter me.

When night fell I left with a saw, my soil, an alarm clock to keep me awake, and a thermos of hot tea.

At first I had difficulty finding the tree in the night. I stayed next to it in order to immerse myself in its essence. There, I did exercises to visualize my life and look for the points in common, and whatever else bound me to this tree.

Immediately images of my life arose in my mind. More than once I wanted to give up. I found it too powerful, too painful. I was crying. But I continued without respite. I took stock of my life all night long. I started at the beginning, I saw the mistakes made, I dissected my behaviors marked by this legacy.

Far into the night I found myself feeling consumed with negativity. I couldn't do it anymore, I was choking, I smelled bad.

Fortunately, the sun came up shortly after. I felt a strong urge to detach myself from this tree and I cut it with a lot of energy. Then I spent a few days with the pot full of my fresh soil and the cut branch.

One day I woke up and I knew that the moment to burn the branch had arrived.

The branch took a long time to burn. I watched the fire with conflicting emotions. At times I felt liberated, then felt tremendously sad. Nevertheless, I concentrated to feel a part of me burning with this branch. I took the ashes and mixed them with soil. I felt ready to go buy my tree. What a disappointment, not an orange tree to be found for at least a month and a half. So, I had to be patient. A daily work began: to be attentive to my fresh soil every day.

Then, without realizing it, I relapsed into aspects related to my mother, which is when I found a small piece of my branch in my car. I burned it right away.

The days followed with many ups and downs, with rather violent alternations. Then, I was suddenly offered work in Paris for four days. I immediately thought of my pot of new earth, impossible to drag along. So I decided to take only some of it.

In Paris I had to share the room. This caused problems because of my intimate relationship with my earth. At the last minute they gave me a room to myself. Phew!

Those four days in Paris were very special. On the one hand I was immersed in a very beautiful, very chic, very feminine mode— and on the other hand, people I worked with corresponded to my materia prima, to the branch that I had cut and burnt. And then my work caused me to move again. This time I was transferred to Seville.

While in Madrid I had to wait for orange trees, in Seville the season was almost over. Luckily I was able to buy one that was very flowery.

I planted the tree at a friend's house. I was very emotional. It's a beautiful little tree with a scent that transports you to a new world, cleaner, happier.

This act is a step toward a different way of living.

EMILY

⇥ LETTER 45 ⇤

From Miguel (fifty-seven years old)

I am both very proud and have suicidal tendencies: "Life is a prison, it is better to die." I asked to be released from that.

The proposed act is in several parts:

Place some very cumbersome growths attached to each of my thighs. Decorate these growths with some samples of mountaineering material, photos of my heroic past as an isolated mountain dweller. Also attach a doll representing contempt for women. Live harnessed like this for ten days. Since I still want to die, go with all that into a coffin and stay there until I'm fed up.

Listen to a requiem at the same time. Once out of the coffin, burn it all, coffin and clothing included. Burn a photo of my father and a photo of my mother, and drink a glass of bitter liquor with a handful of the special ashes. Dress in brand new purple clothes. Prepare on this fire a good meal for my friends.

I made the growths from wood panels, which gave me a burden one meter wide. I decorated everything as planned. For ten days I bumped into things loudly everywhere, it hurt to sit down, and everything caught on me when I moved. In short, discomfort and exhausting harassment were guaranteed.

Ten days of wanting to just quit because it restricted my life's possibilities considerably and my ability to move easily. All my activities were hampered. It got harder and harder to endure. After these ten days I got into a coffin in this state, alone in a dark, hidden room, without an alarm clock or anything to tell time. I listened to Mozart's "Requiem" on repeat.

Stillness soon became torture and I quickly realized that I was better off enjoying life, seeing people. I held on like this for three days. On the afternoon of the third day I got out and burned everything in a big pile of wood, including my clothes. I dressed up in new clothes. It was raining hard. I drank a glass of bitter liquor with a handful of my parents' ashes (after they died in a car accident, I asked for them to be cremated together). Despite the beating rain and fatigue I was able to make the planned meal on the fire and spend a pleasant evening with friends.

I must point out that I have experienced frequent stomach issues that completely block me. Since the realization of this psychomagical act I no longer have such attacks. I admit that I still experience waves of depression from time to time, but they are so much lighter and much easier to control and get over. Thank you, psychomagic.

MIGUEL

⤞ LETTER 46 ⤝

From Raissa (sixty-seven years old)

I wanted to do something to help my sons free themselves from the burden that I make them carry. I was not a good mother. It's my eldest son who played the role of father for me: he often even pulled me out of dangerous situations which I regularly sank into in relationships with violent men. As for my youngest son, I was absent.

The act that was proposed to me was to be carried out entirely alone, in Paris; it was to last for seven days. (In reality, it unfolded over eight days, for the reason given below.) I wasn't meant to talk to anyone about my act. The act was as follows:

Put photos of my sons on my bed. The pictures should be very compressed, in order to see how they were nonexistent for me. Wear a blonde wig. On opposite walls of my room, on one side stick photos of men, and on the other side put pictures of sad little girls.

Also on the wall stick a black leather whip.

Attach a huge penis with big testicles to my stomach, and stick small photos of each son on each testicle. Sleep with it. Place a flat stone the size of my fist over my heart. Sleep with it, too.

On alternating days, live either like a little, narcissistic, euphoric girl or like a small and depressed one. On euphoric days, sleep facing the guys; and on the depressed days, turn toward the sad girls.

For one week, three times a day, for ten minutes, look at the mini-photos of my sons, idolizing them and showing them to imaginary people, both indoors and outside. At the end of these days, keep the photos, and bring together all the used elements: wig, whip, dildo, stone, pictures of guys and girls, and throw them into the Seine. Then show up at my mother's grave at Sceaux in order to affirm my will not to die in hatred, unreconciled with my soul.

Go to my childhood church and have the water blessed. Wash myself with it and purify my chest. Keep some of it for later. During all this time, keep two doves in a cage. After washing myself with holy water, leave with the two doves, to which I will tie the photos of my sons. Go to the Sacré-Cœur in Montmartre. Pour on each picture three drops of holy water, first on that of the eldest, then on the second. After giving the doves a kiss, set them free.

Before starting the act I was going mad. So I submitted to the impulse of the moment, without desiring anything, nor speculating on the results. I knew I must dive into memories to clarify my life alongside my sons.

In Paris, in January, around 10:45 a.m. I planned to stay in my apartment, where I was guaranteed peace. I had already bought the penis in Seville. I bought two male doves on Quai de la Mégisserie. It wasn't the right season, but I still found some. I got myself a long blonde wig. In a sex shop I found a black leather whip.

I took advantage of the energy I still had to get to Saint-Jacques du Haut-Pas, my teenage parish.

The sexton advised me to come back the next day for holy water. I came wearing a wig, which did not seem to surprise him! After a visit to my mother's grave, I had a liter of holy water blessed by the priest with a baptismal text!

My elements were in my possession, the mini-photos installed on my bed.

First day: I'm decked out with the sex organ on my belly, stone stuck on my chest. I'm deformed. How could I not be? A bad mother is not aesthetic. A dove already worries me. I put the name of my eldest son on it; he suffered the most from my selfishness and my infantilism. It's the day of being a euphoric little girl. It gives me nausea and I cry idolizing my sons, inside the studio. Outside, it's harder. I see them sad, receiving nothing from me.

Second day: I didn't play the little depressed girl well. I went to my mother's store, on the Rue des Feuillantines. It's called "Art and Metamorphoses." I see this as a good sign for my sons. Outside, I always have trouble allowing myself to be moved. I still feel blocked by my narcissistic image.

Third day: As a narcissistic little girl, I try to give the doves seeds from my hand. They don't want them. It proves my lack of maternal energy. The doves sing all night long, every hour. I do not sleep anymore. I am overwhelmed. I understand that the selfish mother does not want to be disturbed. I made this observation when my children were young. This is the loving, vigilant, patient anti-mother. Before doing the ten minute exercise I feel a pain in my chest. Exercise is always strenuous on the outside. While showing the photos to an imaginary woman, she doesn't understand why I'm crying—I should be rejoicing in discovering their qualities. They surpassed me with their intelligence and their heart, all the better!

Fourth day: The dildo seems heavier and heavier. The stone hurts me, and this impression gets stronger every day. The weight of sex and a heart of stone prevented me from being a good mother.

Fifth day: Euphoric day, narcissistic little girl. A shock: in the mirror, a horrible witch with long hair, nudity soiled by sex, flayed by stone. The hater . . . !

Sixth day: In Parc Montsouris, during the ten-minute exercise outside, a man hands me a document: "The Way of Hope." He asks me if I believe in Christ, if I have faith. Yes! I feel, day and night, the weight of the stone. "Transforming Stone into Life."

Seventh day: A fever came over me. The doves ask me for something. My tensions increase, I suffocate. The doves are my two sons: their calls for affection, caresses.

Eighth day: Replaces the second day I considered useless. It's almost the end of my act and my anguish is high. I randomly open *The Dance of Reality:* the story of the man whose narcissistic mother cared about nothing but herself and her wrinkles. . . . Yes, that's what I am! I believe a dove broke its foot. I burst into tears, I give it an energetic healing with my hands. Painful observation: lack of vigilance, of attention. After a while, it comes back to life.

I am enraged: I take off all my accessories and I go to the Tolbiac riverbank. My eldest son was born nearby.

I throw the heavy package into the Seine and I go up the stairs without looking back. I feel light and I go to mother's grave in Sceaux. Sobbing, I affirm three times my will not to die in hatred and without being reconciled with my soul.

The doves are distressed. I wash myself with holy water and leave it to dry on my skin. It refreshes me. I purify my chest, which—soiled by hardness—seems soft to me. I leave with the doves in a large box. Around their necks, I hang with sewing thread the mini-photo of each of my sons. It's freezing. The taxi driver tells me it's a good idea to go to the Sacré-Cœur with this beautiful sun. He hears scratching in the box. I tell him that these are doves.

"Ah, are you going to send them to God?! . . ."

"Yes!"

"You are right!"

It's not pleasant to maneuver a big box up the staircase to the Dome! And for 329 steps! An impressive ascent! Well, I climbed seventy steps and I stopped on the first landing. I put three drops on the dove of my eldest son, I took it in my hands, I kissed it, and I set it on a low wall to fly away. I did the same for my other son. I placed them side by side. Now they were both facing their freedom.

The first made a few jumps, flying a short distance away. The other just flew away. I see that the photo's thread got caught in the foot of the eldest. I tried to move it, but the dove jumped and flew away.

I AM AT PEACE, THANK YOU.

RAISSA

⇢ LETTER 47 ⇠
....

From Neus (forty years old)

Dress as a priest, crucifix and all, carrying a lamb's brain in my underpants, with pictures of my father and mother glued to my chest. Take a walk like that for an hour, without speaking to anyone, but looking at everyone with contempt. If someone talks to me, tell them a sermon.

Then remove it all and drop it off at a monastery.

Eat the brains, and drink the ashes from a burned picture of my father in wine, and the ashes of my mother's burned photo in milk. Then dress very feminine.

I first went to look for the cassock. I had no idea if this would be easy or difficult to obtain, nor where to find one. I started in the center of Madrid where after visiting five stores, one street of prostitutes, and being discouraged by vendors, nuns, and spinsters, I almost gave up for the day. But I recalled the words of Alejandro that it was necessary to persist if obstacles appeared. So I walked into one last small store which wasn't any more promising. I hadn't even crossed the threshold, when I asked if by any chance . . . and there, I found the cassock I needed.

It was the only one left in this store, run by a monstrous woman who was very fat and maternal: reassuring, enveloping. The cassock remained because it was small . . . for a man, but ideal for me. I took it without hesitation. I paid without batting an eye at the price, consisting of the number 3, and accepted it with a smile, while noticing a huge selection of liturgical objects. I left. Exactly three doors down the street, I passed in front of a bookseller. Here, I could buy myself an old Bible! The bookseller offered me three of them. I took a classic Bible. I retraced my steps to buy myself a crucifix in a store run by Good Sisters. I chose one and paid. Normally I should have gotten change—a small amount—but the nun cashier felt it wasn't necessary. She gave me a dumb smile and blissfully turned around and disappeared.

I walked into a restaurant where I leafed through the old Bible. Suddenly, I burst out laughing: the Bible was published in 1947, the year my parents got married. The next day I went out to look for a wig. I wanted to make a believable priest and had to hide my voluptuous hair. I also bought a wide bandage to hide my beautiful chest, and very white men's underpants.

The choice of the monastery wasn't easy either, because there are mostly female convents. I chose Los Jeronimos, near Atocha. I wanted to go see where it was, and when I arrived I found an endless line of pious people who had come to adore the "Cristo de Medinaceli" there. I asked an old couple if there was still a religious community there. They confirmed it.

All that was left was to buy the brains, wine, and milk, which was not too difficult. Curiously, the first bottle of wine that fell into my hands was a Paternina. This name suited its purpose well.

Saturday morning. Needless to say the night preceding the act was restless. The next day I got up, dressed, and styled the wig. The brain between my legs bothered me a lot and my father's rather large photo scratched the sensitive skin of my belly. I flattened my chest and fattened my belly with shreds of an old black woolen fabric. I put makeup on to thicken my thin eyebrows and fade my pink lips. The result was scary! I cried over it; I can lean toward the masculine so easily. Besides, this disguise made me grimace very unpleasantly, which made me even more masculine and ugly. And I left like that.

I decided to park in the lower parking lot of Atocha in order to have a quiet place to change and a starting point close to busy areas and the chosen convent. I did so. I found a fairly isolated place, I put on my cassock, and I left on foot with a beating heart. I carried my crucifix, my Bible, and the stuffing. I wore a black scarf around my neck because it was very cold and raining.

The first thing to control: the pace of my approach. I felt like running, but a slow and solemn step was much better suited to my character. And in fact, it helped me dive into it much faster. But initially my legs were shaking. I followed a wide avenue, near the Prado and the Retiro. Suddenly, a small Portuguese family, clearly lost, stopped in front of me and asked me where the museum was. I waved my hand vaguely and sent them in the opposite direction growling a few incomprehensible words. I carried on walking. Horror! Five minutes later, we found ourselves face to face at a crossroads, them being still lost obviously. They asked me where the museum was. Again, I made a contemptuous and vague gesture telling them to keep going straight.

Then I found an entrance to the Retiro and I took it. It was marked: "Portal of the Fallen Angel." I walked down a wide alley. I walked—forcing myself—in the middle of sidewalks to oblige passersby to move aside as I passed. When I saw a group in the distance, instead of avoiding it, I rushed straight toward them. Surprise, people reacted by stepping aside with a certain respect, others with apathy.

I felt real in my parish priest disguise—deep inside, the role was easy for me to play. A group of Ecuadorians looked at me with a certain reverence, to whose gaze I responded with the greatest indifference. After an hour I was very cold. On my way back to the car a stupid young woman stopped to look at me.

I took everything off, slowly. I took off my makeup, restyled my hair. I put everything in a bag, I kept the photos and the brains in the car, I went to the toilet to take off my underwear, which I had also put in the bag, and I left for the monastery. When leaving the station the sun was out, shining bright. And there I began to feel the first effects of the magic act. I was overcome by a very intense emotion linked to the woman who I really am once I take off this thick masculine skin under which I've been hiding all my life. I was stripped of what always protected me and gave me a false reassurance. And I felt extremely fragile, small, and vulnerable. I cried until I reached the monastery.

I did not encounter any obstacles to leaving my bag with the cassock, crucifix, Bible, underpants, wig, scarf, and even the bandage and shreds. I heard a voice behind the door, so there was someone there. I went back to the station and while I cried on the way there, on the way back I was sobbing.

AMEN,

NEUS

⊹ LETTER 48 ⊱

From Roland

Toulon, July 3, 1999

My name is Roland. During your last seminar at the end of the month of May in Toulon I told you about the canker sores I've had in my mouth since early childhood. I explained that my mother never wanted me to be born and did everything possible to avoid it.

You asked me about my profession and I answered that I was a submariner in the National Navy. You then gave me this psychomagical act which I carried out two weeks later, to the letter, as it should be. I remember that I was already living it little by little as you were dictating it to me.

Here is my story:

I bought a statue of the Holy Virgin, rented snorkel gear, and bought a camphor tree for the accomplishment of my deed. On Friday, June 11, 1999, I descended into the sea with the statue of the Blessed Virgin. Once at the bottom I let my anger erupt, releasing all this violence which was in me while piercing her ears. I lost track of time but I think I insulted her for a long time during which my emotion was intense. Once this anger was expressed, still at the bottom of the water, I kissed her, entwined in my arms. Then I took a little walk with her on the sea floor. I felt good, almost like a baby in the mother's womb, happy to come out to the world soon.

I then came back to the surface and I took her out of the water. Something surprising happened while surfacing. I was not far from the shore. I saw a statue of the god Neptune on the edge looking in my direction. I didn't realize his presence before getting into the water. The next morning I had to finish my act. By chance my son Alexandre was with me and I had to take care of him. However, it did not interrupt my act. We were in the car on the way to where I decided to bury the Virgin (at Notre-Dame of May) when he asked me, "Dad, is this statue your mother?" (Alexandre is five years old.) I answered him that yes, this statue represented my mother. Satisfied with the answer he said nothing more. I felt that my son was happy to accompany his father, that it was apparent on his face.

We arrived in a place that I was not familiar with.

There, stuck on an umbrella pine, was a sign that read: "Here, school children have participated in reforestation." There was also the WWF panda on a small signpost. I thought that was the ideal location to complete my act. I dug a hole in the ground and I placed the statue of the Blessed Virgin.

I fashioned a small phallus with a bit of marzipan. I placed it between my lips. I lowered my face to the belly of the virgin and put the phallus there. I spoke these words: "Now I find the verb, I find life."

Alexandre watched me without saying anything. He understood everything. Otherwise he would have asked me a whole series of questions. He was assisting there at his father's birth. He watched the scene, sat on his little legs smiling at me tenderly. I then buried the statue and planted the camphor tree.

Alexandre then insisted on watering the tree with the water provided for this purpose. He told me that he wanted the tree to live, so he insisted on giving it a drink himself.

Since then, I haven't had canker sores in my mouth and life has new flavor. Maybe I will have the pleasure to thank you in person in September in Toulon.

THANK YOU, A THOUSAND TIMES, THANK YOU, ALEJANDRO.

ROLAND

→ LETTER 49 ←
....

From Daniel

Barcelona, June 29, 2004

Dear Teacher:

My name is Daniel. I was in Paris with you on December 4, 2002, at Le Téméraire. My patient number was 17. Finally, almost a year and a half after our meeting, I decide to write to you. As you say, writing you a letter is the only payment you ask in return. Something as simple as that took me all this time. Many might think that just to write in exchange for something that was given free is simple, but it is not at all.

I've done everything you indicated, and just the way you told me. After performing the psychomagic act, I was full of questions. Have I done it right? It was very difficult for me to overcome the temptation to call you by phone or write you an email or go to Paris and knock on the door to your house. I have family in Paris—it's very simple to go there! But as I read somewhere, "The Master only speaks once!" I have strictly adhered to this. I am satisfied. I've received more than I could ever imagine.

My question was the following: "I have an autoimmune disease called psoriatic arthritis which causes inflammation in the joints and peeling skin, in my case the feet, head, genitals, and anus. I want to heal myself."

The first thing you said to me as you saw me was "You have to forgive your father." This was before I even cut the deck and laid out three cards. You asked about my family tree. My father was a brilliant man and a politician, but he ended up an alcoholic and a psychiatric patient. At one point he lost the family assets. He was never a close father. You could never talk with him for more than fifteen minutes.

Today he suffers from Alzheimer's, despite being a relatively young man, sixty-one years old. I told you that his father committed suicide. Concerning my mother's side, I told you that my maternal grandfather had killed my maternal grandmother when my mother was barely three years old. I was afraid of reproducing a familial disease, to a lesser degree, but a disease nevertheless. I am the oldest of four brothers, the first child of my generation, born into that family after a series of violent deaths and diseases.

The cards that came out were the following: The Sun, Death, and The World. You explained something like this: The Sun (the father), Death (the disease), and The World (the body).

The proposed psychomagic act was as follows: I had to cover my body completely with red pottery clay, and do the same with my wife. Then I was to cleanse myself with holy water, and drink it too. Afterward I had to cover myself with acacia honey and my wife and my son had to lick it off me. Once clean, I had to put on new clothes. All underwear had to be white. I had to buy a plant and water it with whatever remained of the holy water.

It took me about twenty days to acquire everything. The clay, the clothes, and the plant were easy. Acacia honey led me to visit several stores before I found it. The amazing thing was the holy water. I had to clean a huge amount of clay, not only from my body, but also my wife's. At one point, I thought of going to steal holy water from churches, but I could only take very little. Finally, I opted for the unbelievable. I bought a bottle of water (about five or eight liters), I went to the church near my house, I spoke to the priest, and after protesting and warning me that it had no magical powers, he agreed to bless the enormous carafe of water (at no point did I give him any explanation). It was funny looking at that man blessing a big plastic bottle, alone in a small room with someone he had never seen before.

Once I had everything, on the 25th of December, I decided to perform the act just as you indicated.

All my clothes were new, immaculate. What I couldn't get was shoes. The night before, on the 24th of December, at the last minute, I finally got to a store that was about to close and bought some new slippers. When I performed the psychomagic act, it was these shoes that I put on. I was like this for several hours in my house. I'm still using them.

Both arthritis and the skin problem are still there, but they do not bother me anymore. I feel like I can cure myself of it. Maybe I just need a bit more time.

In the hours I spent waiting for you in the Café Le Téméraire I wrote like never before. Today, a year and a half later, I have read what I wrote. In those pages I was surprised to read a dream that I had before and wrote down: "I was on a beach, looking at the horizon of a sea and clean blue sky. The sun was warm but not burning. Jodorowsky appeared and stood next to me. Somehow we looked to the left where the beach ended. Jodorowsky picked up a stone and began to remove the crusty layer. It fell away and a shiny black stone with greenish shades appeared, as if it were cobalt."

Why am I writing to you now? I have forgiven my father. I returned to Uruguay (I was born there) and I saw the man my father is. He is very physically and mentally impaired. His body is full of toxins. He gave up alcohol, but his smoking is the worst I have ever seen in a human. He is a smoking addict just as one can be a cocaine addict. You can hardly talk to him, since in addition to his autism, he suffers from Alzheimer's.

However, while there I found myself saying: "I must forgive my father." On the last day, when we were going back to Barcelona, my father thanked me for spending "ten unforgettable days" with him, saying "maybe we won't see each other again." When I hugged him to say goodbye and I had his head in my hand, I felt him as a child, and I felt a great pity, as well as a great love toward him.

WITH LOVE AND RESPECT,

DANIEL

⤙ LETTER 50 ⤚

From Claire

Nice, July 24

Hello,

During a workshop on the Family Tree, I asked you for a psychomagical act for the verbal abuse that I was subjected to as child and teenager from my mother. This has continued to bother me in the present, as it is very easy for me to feel blamed verbally. The day before I left, while spending a few days with my parents, I decided to carry out the act. Thanks to a recent event that was symbolic of this verbal abuse I was able to address the feeling these exchanges caused. I was embarrassed to feel my mother's aggressiveness toward me and my difficulty in making my point of view heard. It was also my desire for her to understand that what I was doing or saying was not against her, but rather was a way to express and respect myself. I told her that I wanted a sweeter relationship, and to symbolize this exchange with her, I wanted to materialize it through an act that I explained to her. She agreed, telling me that it didn't bother her too much to kiss me on the mouth and . . . that she wouldn't talk about all this to my father (she who tells him everything normally . . .)

So I coated two fingers (index and middle finger) on my right hand with honey, and I put some on her tongue, the inside of her mouth, and her lips. She was a little reluctant to open her mouth. Then I smeared honey inside my mouth and we kissed. I finally thanked her for participating in this act and kissed her while taking her in my arms. It is true that I thought that she would accept this act, while I remained afraid of this kiss on the mouth because I had real disgust of my mother as a teenager, even being unable to stand the smell of her skin. She always conveyed sexual dangers, taboos, and judgments that have greatly hindered and weighed on my own sex life. This kiss between two women could be qualified, somewhere in me, as lesbian sexuality.

When I kissed her, I was surprised by the softness of her lips smeared with honey and the total destitution of sexuality. This act happened quickly enough. I experienced in myself the discomfort of the uncertainty of my feeling, and sensed in my mother the jubilation and embarrassment of a little girl who is about to do something she shouldn't be doing.

I, who was distant and could not bring myself to touch her too much when I kissed her, was able to carry out the act, take her in my arms, and kiss her. My defenses and my repulsion had dissipated. I was at peace in this embrace. I'm done imagining her words as venom. I can finally feel the sweetness that is in her.

Thank you for entrusting me with this act.

The relationship with my mother has been permanently transformed.

THANKS,

CLAIRE

→ LETTER 51 ←

From Emmanuelle

Hello Alejandro,

During the February seminar (February 12–14, 1999) I told you that I had been HIV positive for seven years and that I wanted to test negative.

You answered me that you could not do anything but that you could give me an act to help me better experience this seropositivity. You advised me to make a yellow star on which I had to write "I am seropositive" and wear this star every day until I felt good.

I remember with laughter the days that followed so much; it seemed hard to me. I imagined myself wearing this star in the street, and at work (I am a nurse). "I will never make it!" The days passed. And the more time passed, the more this act seemed hard to me. But I knew deep down that I would do it.

More than a month later, on April 6, I stopped thinking and made myself a few stars. I had this feeling that there was no point in thinking about it, that you have to go for it and that I would feel better afterward.

On April 6, getting up to go to work, I put on my star. I was going to come across these few people who I meet regularly on my way, people I don't know, I was going to tell my patients that I was HIV positive . . . my legs started shaking. It's the second time I was scared to the point of really having my legs tremble.

I left, my head a little low, forcing myself to lift it, to confront the looks, to drop my shoulders. I was afraid that people would attack me or reject me. Afraid of the average Joe, a little too sectarian, a bit too dumb, whose reflections could have hurt me after all. But everyone close to me has nevertheless known for a long time!!! So what do I care about the potential judgment of someone I don't know?

And can we predict the other's reaction? Of course not. So go, Emmanuelle, do it and you'll see! I had to learn to defend myself and not be affected by the opinions of others.

And then curiously, that first day when I wanted to be alone during my travels, I did not encounter any aggression. But it took a lot of energy simply to lift my eyes, to straighten up and dare to look others in the face.

The days followed. Each brought an additional challenge: the bar in which I drink my coffee in the morning, walking around the city, shopping, the horse-riding club, restaurants . . . Most people said nothing, did nothing, just pretended not to see anything—not knowing, I presume, what to think or how to be. And that's when I realized that I needed a more direct, stronger reaction from them to help me better accept my seropositivity: they would have to help me get angry so that I could defend myself.

So to those I knew vaguely and who were trying to run away, I told them what was written on the star, in a provocative way. People then expressed their own fear with rejection or apprehension. I did not feel attacked and just answered them that it's been seven years! I also added that to the star. And then indeed, after a few days, I began to mechanically put on my star in the morning only to remove it in the evening.

Some people had more compassionate attitudes, asking things like, "Are you okay?" So rather reassuring for humanity. But I didn't care. I did not have or no longer had the need for this sympathy.

I'm not made of glass, I'm just seropositive. That's it. And I no longer have the need for their so-called compassion, their sadness . . . I just want them to watch what I am, me, Emmanuelle, who yes, is seropositive. And it's not because I am so that I am made of sugar or tired or complaining.

It's because I was defenseless that I am HIV positive; to be negative here right away won't solve my defense issues.

On April 15, I put down the star for good. I'm glad I wore it and removed it.

Once finished, I did not want to pick up the pen immediately. I waited for weeks, and now months have gone by. I felt guilty for not being able write to thank you. Then I let it go. The guilt is gone. And then I realized that I couldn't write because my request remained to test negative. It's only been a few days since I really started to feel indifference to HIV. Yes, you explained to me that you could not do anything to make me negative. I heard it but I did not accept it.

It was so important to me in my romantic and sexual relationships to be negative . . . I lost myself.

And seropositivity doesn't pose a problem to me for now aside from my desire to have kids and natural sexual relations.

Today I came to respect myself more in front of my companion by choosing not to use a condom. As for motherhood, it is an increasing desire that still needs some time from both of us before it can be satisfied the way I want.

So yes, today I want to thank you for this act which let me better accept myself, my seropositivity, and therefore who I am, and allowed me to move out of the eyes of others in order to be more in tune with myself. I am gently moving along this path that has been mine for two years now. And what I always believed in, to manage to live fulfilled with a man and build a personal life and family, is right there in front of me. And it's the encounters like yours that help me stay on the right path and yes, I will achieve what I have always believed.

Thank you for your act, thank you for simply existing with your honesty and your energy. Thank you for this opening to the world and to ourselves. Thanks for this star, thank you for being there.

EMMANUELLE

↝ LETTER 52 ↜

From Rachel

It was Wednesday, January 29, and thanks to you, this date will mark an event in my life that I can compare to a new birth. That was the day I decided to push open the door in front of which the path of my quest had stopped. A door in front of which I had accumulated words and words—written or spoken—to hide the scary and sealed panel. Words blackening hundreds of notebooks, lyrics dumped in the cabinets of psychiatrists or along the corridors of mental asylums. It was like make-believe: to make up this door that I couldn't open and behind which I sensed the *black secret* that I used to talk about in front of my psychiatrist, with no helpful advice about the gestures necessary to open it.

Making up the buried knowledge that no talk therapy could bring to awareness constituted the main activity of my existence—solely to survive. Instigated by your translator who told me about your works, your power to resurrect the awareness of trauma carefully buried in the unconscious, and of psychomagic acts successfully delivering sentient beings from their suffering, I came to find you this January 29 at the Café Le Téméraire where you do your tarot readings.

At your request, I spelled out the reason for my consultation with you in these terms: I come so that you might help me find an event that occurred in my childhood, the ignorance of which prevents me from living and being free. This is a violent event of which I have more than an intuition, a conviction, but one I cannot bring back to my memory. You invited me to shuffle the cards and draw blind in order to turn them over in front of you. You explained to me step by step: motherhood—the father—the lover. You invited me to formulate the question I was asking myself, and after a few sentences in which I mentioned a probable act of violence by my father against me, you took over to reveal that, indeed, my father, denying my sex and my birth, had committed a criminal act meant to destroy what I was. He did this in the presence of my mother who did not step in to defend me. "Non-assistance to the person in danger," you commented. Then you asked me if I wanted additional details about this event. I wanted to know my age when this act was committed. You read on one of the upturned cards that I was three years old. Next, you asked me what I was going to do now that I knew what the hidden door had been hiding all this time.

My answer, very revealing of the guilt that I carried for forty-three years at having felt an accomplice in this destructive act ("ask my father for forgiveness") determined the form of the psychomagic act that you suggested to me: take a pétanque ball, paint it black, and wear it on me for a period of twenty-one days, a period which represents the time it takes a chick to hatch from an egg. This image moved me all the more because I often compared myself to a being imprisoned in an egg whose shell it could not break without help from the outside, which it could not find. At the end of the twenty-one days, I had to go to my father to give him back the pétanque ball, saying: "I return to you what is yours. If you don't understand now, you will understand later; now I have to go." And I would leave my father with this object which will allow him, or not, to become aware of the act he committed. I followed the prescription of the psychomagic act to the letter and I carried the pétanque ball painted black for the planned twenty-one days. On February 20 I took off the ball and that night a high fever kept me awake, a fever which I interpreted as a spring cleaning from the depth of my being. Eventually, because I didn't happen to be where my father lived, I went to his house to return the ball, saying the words you indicated to me. As I turned away to get on my bicycle, and retrace the twenty kilometers in the opposite direction, I heard him mumble as if to himself: "That belongs to me, does it?" This impromptu visit with the object that I brought could only arouse boundless astonishment. However, a few moments later, he alerted some members of the family to ask them for explanations of the gesture that I just made, and of which he had understood the symbolic character. During this time I returned home, perplexed and scared as I seemed to have made the gesture that was at once the craziest and the most reasonable in my life. Once settled, I was hungry and I went to buy myself a fillet of meat, which deserves to be mentioned because I never prepare myself a meal of this type. After resting, I slept for an hour. However, it was only the next day that I realized that I was delivered from the weight of guilt and I felt a kind of freedom that I hadn't known. I discovered the lightness of no longer feeling guilty. I also realized that I needed to learn this world that had remained alien to me, learn the meaning of gestures and inscribe my own gestures into a reality from which I had remained absent. The warning light constantly lit in me could be turned off. Today I feel that my life is in my own hands and it is a joy that I owe you.

Epilogue: to sum up, I give you a glimpse of what my relationship with my father has become. He phoned me the day after my visit to ask me about my news and I replied that I would gladly do it again with my son and bicycle, the very pleasant country lane that leads to his house. He immediately fixed a day for a family lunch. Peace is therefore assured. He will or will not go the way that the black ball indicates to him but I did not need him to do it to be free.

As for my mother, she sent me a letter advising me to seek treatment, to see a psychiatrist (my parents are divorced but she has got wind, certainly, of the psychomagical gesture); but at the end of her letter she wrote the three words that I stopped waiting for, forty-six years after my birth—"I love you"—which, even if they no longer mean anything, are words of reconciliation. Each of the two actors who destroyed my life opted for the neutral attitude that preserves a form of peace and exempts me from family turmoil that I don't have the desire to manage, busy as I am thinking about and organizing my life to come, simply my own life.

I know that the psychomagical act will not be fully accomplished until this letter reaches you, informing you of the progress and the outcome of the operation. So here it is and with it, the expression of my infinite gratitude.

RACHEL

⇥ LETTER 53 ⇤
....
From Mahel (Ex-Pierre)

My name is Pierre. I attended the seminar of May 29–30, 1999, in Ollioules. I am a student of Yvan, to whom you asked me to convey your regards but he died before I could do it, on June 18 of this year. You gave me an act that included acquiring a cow vagina so I could introduce a stone (my first name) into it and then bury it in a beautiful box above which I would grow a plant, after which I would change my first name. The kosher butcher was not able to get me a vagina. I turned toward a biodynamic group from Ariege that uses the organs of the animals they raise. I received an answer that because of the provisions relating to mad cow disease, for health reasons the authorities systematically confiscate organs that are not intended for sale. At least that's what is claimed officially. All cows must be slaughtered in slaughterhouses, which are under their control. This legislation does not affect other animals.

Friday, September 12, 1999

I'm still eager to accomplish the task that you suggested to me. What am I supposed to do? You can answer me by email or by mail. Thanks in advance for your time.

Friday, September 12, 1999,

Dear Pierre,

I did not know that there was such a shortage of vaginas! The reality is our own dream. In your dream, it is impossible to find a cow's vagina. The difficulties you encounter are the ones you impose on yourself in order to get rid of your mother. The patient goes to the doctor so that he cures him, and when the treatment begins, the patient struggles so as not to heal. That's it. I could tell you: find that vagina even if you have to go to the end of the world! (Maybe in Africa you will find it! Or in Japan? Go find out . . . where your dreams will send you.) However, for you I will make an exception—but, it gives me the impression you have a homosexual drive. Look for the best florist in your city, order his most expensive orchid, and use it instead of the cow's vagina.

Then don't forget to send me a thank you message!

ALL THE BEST,
JODOROWSKY

September 12, 1999

Dear Alejandro,

Thank you for your response regarding my inability to find a cow's vagina and especially my inability to want to heal. Your message hit me hard. So I pushed to accomplish the first act. I managed to find a vagina from a veterinary service, claiming scientific work. Since it was not kosher I introduced a Jewish star in gold and I buried it in a beautiful box with a plant above. I taped a business card with my new name to an open jar of honey. For the anecdote: I found a beautiful but very light box, and the seller told me: "You're not going to put stones in it." Also, the day before I left for Toulouse, where my mother is buried, my friend's wife offered me a pot of honey wishing me a good trip. We mustn't confabulate but it seems that these little signs perfume the path. Thank you again and see you soon.

MAHEL (EX-PIERRE)

→ LETTER 54 ←
....
From Philippe

Alejandro,

I had idealized my father as God, the Father; I had a Christ fantasy. You asked me to do the following deed: In my garden, dressed as Christ, with crown of thorns, loincloth, and stigmata, I crucifed myself by attaching my wrists and ankles. Three women—Mary, Mary Magdalene, and Jeanne—dressed in long white dresses and accompanied me during three hours (lord, my shoulders!). A man with a white face with a brown beard, Joseph, then untied me, wrapped me in a white shroud, and carried me into a deep hole which closed with a large plank (a door) on which they laid a stone. The man and the three women, one in each corner, watched over me for an hour. Coming out of the sepulcher, they washed me with seven liters of wine, seven liters of water, and one liter of lavender scent. I was exhilarated. The next day I buried the shroud, the loincloth, the crown of thorns, the sign INRI,* and a cicada chrysalis. NB: I planted the cross an hour before the act. A cicada larva took advantage of it to climb in and accomplish its metamorphosis. The cicada accompanied me and was my guide during the crucifixion. I thank you from the bottom of my soul.

PHILIPPE

✦ LETTER 55 ✦

From Philippe

Alejandro,

I told you about the psychomagical act regarding my Oedipus complex. You asked me to add reparation and gratitude. You gave me instructions on May 28 and I did it on July 6. All I had to do was to give three candies to my mother and three red roses to my wife. My mother lives a few miles from us and I managed to get them sent by post to Stockholm where she was on vacation for three days. Unheard of!!! She received them. I initially resisted giving the three red roses to my wife Valerie. Today I am delighted.

ALEJANDRO, THANK YOU, THANK YOU, THANK YOU.

PHILIPPE

✦ LETTER 56 ✦

From Bruno

Alejandro,

I was able to go to the Café Le Téméraire on Wednesday, February 12, to meet you. I tried in a few seconds to tell you about me, my experience, my research, and my work of analysis (Jungian approach since 1996, recently completed by mantra therapy/emotional dynamics work).

---

*INRI stands for *Iesus Nazarenus, Rex Iudæorum,* Latin for "Jesus the Nazarene, King of the Jews."

A journey that helped me understand and assimilate so many things. But with my mind, without it really being possible for me to touch the depths of my being, the repeatedly wounded child remained hidden under a thick blanket of a very resistant material. I tried to present you my experience and what I consider to be the greatest test of my life. The limited time made this task impossible so I was very clumsy. My ordeal is the consequence of last year's rupture of a relationship with a woman whom I had believed to be my soulmate. As soon as we met, I was transported, miraculously, on the way to what I thought was finally the opportunity to achieve and find my rightful place in this life. Unfortunately, our story was a series of great interior sufferings that I didn't want to listen to, an impossible love that lasted several years when I always hoped to receive what she could not give me. It's also likely it was this way because I carried the hurts and lacks of the past inside. I only recently realized that I had physically idealized a person who had always been forbidden to me as she was separated but still married throughout the period of our story.

A year after the breakup that I myself initiated, I still suffer terrible feelings of betrayal and abandonment, sometimes even jealousy, imagining that the one who hurt me so much is happy while I suffer. After this rupture I realized that I needed to understand why I had this encounter. It had to have meaning, I must have chosen this person to live a crucial lesson. Among my readings on synchronicity I read that "the most important doors of our existence are opened by people who do not go through them with us." That spoke to me. I have received responses with no real sense of healing, still clinging to this archetype that haunts me. Apparently I can't seem to forgive myself. Plus I lost my job at the end of the year. Another difficult test. Three years ago I wanted to change jobs to try to join a sector related to my personal affinities. Not being able to enter through the front door (as it always has been) I planted a seed that bore fruit. My girlfriend had strongly criticized my change at the time, which surely contributed to the instability of our relationship.

Having more free time for a few months, I was able to deepen my analytical work, bring to light wounds from the past, but especially intellectualize a lot. Without healing. I will be forty-two this year.

Often I have the feeling of having missed everything and being lost in the desert. I followed ways that did not suit me, feeling the need to prove that I could succeed. Once the goal was reached I had to find something else to prove myself again. I realized that I didn't find my rightful place. I was given nothing to get there. It's without a doubt the reason my encounter with this woman seemed liberating to me. I was wrong because there was no place for me by her side. I thought I could meet you and, as you mention in your book, have the opportunity to talk to you during a long session. I already consider myself lucky to have been able to see you last Wednesday.

The cards seemed to reveal to you repetitions, the number 16 being dominant—at one point I even drew the 11th card, then the 5th. You asked me what was the biggest love possible. I did not know the answer. "Cosmic Love." You prescribed an act for me to carry out. I had to apply acacia honey on my chest, paint the right part of my forehead in gold and the left part in silver, put rouge on my nose, and dress myself in a white suit with wings and white gloves. The shoes would be gold and silver. I had to go and meet twelve children and offer them twelve bags of marbles. Finally I had to bury the suit and plant a plant.

I admit I was deeply distressed at the idea of walking the streets in such a costume, afraid of being ashamed, afraid of being teased, of being singled out and judged. I was very afraid to do it and afraid of not doing it. I had to go through an initiation. So I found some wings made of beautiful feathers, a sweatshirt, gloves, and white pants, shoes I had to paint, gold and silver paint for the face, and very beautiful marbles of shimmering colors. I was anxious imagining the place where I could go to meet children without their parents. I thought it could be possible to go my godchild's school on Friday, February 21, for the return to school, but after talking to his father without disclosing everything, it appeared difficult because of the neighborhood watch and the authorities. Having brought together all the elements on Saturday the 15th I decided to go to the Luxembourg Gardens the next day to meet children. Later I realized that it would be the 16th, the number highlighted during my reading.

I got up, shaved, and took a hot shower to warm up. I applied the honey abundantly on my chest. The fairly low temperature, despite a beautiful and sunny blue sky, prompted me to put on two white t-shirts (but already worn) before putting on the sweatshirt too thin for the day's weather. I went to the garden realizing that people still queue up to see Modigliani's exhibition entitled "The Angel with the Serious Face." It was past 9:30 a.m. The day was worthy of a Sunday winter in New York. I walked slowly toward the children who I saw, and without knowing if I had to say anything in particular I let my heart speak. One of them did not want my present since he said he had marbles already. I suggested he give them to his brother; he did not tell me if he had one but he accepted my gift, thanking me. Another child stretched out his hand; he was still too young to play marbles so I offered my present to his mother suggesting she give them to him when he was older. A young man seeing me approaching, smiled, calling me "the Angel Gabriel," so I offered him a bag of marbles "for the child within you." He accepted with pleasure; perhaps it was not in the rules of the act, but it was spontaneous. At one point, a representative of the security services approached me to tell me that I couldn't do it, that it was forbidden. I expressed my desire to give gifts to children, without success. As he pushed me to get out immediately while diverting his look I told him he shouldn't be ashamed of looking at me. Raising his voice he replied that he "was not attracted to men." I smiled and left the garden. I had to walk the surrounding streets to offer gifts to other children.

Straight away I no longer paid attention to my anxieties; I walked like an angel among all these people wrapped up in their warm clothes. Some turned heads and I nodded at them. Others looked away. Joggers and the like would look at me, smiling mostly, I believe. There was "an angel in the Luxembourg Gardens." Before meeting the guard, while I was still close to the central basin, with my back to the sun I saw my shadow and the big wings beyond me. It was me. After my last gift, I came back to my car. I was freezing. Honey had me well protected from the cold (I wonder about its meaning, as well as that of gold and silver on my forehead and on my shoes). I went home to take another hot shower. Then I hit the road to go a hundred kilometers from Paris. I thought about burying my clothes not far from where I was baptized, where there are beautiful forests and lilies of the valley in May. I chose a plant among the golden orange trees from Mexico that I bought to flower my windows before the end-of-year celebrations. This plant made me think of you and of Pachita because of her supposed Mexican origins. I ended up choosing a place just behind the twelfth-century Romanesque church in which I was baptized, thinking that in the future, when I return, I will be able to see the orange tree grow.

One thing is certain: I overcame the anxieties that were inside, injuries and fear due to negative judgments, wounds and fear of shame, wounds and fear of teasing. These anxieties were fruits of pride that I built in me and residues of my past as a child cut off from the world. Before this initiatory act I thought myself unable to wear a costume to go to a party. I forgot everything while putting on my wings; I didn't care if I was being judged or made fun of. I stood out by being other than myself, the one we often perceive as dark, even superior or unapproachable. Who is not me. Recently, I realized without understanding why people would make a false opinion of me, often a negative one. My only desire is to be loved for what I am and not for what I seem to be. I know the act changed a part of me and helped to enable me to bring me closer to a feeling of interior peace. Maybe others will be able to perceive the real me henceforth.

Another thing: I think I can no longer let anybody hurt me like in the past. A beginning of healing took place in me. I know there are other wounds that I will have to heal, and ties I will have to cut. Despite the uncertainties regarding my future I know there is still the energy in me—but will I finally find the right path? I hope to see you again for a longer visit, to progress further. I am very grateful to you for your kindness.

BRUNO

→ LETTER 57 ←
....

From Amedee

During the Tarot course and following the Family Tree workshops in Bordeaux from February 25–27, 2000, you performed a psychomagic act on me.

Here are the details: When my father was in a coma, he awoke for a few minutes shortly before his death and asked me with his eyes to unplug him. I took advantage of an opportunity when I was alone to unplug him, and he was gone not long after. Since 1967, the date of the death of my father, my right knee has made me suffer horribly. You "operated" on my right knee, wrapping it with a paper on which was marked "Guilt." While washing my knee with water, you asked my father to get out of me, to leave me, shouting: "Get out of there!" (This was because I felt guilt inside me.) A participant, covered with several layers of clothes, knelt beside me, and I slapped his back very hard, shouting: "Get out!" And with each layer removed I slapped again, etc. And then I burned the paper on which was marked "Guilt." Afterward everything stopped. My knee doesn't hurt me anymore. Thanks again.

KISSES,

AMEDEE

→ LETTER 58 ←
....

From Alexandre (twenty-eight years old)

About a year ago I began studying my family tree. The silhouette clearly showed that over several generations, until my birth, a main branch had never held: that of the fathers. You could read there cyclically: father unknown, father missing, deceased father, father abandoning his family. Without a dad, I was also abandoned very quickly by my mother.

Today, on my fragile branch, under the stern gaze of my ancestors, and knowing the sap that runs through my veins, I'm aware that it won't be easy for me to be a father and to follow another path. However, my desire to change is strong. I know that since childhood there is a desire in my unconscious to be a woman. The male is unreliable. While being a woman I could make myself loved, especially by my mother, a woman with blonde hair. Métis,* complexé prisoner in the skin of an unloved being, I prefer to see myself as a tall blonde. In my dealings with others, in my relationship, I always cling to this feminine ideal and I can't be a man. Today my fear is the following: Will I remain a woman while Django, my future son, expects to have a father? How to become a man? How to be a father, a stable and reassuring male presence? My wish is to no longer consider myself a woman but to learn to be a man.

One night I woke up from a nightmare clearly speaking of my female identification and my desire to do the same with my son. In short, I was preparing him to tell himself: it is not worth it being a man. In this dream I saw the birth of my son like the arrival of a great lady. I could not be sure of the interpretation but I was gripped by an emotion motivating me to act. An intuition came to me:

You could dress as a woman and walk the streets singing. You would carry two eggs in your underpants. You would strut about like this until a man shouts to you: "Hi, beautiful!" Then you would take off your disguise. You would carry the eggs until the birth of your son. As soon as he's born cook the eggs, separate the yolks, and eat the shell.

Then give a taste of the cooking water to your son, explaining the reason for this ritual to him.

Waking up from the nightmare around 4:00 a.m., I immediately made the decision to carry out my act, urgently. "I can no longer be a woman."

I managed to collect things belonging to my wife and my mother-in-law, who was living with us at the time. I put on a pair of stockings, a bra filled with large apples, boots, and a fur coat. I put on makeup.

Here I was, going out at 4:00 a.m., in the deserted streets of the village where I live near Madrid. Not a soul, of course, only a December

*Mixed race.

cold that made me tenser as I tried to wiggle seductively in too-small high heels. The two eggs that I had delicately stuffed into my underpants bothered me enough. On one hand I was fearful to break them, as they seemed abnormally heavy; no doubt I really felt like a man, but the egg weight caused an absurd dissonance with the feminine clothes that I was wearing.

I walked for a good half hour before seeing anyone. I wandered back and forth whistling Whitney Houston's "I Will Always Love You" to attract attention. My song intensified and I gained confidence. Then some cars, some alarmed looks.

Suddenly, on the sidewalk opposite the bakery, I heard a *psst*. A fear rose in me and I didn't dare to look. From behind his door the baker hissed at me with interest. I turned around then to give him a tender sign. The hisses intensified and the baker sneaked out of his cage to approach me. "Psst! Come here!" I hurried on a bit like a scared doe. "Psst! Come here!" I did not really know where he was coming from, but my style seemed to excite him. I did not imagine that his intention was completely serious. On my side, I felt like a woman, with the powerlessness to defend myself if something were to happen.

The baker quickened his pace, looking around for potential witnesses.

"Psst, come over here!" But no "Hello, beautiful!" Two steps away, trotting to catch up with me, he was suddenly surprised as I turned and he discovered with horror that my legs were not so sweet and attractive as those of a woman.

With fear the expression of my face must have hardened, my gait became heavier, and with amazement the baker stopped, quickly glancing to see if anyone had caught him. Frightened, he turned back to his lair, ashamed, disgusted with himself for having pursued a transvestite.

It took another good half hour until a car of students stopped and came to my rescue, shouting so clearly at first: "Hi, my darling!" and finally the magic formula: "Hi, beautiful!" I went home surprised at how quickly my wish was granted.

I found a banana and ate it immediately, feeling the pleasure of integrating my masculinity.

Then for about three to four weeks I carried the eggs, both day and night, while teaching, and in bed with my wife. I agonized about breaking them at any moment. I had never granted so much importance and delicacy to my eggs when suddenly disaster struck. About a week before the birth, going to the toilet, an egg fell and cracked. I was gripped with terrible anguish, thinking that my act had just failed, leaving me no further recourse. At the same time, I felt the sadness of a man who has lost something of the greatest value. Screaming in rage, I begged God for a few seconds to offer a solution. Before going to the bathroom I had automatically picked up a book entitled *Subtle Body: Essence and Shadow*. I opened it at random and came across this sentence: "The healer can use soul energies. It is important to clearly visualize the process and stay focused on the path till the end of the healing work." If this was the message, I thought to myself that I could only try to continue by staying focused on the energies and, above all, by not losing faith. I tasted the egg yolk and ate the shell as dictated in the recipe. A week and a half later my son was born.

One evening, I cooked the egg, ate the shell, and gave my son a taste of the water. All that while explaining the history of fathers in our family, and our desire to change things and create something else. Then I added these words: "I'm glad you're a boy, and I'm happy to be your dad." A few minutes later, when my wife was about to change him, he peed a stream of urine on her. I thought it was primarily a male explosion, following the act in which I implicated him. However, days later some violent dreams appeared, also warning me of the danger of using my son and us uniting against women to destroy them. That same day the urine stream was returned to me while I was changing him. Django and I learned to integrate the masculine.

MANY THANKS,

ALEXANDRE

⤍ LETTER 59 ⤎

....

From Alice (fifty-nine years old)

My father did not appreciate me, and my mother "owned" me. I only lived through others, through the eyes of others, the lives of others. I haven't lived my life and I have reproduced my mother's pattern with my relatives. I wanted to experience a liberating shock by this psychomagic act.

The design of the act was as follows:

Write a letter to my father and a letter to my mother (both dead) with all my unspoken criticisms. Go begging in the streets for two to three hours, begging for a look. Ask to be recognized as a perfect mother (it took me a while to accept seeing the reality of my daughter, and recognizing that I had reproduced, in an even worse form, the pattern inherited from my mother). Go as a beggar into the mountains, screaming my hate into a black bag. Burn it, collect the ashes. Throw all my beggar's clothes, together with the ashes, into the current of a river. Burn the two letters and collect part of the ashes to drink—those of the father with a glass of red wine, and those of the mother with milk.

First I wrote a violent letter to my father. I insulted him while screaming and crying: my unwanted conception—a shock received in my early childhood (which killed everything in me)—his fits of Catholic fanaticism in my youth, our last failed encounter before his death, the beggar I am today.

It was done at once: direct, strong, full of sad rage.

The letter to my mother was more difficult. I discovered that the revolt toward her was painful, and I felt like it must have been painful for my own daughter to manage to rebel against me. This reproduction of the inherited maternal pattern that I projected on my daughter was insistent while writing this letter.

For my father, I was enraged right from the start. But my mother's wickedness was both much more subtle, and more violent!

I understood, while writing, my present fears toward some women. I kept going anyway, step by step, because I wanted to see it through.

But as a woman toward her mother, I still protected myself. I should have screamed, a primal scream; I felt it but it was not ripe.

I had prepared everything carefully to beg, without trapping myself because I was very scared. Signs helped me at all times. I was immediately taken for a real beggar (since I was). A woman asked me questions then showed me an address where I could eat. I was given money. Another woman asked me about my children (since I wore a sign around my neck saying that I had been a perfect mother and repeated it). Others laughed at me: "A perfect mother! Me too!"

But most would look away. I reclaimed, consciously, the gaze of my dad. I beg for the beautiful image of me. "Please, please . . ." To go to the limit of this madness. To recover strength, I walk, I scour the neighborhood calling to people, and when I feel more centered, I stop begging for them to see me.

I avoid the police and the other beggars, so as not to create incidents that could be pitfalls.

I want to live it to the fullest to be exorcised from it. I was in shock until the next evening. But I feel it's an exorcism, I feel my fear was related to this begging. I feel released from a large part of my fear/hate. And it's still working, I feel it won't stop now.

Screaming on the mountain was less strong because, under the shock of the begging, I was doing everything in a daze. I believe that one day I will have to go scream—not necessarily out of hate, but out of pain and life.

At the river, I'm glad it's all gone, and I am happy to revisualize this strong river that understood what I had to throw in there.

I burned the letters to my parents in earthen pots which became like funeral urns and, one evening, I played Mozart's "Requiem" for them because this phrase came back to me: "May they rest in peace." And I drank some of the ashes, those of my father with red wine and those of my mother with milk.

THANKS,
ALICE

⤖ LETTER 60 ⬳

....

From Alison (thirty-three years old)

I have always been very rigid in my way of thinking as well as in how I move. This stiffness is related to control of a very powerful part of me, of which I dreamed and which manifests as much in my unconscious as it does in my physical being (via health problems, my relationship with men, or with others in general). This part of me, which corresponds to a very destructive personality, appears as a psychopath, producing a very strong hatred of both men and women. I have three brothers and I am the youngest. I have always hated to be the last and what's more, a woman. My hatred was projected on my brothers and on myself. In fact, I have a deep hatred for every human being. All this is linked to the relationship, also negative, that I had with my father (a proud officer, authoritarian, contemptuous and alcoholic), with what he wanted me to be. This rigidity, this control, this desire to bend to my father's wishes generated a lot of rage, rage at not being perfect, and this need to hide my psychopathic personality.

In my psychomagic act, first I must experience this rigidity fully: Spend two days with a "harnessed" body—a collar around the neck, and splints on my arms and legs—reducing my movements to practically nothing, to that of an automaton under control. The evening of the second day, my older brother (on whom I invariably project my father) will visit me and, without saying a word, I will tear off my neck braces and splints in front of him, screaming my rage, my rage toward my father.

Once rid of all that harnessed me, I'll put on my psychopath clothes and I will carry a beautiful knife purchased for the occasion, stuck on my chest, a symbol of destruction. I will live as this psychopath for three days. During these three days, I will have to go in front of, and finally enter, a mental asylum, home of the psychopath.

After these three days, I will remove the psychopath clothes and knife, and I will massage the latter with honey, for two hours, singing.

Then I will burn the clothes, the splints, and the neck brace; I will keep some ashes and bake a cake, adding the preserved ashes. I will eat it with dear friends, I'll cut it with the knife, and, finally, I will offer this knife to my older brother.

The act went as follows: I built my splints and a very close friend helped me put them on. I was left alone, stiff as a post, unable to move. I tried to lie down, but was unable to bend my legs or arms. Every movement was painful to me, slow, like I was an automaton. I couldn't walk other than like a soldier on watch (my father would be happy!). Impossible to eat too: I had the choice between drinking with a straw, or eating with my head on the plate, all upright. I isolated myself; I saw no one. I couldn't do anything normally. During these two days, I felt quite asocial. I was physically diminished. I was an empty shell, without interest, nonexistent.

On the evening of the second day, my eldest brother came. I tore off my splints and my neck brace, and I screamed all my rage, my anger, my humiliation at feeling less than a beast. I screamed, cried, I let off steam, until I couldn't anymore.

My brother left. Little by little I let my psychopath personality take over. I was prepared: I stuck the knife on my chest. I put on the prepared clothes (black pants, red sweater, cape, hat, and black gloves). I no longer felt like a powerless automaton: I was a psychopath, nothing affected me, nothing moved me. I was antisocial but I didn't care; I no longer suffered from it.

Throughout these three days I lived with a psychopath in my head. I felt a deep hatred toward everything I came across, which had less than a zero value for me, ants to be crushed. The feeling of having the right of life or death over others made me feel strong. I was no longer afraid of anything, of anyone. While walking—and I walked a lot, spending my days outside in fairly isolated areas—this strength filled me. The knife began to be a part of me, like an additional organ. I no longer felt it; it was in me. I was a destroyer; I could destroy what I created. I felt a terrible power: "I destroy what Life has created, I am above Life!! And I have this ultimate power to destroy myself, me, Its creation! I am above all."

On the third day, I went to a psychiatric hospital. I was able to enter thanks to a little lie, and I settled in the cafeteria. I was home, in the house of the psychopath, surrounded by madmen. These madmen had no more value than normal people for me. But this was beginning to weigh me down, this emptiness, this lack of humanity in me. The hospital was nevertheless impressive: the cries of the mad, the bulging eyes, their attitudes and movements.

I left very quickly. I was completely empty and took a train to get away from it.

Then I went home. My psychopath was getting heavier and heavier. Finally, that night I left my psycho clothes and I massaged the knife with honey for two hours. I let my voice come. I did not sing in an articulate way but melodies appeared. Everything was quite magical because I didn't recognize my voice; these sounds came from me while being unknown to me. I really liked this moment and these melodies made me vibrate. I could carry on for hours. I felt human again. I burned my clothes, my splints . . . and I kept some ashes. The following weekend I made a cake that I ate with dear friends and my older brother. Then I gave him the knife, which he liked very much.

ALISON

✦ LETTER 61 ✦

From Amalia (thirty-five years old)

My name is Amalia. I am thirty-five years old and have a partner and two daughters, which obliges me to be a woman to my partner and a mother to my daughters. I have many difficulties achieving this.

The aim of my psychomagic act was to free myself from my maternal need caused by the fact my mother didn't love me. Free myself from the feeling of being a nullity, null as a daughter and null as a woman. I behave like a vampire beggar who feeds on people who live around me, asking them constantly for love, attention, etc. I compensate with great spiritual pride and high self-confidence. To sum up, I isolate myself from the rest of the world thinking that no one understands me and that I'm always right. I carry on being a little girl and my need is so strong that no one can satisfy it. This causes great frustration to which I respond with a lot of aggression and a very bad temper, making people run away from me. I live locked inside my head, cutting myself off from my emotions and others.

The psychomagical act consisted of dressing up as a saint representing my spiritual pride. On my head I would wear a tight helmet, to symbolize my crazy mind. To that helmet I would attach:

1. A pacifier, to indicate my maternal need to beg for love and my status as a little girl.
2. A band, on which I would write, "I am the best, but no one knows." This would be my "unknown genius," my overestimation.
3. A plastic knife, to symbolize my rage and aggression toward life.

In my mouth I would put vampire teeth to represent my vampiric and beggar side. I would keep a picture of my parents on me to feel that my relationship with them is the basis of this neurotic construction.

Dressed like this I would go to the street. I would go up on a pedestal for an hour and I would ask everyone passing: "You love me, right? You love me?"

Then I would change and burn the photos of my parents, putting my father's photo's ashes in my right shoe, and my mother's photo's ashes in my left shoe. I would kiss each shoe.

Next, I would gather everything used for the act and throw it into a river without looking back.

I would then go for an hour's walk, caressing a rubber heart that I would carry in my pocket. I would then go to a busy place, and still touching the heart, I would wait until someone spoke to me. Without any expectation I would listen and ask questions about them, without ever talking about myself, continuously touching the heart.

Once everything was ready, I first dressed like a saint. I put on my helmet with everything hanging and on my chest the photo of my parents. I took my car and drove toward the pedestal in the heart of Madrid. It was freezing. First, I took a walk dressed as a saint in the city center, until I reached the pedestal, right next to a crossing, surrounded by three lanes of cars. I climbed onto the pedestal. I was immersed in the emotion of the act and felt clearly all these aspects that prevented me from being a mother, a companion, a friend, a human being. I deeply felt my madness. Tears welled up when I felt a great pain that came from my innermost self.

I asked everyone if they wanted me. Few answered. Some people were scared, I understood that I had even changed physically for this occasion. I am dark-skinned, but that day I was pale as a vampire. Some laughed and others looked at me thinking I was a madwoman—or better yet, a *madman,* because I looked like a man.

Above where I was there was a sculpture of a big eagle with open wings. I was there for an hour. In the last minute I was approached by a very nice man. I asked him if he loved me and he replied that of course, it was unthinkable not to love me. He shook my hand and walked away smiling at me.

When the hour was up it started to rain. I got off the pedestal and headed home, where everything was prepared for the next stage. I changed and burned the photos of my parents, putting the ashes in the respective shoes. I kissed them and then I picked up everything that I used for the act.

I headed to the river and threw in everything without looking back. I started to get a bit upset thinking I should have thrown everything behind me so I would not be tempted to look. Then I started caressing the heart, warming it up and thinking about my cold heart. I walked for an hour. I planned to sit in a park but I couldn't because it started raining again. I went into the Orient Café. I waited and waited for three and a half hours in which I did not stop caressing the heart and in which I had moments of anguish thinking that I would spoil the act.

I was going mad thinking that everything had gone well but that at last moment it could fail.

Finally a very nice guy started talking to me. I started asking about him, without talking about myself. He told me about his illusions, his fears, his life. I listened attentively. He thanked me for talking to him. I saw a book in front of me with the title *In Him Is Life*. I felt a great warm force enter me. When I finished the act, it stopped raining.

THANKS FOR EVERYTHING,

AMALIA

✣ LETTER 62 ✣

From André (fifty-nine years old)

Objective of the act: free myself from my parents. My mom has always been a servant since she was ten. She hated her superiors and everything beyond her. She rejected the woman and the feminine in her. She loved her father, paralyzed from the age of twenty-seven, even though she was not his favorite. I myself suffer from a developing condition which prevents me from using my hands well and which frequently causes me a lot of pain. My mother hated men. I'm fifty-nine and all my life I told myself I was her favorite, while I have always been a loser, a failure. I never managed to make myself loved by her. It always made me want to die. My father, a weak man, died of an embolism when I was five years old. I have no emotional memory of him. He used to smoke. After his death, as a child, I smoked his cigarette butts. It is from him that I hold this vice (which I just got rid of), this suicidal will.

I want to give back to my parents what they gave me! I will go to the grave of my mother in Le Roux. She wanted a little girl, so I'll go dressed as a little girl. I will attach pig's feet to my hands, dead paws like the hands of my paralytic grandfather who was loved by all his daughters. There were five of them including my mother. In order for me to be loved, my hands and my feet are being destroyed. Then I will release myself (scream, spit, urinate . . .). I'll clean up, dig a hole, put everything in it, fill it up, and plant a rosebush. I will then go to my father's grave.

I will put a mask of servility on my face—in his image—from a photo taken of my "servile" face, I'll have a cigarette in my hand and once more I will free myself (shout, spit, urinate . . .). Then I will clean up, dig a hole, and put the excrement there along with the mask and a pack of cigarettes. I will fill it up and plant a rosebush.

I arrive on Monday morning by plane. I rent a car and drive toward the village. The first views of the countryside move me a lot but very quickly my old impression begins to dominate. I arrive where I lived when I was very small—a place that my mother considered idyllic because they had a small house for themselves. But I realize that it was very far from the school, for my brother and my sister, and that without a doubt it was a very selfish choice. I pass through Le Roux. The village square, my grandmother's house, and the cemetery are all the same. Everything is decrepit. There are only a few new houses just before the cemetery. On one side an addition has been added, a small meadow.

I find the tomb of my paternal grandfather, then, below, that of my maternal grandparents, and next to it the grave with my mother and my father together! However, my father was near his father. I guess we had to relocate him. It is a slab with an erected nameplate. There are several bouquets of plastic flowers. From the tomb we clearly see the window of the first floor of the nearest house. There are no tools available. The cemetery seems permanently open. I have a shopping list. I find everything without a problem. I take a room at the Hotel des Flandre opposite the Namur train station, near where I lived as a child.

I sleep badly; it's too hot. The next day I go straight for the goal. It seems to me that nobody lives in the houses near the cemetery. I am aware of the importance of the moment. I religiously pull out my tools and carry everything close to the grave. The sky is overcast but bright. It's cold and the wind is strong. First I dig on each side of the head of the grave. Right side for my mother, chosen without thinking, seems normal to me. The earth is humid. I dig without a problem. Next I clear the surface of flowers, plates, or porcelain pieces that say "I love you, mom." I lay everything on the neighboring tomb. I put a newspaper on the grave (I'll be in socks), the water bottle, and the brush to clean. I get changed. I have red socks, a red t-shirt as well (I am a girl who likes colors), and I put on a green sleeveless dress that buttons up at the front. I tie pig's feet to my hands and feet. I'm ready. I hear hammering in the neighborhood. I think about Boris Vian and his "I'll spit on your grave." If that's strong, what I am about to do is unspeakable! I squat against the column and I spit, I shit, and calmly I clean. The hole is too small to accommodate a dress, four pig's feet, and a t-shirt. I have to enlarge it. I finally put in the first plant and refill it. It's my father's turn. I slip on the mask I prepared in Madrid. I hold the cigarettes in hand, I spit, cleaning again, and I lay down the second plant, putting the soil back and the gravel on top. I reinstall all the objects that were there. The grave looks beautiful. Facing it, standing up straight, I feel strong and free and I can make my official statement: I give back to everyone their physical absence (especially to my father who preferred to die—and as for my mother, I think of her laughter and what she used to say: "Ah, what a quiet child who plays for hours alone without a problem, we even found he ate earthworms"); I give them back their lack of love and my guilt for not having been able to make myself loved, which made me a loser, useless, and suicidal. I think of the little girl she wanted and who I tried to be. I am light. I thank my guides for the magic of this act (I haven't been disturbed, I thank them also for that). I am aware that it is an important first step. I return home, happy.

THANKS,

ANDRÉ

✦ LETTER 63 ✦

From Barbara (forty years old)

Objective of the act: to work on my obsessive search for affection related to my mother.

Conception of the act: Disguise myself as all aspects of my mother present in me, as everything I developed to satisfy her: a clown, the little girl, the bourgeois, the trickster. Spend a day in this costume in order to see and feel the true love that my mother has given me and what I have become only to please her. Once my act is done, I should make a big package out of my costume and send it to my mother.

Development of the act: Each element that I used to disguise myself had its meaning. I was surprised to feel how thrilled I was with the simple preparation of my act. First, I stood naked in front of the mirror and I saw a beautiful woman who little by little turned into a grotesque woman, a puppet full of fear, something outside of reality. The clown wig that I used overwhelmed me; it was as if it dimmed my ideas. I decorated the wig with ridiculous trinkets that mothers buy you on occasion so you don't forget that they love you. And you, in gratitude for that gift, wear them garnished with pride and you melt like chocolate in the summer, feeling it in the depths of your badly loved child, the child being loved in a humiliating way. I put rollers in my wig to symbolize the endless movies that show the house-proud wives who dedicate all their time and energy on cleaning, rubbing, polishing. The wives who devour you when a sad crumb of your bread falls on their immaculate carpet (I remember how my mother washed it on her knees and cleaned its fringes with passion—I suffered if I stained anything, including myself, and to my misfortune I always had a stain on my clothes). My face was a poem. I made half of it as a silly clown, half as a little girl with a troubled face. I wore a black-laced jacket that my mother loved (perhaps because it was stiff, narrow, and expensive).

I painted white polka dots on my pants, which were symbols of elegance for my mother. I was lame on one foot with a sandal full of coins, to remind me of my tricky side. On the other foot, of course, I wore a black shoe, brand new to keep up appearances. It occurred to me to start my act at 9:00 a.m. and finish at the same time at night. I was even more convinced to make this decision when I learned the meaning of this number in the tarot. I asked a friend to interrupt my act at 9:00 p.m. and leave me a golden robe she owned, worthy of a shaman. I put on drum music and the savage that I have inside bewitched me. I danced and started to feel it intensifying my love for life. It was at that time that I realized that a part of the ill bond I have with my mother cracked.

BARBARA

⇾ LETTER 64 ⇽

From Charlie (forty-three years old)

Objective of the act: my father within me. He was an officer of the air force and wanted me to follow his tracks. Even if concretely I did not do it, psychically I was ready to do anything so that he would recognize me and love me. Finally, I became like him.

Design of the act: I would have a uniform tailored and I would wear it. Underneath I would blacken my skin from head to toe and I would stick my father's crap to my body: diapers with *Playboy* pictures, pacifiers, a pipe, wine-bottle labels, a handkerchief soaked in whiskey, and a stone. I would stay silent, draw a portrait of my father, and make him an altar where I would worship him and pray to him: "Oh my Father, help me, poor sinner, help me to look like you." I would caress the stone, then I would use it to clean myself of the black and to crush all the objects that I wore on the body. I would take part of this powder and drink it in wine. I'd use the rest to make a candle that I would offer to the Father, to God, during a sung mass. I would take part in the singing of the mass, give the uniform to a theater or a drama school so that it would be useful, I would look for a building site, and I would place the stone in its foundation. I would buy a lamb heart and would place it over my heart while I crushed my objects and prepared the candles. Then I would cook and eat it.

The preparation: I'm looking for a military tailor. From store to workshop, they direct me each time to another place, until I find myself in a street where I can't find anything anymore. An old woman walks past me with small steps. Suddenly her wallet falls to the ground. I have an impulse to turn around and pick it up, but I stop: she is already reaching for it. I think it's not worth it and I continue on my way . . . immediately stepping in dog shit. Screw that! I see how I gagged my positive impulses; I was making myself smaller! It struck me because I realized it had become a daily behavior, an automatic behavior: I see something I want to do and I end up not doing it. "What's the point? It won't make any difference!" And as a consequence, it allows me to stay in my negative pattern. I saw myself again as a child, very motivated, attentive to others. I would not have hesitated then. I know that at the time there was a huge need behind all that. I wanted to be acknowledged, loved, to receive a positive image of myself. I also saw all these times when I grumbled at others because they weren't paying attention and gave no response. And the attitude: "Since they won't do it, neither will I!" In short, I was confronted by all my pettiness and hatred. What clearly came to me was that I was neglecting and despising my positive aspect. The first person I deprived of it, even before others, was myself. Believing that others do nothing is aberrant: in fact, they see and pay attention to things that I don't see! It is by acting each in their power that harmony is created. Since I couldn't find anything, I told myself I wasn't looking from the right angle: before the uniform, I had to first find the black paint! I went to get it.

Then I go to a tailor who I had overlooked earlier, "El Corte Militar" on Plaza San Nicolás (the day of my birth). I thought I could buy a ready-to-wear uniform, but there are none. What's more, to be able to buy a uniform, you have to be in the military. I see on a mannequin a superb dark-blue uniform. It is the grand dress uniform of a lieutenant colonel of the legal corps. It's him! The next morning I go back to the tailor. He takes the measurements and little by little the vision of a military uniform emerges, but without the specific attributes of the Spanish Army. He suggests smooth golden buttons. For the collar and the cap, he asks me if I would like to design the coat of arms myself. At first I refuse since I can't draw, but because what he offers me (the palms of the marching band or the Maltese cross of health corps) doesn't suit me, I change my mind. Leaving, the excitement sets in. But, of course, I will be an officer of my own military corps. What stands out first are the family initials: "R.L." In my father's family, for generations, the first child takes a first name beginning with "R" (Rene, Raoul, Renaud, Romain). My mother did not want that. Then, little by little, everything falls into place. My coat of arms: wings (my father wanted me to be a fighter pilot); a dead branch (in our last conversation, he dismissed me with: "Go away, you no longer exist for me, I cut off your branch of the family tree"); a screwdriver (in one of my dreams, it represented my pride and my obsession with the power that turns into vice); a blue diamond to represent my stone, my coldness; all that topped with a rain cloud to mark my gray mind, the destroyer, the weeper. My rank: lieutenant colonel (my father wanted me to succeed where he had failed and become a senior officer). My stripes are symbolized by two ice crystals to mark my coldness. On the sleeves two buckles mark the endless circle of the family.

The next day the final details are settled. Suddenly, the tailor tells me to look out the window: a wedding is taking place in the church across the street, and several officers in full uniform are there. He shows me those who wear the same dress uniform as the one I just ordered. I find it beautiful! Little by little, I feel within me the excitement of wearing this uniform, no revulsion or disgust at all. On the contrary, pleasure, jubilation. I feel my whole frustrated family part looking forward to my wearing the uniform. It scares me a little. It reminds me of what my analyst told me: "You will never wear the uniform—otherwise you're lost! The attraction is too strong." This is why I chose conscientious objection at the time of military service. Now I almost feel this attraction physically. I feel that I should dive deep into it. When I call next week to get the news, I learn that the tailor fell ill the day I went there. He remains absent for two weeks and I begin to worry. No news about the uniform for two weeks. One Tuesday, I call and they tell me it's ready. That's it, everything can begin. I quickly go to buy everything that remains and I begin the act.

I cover myself in black from head to toe, everything I can reach. I put on a diaper and inside I slip the *Playboy* pictures. I put my stone on the right side, just below the ribs, and I hold it in place with a black sheath. I put on a shirt with wine labels and a pacifier pinned to it. Then I put on the uniform. I draw the portrait of my father. It is impressive. I thought that since I don't know how to draw, I wouldn't be able to represent him. But no, he is there, he showed up under my fingers. I put up a small altar: his effigy, two candles. As incense, his tobacco. I fill a pipe with it and I light it.

As a perfume, his whiskey. I sprinkle a handkerchief that I breathe into deeply. I put a mirror next to the altar to see myself. I pray silently.

Among the accessories I bought there was an *Interviú* magazine with an erotic video, "Adolescent Fantasies." I saw synchronicity there and I followed it. A whole part of my mind has remained stuck precisely in these "teenage fantasies," and regularly I fall back into the temptation to flick through a magazine or skip channels to find erotic images there. I watch the film without sound: it's a series of encounters, repetitive couplings. I force myself to watch till the end. I feel empty. Regularly I return to the altar to seek paternal blessing. I also force myself to browse the entire *Playboy,* page by page. I also acquired military magazines that I leaf through, stopping on planes and uniforms. Then I assemble an airplane model: a YF-16, the last plane my father flew. I feel outside of time. Finally, I undress and go clean myself. The black makeup comes off with difficulty; I use the stone to scrape myself clean. The bath is very hot, the black won't stop coming out, the water is completely black, I wash in black, I rub myself in black. It's very hard. It will always be the hardest moment when I see more clearly what I immersed myself in. I come out of there exhausted, knocked out, completely empty. Afterward I caress the stone.

The same scene will take place, day after day, for the whole week. The first day there was the excitement of beginning the act; I was sort of fantasizing about it. But from the second day on I feel the weight, the emptiness, smallness, boredom. The despair and self-loathing too, as I realize that these pornographic images are still having an effect because I also feel my narcissism, my attraction toward the uniform, toward this entire fake masculinity. I rediscover the child and the teenager who played alone in his room facing the mirror, inventing heroic exploits, strutting, admiring himself, challenging himself in the mirror. In the end, nothing happens in this space; I go round in circles, repeating the same gestures, succumbing to the same chimeras. To escape boredom, the void, I disconnect myself. It reminds me of the image of that lab rat mechanically pushing a button to activate his brain's pleasure center. Covering myself in black every day provokes more and more emotions: despair, nausea, rage, the will to reach limits. And stripping myself each time leaves me in a greater state of shock. I'm sick of this black, it never stops coming out, it's everywhere. Rubbing it doesn't make any difference; it clings to my skin. My pores are blackening, my nails are darkened.

My anguish was not to start the act, but to get to the end of it.

I ordered a lamb's heart for Saturday, and I had a list of theater schools, but I still needed a church where I was sure to celebrate a sung mass. Friday morning, when I called the theater school, they told me to come directly to see the costume designer who works from 9:30 a.m. to 2:30 p.m. I'm shaken. I was still thinking of spending an evening with my uniform, but if I want to finish this weekend, it's now or never. It takes me by surprise, I realize that in fact I was ready to continue like this for a very long time; taking off my uniform takes its toll. I leave immediately. I donate the uniform to the Royal High School of Dramatic Arts (RESAD). I really like the name, and the address: Nazareth Street. When the costume designer sees the uniform her eyes shine; I feel a pang in the heart. If she takes it it's over forever; I can't wear it anymore. I hear two voices within me, one who would like to keep it and be able to keep putting it on and the other who is fed up with all this, who wants to be freed. When I leave, I go to a religious bookstore to buy a book for making candles, where they point me to a church where masses are sung.

The next day I go to pick up the lamb heart from a halal butcher. While paying the butcher nods to me. It moves me. I come back home. I put the heart on my heart. I use my stone to grind everything. It's difficult. I realize that there are a lot of things: I first crush the portrait of my father, the photos that I put in my diaper, the labels, the pacifier, the plastic airplane, the pipe. Then I tear the magazines into a thousand pieces. I break the pipe, I add the tobacco.

Seeing the volume, I decide to burn everything: I pour the rest of the whiskey onto the heap and I set it on fire. It takes time to burn, especially the diaper, but finally everything turns into ashes. I go back to grinding the ashes with the stone, to obtain very fine dust. I melt the wax and make the candle: I have so much wax that I make two of them; with the ashes, they take on a gray-black color. Then I prepare the lamb heart with sesame oil and honey. I eat it, accompanied by a glass of wine in which I also put the ashes.

The next day there is excitement. I get up, leaving early, thinking I will find a house under construction before the mass. I locate the place, then I look for a construction site.

As I find nothing, I go to the basilica. I was told that at the Basilica of the Santa Cruz del Valle de los Caídos the monks sang the mass. I had never been there and I naively thought that the monastery was separated from the Francoist monument. The closer I get, the more I feel discomfort. I try to calm down, but it's getting worse. Finally I get to the top and see the entrance to the basilica under the gigantic cross. I don't like the idea of locking myself underground in order to open myself to Father. I plunge into the corridors and, once at the center, I discover the tomb of Franco and de Rivera. The unease is accentuated, it is physical. I feel worse and worse and I run out. I don't know what to do; I don't know where to go. At first I wanted to go to the Basilica of the Real Monasterio de San Lorenzo de El Escorial, but there was no sign of sung masses. I decide to go there. A guard tells me that normally the 1:00 p.m. mass is sung; a phone call confirms it. I go back in search for a house under construction. I crisscross the whole village. Sometimes I come across a building site, but either it is already too advanced and the walls are already built, or it has just begun and there are no excavations yet. Too bad, the time of the mass is approaching, I decide to put down my stone afterward.

First I leave the candles and light them. The basilica is full of visitors and my heart is beating. It's absurd—I'm not trying to commit a crime. I find a stand filled with small candles. I like the text inviting visitors to meditate: "Lord, you are the light that shows eternal life." I put down two black candles and light them. Then I go to sit just under the rostrum where the choir is going to sing. The mass begins. Every time the choir sings, I sing with it; my voice is not strong, I do not always know the lyrics, so I muse and I feel myself vibrate with the voices. At the end of the mass, the sun passes through the central dome and I bathe in its light. Especially since the mass was dedicated to the theme of light. I leave and go looking for a worksite. It's going to take me some time but I want a real construction site, a real foundation. Finally, after having scoured the surroundings of Madrid, I find it. It is of course fenced in. I go around and just where the concrete has not yet been poured, where there are still only the excavations, I notice an opening in the fence. I slip through it, jump into the hole, and sink my stone into the sand. Coming back, I tell myself that I still have a garbage bag filled with ashes as well as the black shoes that I wore with the uniform and that I no longer want to use. I do not want to just throw them away; it doesn't seem right. I then decide to bury them and plant a tree. I go to the countryside to dig a hole, scatter the ashes there, deposit the shoes, and plant a pomegranate over them, so that the remains of my alcoholic elite soldier feed a fruit tree!

CHARLIE

⇢ LETTER 65 ⇠

From Francois (forty-five years old)

Objective of the psychomagic act: help me integrate the figure of my father and the positive aspects of the soul he represents that I rejected to satisfy my mother's wishes.

My family comes from an extremely poor layer of society. The origin of my neurosis resides in the huge social complex I inherited from my mother. This complex has been my driving life force, the engine of

my race against life and others. The result: I live only to achieve good
social standing and I see others as competitors and enemies. Countering
this pattern is my father, who was extremely poor in his childhood and
youth but knew how to see life in a much more positive way, with the
eyes of an artist.

The act should help me stop identifying with the world of possession, with the world of appearance, and develop the world of the soul
so I can balance my life. It is important to note that I did this act a few
days before an operation on my left hip to correct the effects of a disease
inherited from my father.

Conception of the act: I had to find out where my father is buried.
He passed away thirteen years ago. I had to get three tattoos on my
arms just like the ones he wore and that my mother disliked so much:
a naked woman, a bleeding heart, and a flying dove. Likewise I had to
find Spanish music, the music that my father sang when he felt happy,
and, most often, when he worked. My father liked wine a lot; therefore I should buy a bottle of good wine. Along with all of the above,
I should have a copy of an article that appeared in a newspaper, at the
beginning of my professional career, on a lecture I gave at a meeting in
Valladolid. This article represents the beginning of my identification
with the material world of power and appearance.

With all the elements mentioned above, I had to confront my
father's tomb. Once there, I would put on the music, open the bottle
of wine, and pour two glasses—one for him and one for me. With the
wine from his cup I had to wash the headstone on his grave. Afterward
I had to burn the article, put the ashes in my cup, and drink them with
wine. After having done all this, I had to go see my brother Carlos in
his workplace to offer him a bouquet of red roses as a gift and invite
him to a good restaurant.

Preparation of the act: During the trip to Madrid, when I stopped at
a service station, I found a tape of the music I was looking for, Spanish
music by Antonio Molina, one of my father's favorite singers. To find
out the exact place of his grave I asked my mother. She was surprised

by my question because she knew that I had never been interested in going to visit my father's grave. To my surprise, she told me that she hardly ever visited. She knew how to get there but she couldn't give me the exact directions. I had to call my brother who didn't know either, but he told me where to find them: Cemetery South, row C7, tomb 34. The next day I went to get my tattoos. I visited dozens of places but none of them did tattoos that were not permanent. I walked into a place where, as in the previous ones, they refused. I felt that in this place was something special and I asked to speak with the artist who created the displayed designs. I noticed that they were a little annoyed by my insistence and they gave me the reasons why they didn't want to do the tattoos I asked for.

They assumed I was a model and that I wanted the tattoos for a photography session, and for this purpose, tattoos drawn only on my skin wouldn't be suitable. I explained that I wanted to pay homage to my father, that he had those same three tattoos. Afterward they agreed immediately and an hour later, a true artist was painting a beautiful dove, a realistic woman, and a heart that, although bleeding, reflected joy on me.

The psychomagic act: The next day I took the metro to Plaza de las Acacias. Once there I had two options: either take the bus to the cemetery or walk about a kilometer. After tossing a coin, it turned out I had to go by foot and I began walking, very focused. As I walked, my ailing leg started to hurt more and more. When I saw the cemetery in the distance I felt a very strong emotion growing in me. I got to the entrance and immediately recognized the place. Enormous sadness possessed me when I remembered my pride on the day of the funeral thirteen years ago, and the loneliness in which my father must have died when he called me while I was miles away with no desire to go to the hospital. I entered the cemetery. It was immense, it was very cold, and there was no one there. I was completely alone. I went to look for his grave: row C7, tomb 34.

As I approached I couldn't contain the tears that overflowed when I saw the tombstone of a niche engraved with "Dionisio A." It was a beautiful and well-kept place, but the tombstone was dirty and almost abandoned. I felt the abandonment I caused my father to feel. I was very emotional, I cried without being able to stop but also did not want to stop. I put on the music of Antonio Molina. Softly at first, then little by little, I turned up the volume. The music sounded beautiful and strong. I opened the bottle of wine, thinking that my father would be very glad to be able to share good wine with me. I served the two glasses and with the wine from his I started to clean his tombstone. There was a strong smell of wine. I remembered that when I was little I hated it, but now I liked it enormously. My crying became more intense. I poured the tears that I had not shed, the tears that I kept and that out of pride and hatred toward my father did not want to spill. When crying, I did not feel relieved; on the contrary, I felt sad for how I was apart from my father and what he meant. The site was still deserted. I was alone. I then burned the article and drank the ashes. I continued cleaning with the music and the tears. I had no notion of passing time. I decided to go, but it hurt; I felt good in this place. I got ready to leave, I turned off the music, I put the device in the bag, and I started walking. Suddenly, the music started playing without me touching the device. I started laughing and let the music play again next to my father's grave. Then I went to see my brother. I went to look for him at his office with the bouquet of roses for him. I felt that he reacted with a certain embarrassment. He asked why I gave him those flowers. I said that I gave him very few gifts in my life and when walking by the florist I really liked the roses and I really wanted to give them to him. I felt that at that moment Carlos was glad. We went to the restaurant. Everything was going very well, we were happy and relaxed. In the middle of the meal, the director of the company where he works entered the restaurant. My brother got nervous and asked me to eat as quickly as possible since his bosses do not put up with a subordinate eating in the same restaurant as them. In the evening my mother called me to tell me that she talked to Carlos and he was very happy because I gave him a bouquet of roses.

FRANCOIS

⇥ LETTER 66 ⇤

From Gregory (forty years old)

The purpose of the psychomagic act was to lighten up, to free myself from the *weight of the mother* and my unloved child personality. Youngest of a family of three, I joined an already established family dynamic: my mother took care of my brother, who was a difficult child, my father having set his sights on my sister whose intelligence and school achievements he valued. I chose to hide, to be invisible in order to be accepted, and I installed a loser mindset inside. It became a way of life: inaction, isolation, avarice, and in compensation pride and a ferocious rage against those who manage to develop in life.

The act was designed as follows: First, record on tapes crazy thoughts that I have or had in the past. Also buy some heavy metal CDs, and make a headless doll with fabric and stuffing to represent my hatred toward my mother that is projected onto other women. Also make a small hot air balloon with balloons and a basket to represent my pride. Take a blank diary from which I would tear seven pages to symbolize my inaction, and a children's little hero book to represent my infantilism. Buy a Scottish blanket to represent greed and a revolver of black plastic to represent my suicidal side. Also procure large drawing paper and acrylic paints.

Settle down for two days, during a long weekend, in a room where I close the shutters, with a very weak artificial light. Install a sofa in the center of the room and cover it with the Scottish blanket. Scatter CDs and tapes on the floor around the couch. Glue the seven blank pages of the diary on the walls, put the black revolver in front of the couch, place the doll in the tub. Spend two days alone, telephone switched off, stuck on the couch repetitively reading the same page of this hero story and listening to the cassettes with the recording of my mind. Tie my hot air balloon to one or both wrists.

On the third day at sunrise, destroy the CDs and cassettes with a hammer, pierce the balloon with a CD shard, and wrap it all up with the doll, the seven blank pages, the little book, and the revolver in the Scottish blanket. Then go to a quiet corner in the countryside to burn it all and bury the remains. On the way back, clean my whole body with salt, lemon, and lavender soap.

Then go to a park in the afternoon and sit on a bench to paint in bright colors. Give the painting to someone who likes it in order to pass from my black-and-white world to a colorful life, from avarice to generosity. Also take advantage of this time to talk with people stopping by, to learn to leave my glass bubble. Go back several Sundays, maybe seven for the seven days of the week, to solidly establish the idea of constancy, regularity.

The preparation for the magic act happened without difficulty, except that I realized that balloons inflated without helium do not float and my balloon was therefore not flying. The making of the headless dummy and the recording of my thoughts on a tape brought out a lot of sadness.

On Wednesday morning I installed all the elements in the room: pistol, CDs, white pages on the wall, shutters closed, the balloon attached to the wrists, the Scottish blanket, and in the bathtub, the dummy. Then I settled on the couch covered in plaid. I started to read the page of my children's book. I had found a Peter Pan book, and the page had a very short text: "Peter Pan and his shadow flitted around the room. The shadow seemed in no hurry to rejoin Peter. They hovered above and below the children, dodging furniture and toys until the ruckus woke up Wendy. 'What are you doing?' exclaimed Wendy. 'I see, you try to recover your shadow. Come on, let me help you.'"

In between reading, I listened to the recorded tape. Twilight, the severe nature of the space, and my voice expressing that stupid mindset created waves lasting all day.

Waves of anger and rage, not really defined, against my stupidity, followed one another.

I had already experienced this rage. But this time, thanks to the Seitai sessions where I realized I was physically blocking my emotions,

I was able to let them out more freely and go further than mere rage. Other waves followed, where the desire to live in the present emerged. Out of this mind that swayed me from past to future, as if I had always forbidden myself to exist, was stuck my pride and hatred. I tried to reaffirm my voice, realizing the fragility of my awareness facing different currents that show up and invade all my interior space too easily. As the half-light fatigued my eyes, I had to close them regularly and would immediately see images. I didn't give them too much attention to avoid plunging into another train of thought. Later, I uncovered a painting with three women seated on a sofa, just in front of me. I told them about my desire to live, to feel, to love. The next morning I had quite a different impression, as if what happened the day before was a step, but that I had to go further now. It was no longer just about an exercise expressing positive or negative emotions, but about an act and the fact that change had to happen. It was more pragmatic and also harder because there was a requirement of an outcome. I listened to the tape again and read my book to follow the program, but I also listened to my mind at that time and above all tried to create silence. It was my job all day long, to install this silence not as a moment of meditation, but as a new state.

Only one wave came at the end of the day. I shouted "Mom!" all possible ways, and afterward I expressed the desire to be able to love women, to get out of this pattern in which they are only mothers from whom I expect everything or nothing but a castrating attitude, and on whom I cast my shadow. At the end of these two days, I lived a feeling of joy, without euphoria, because I felt like I already accomplished something. I had one more day to go and of course my loser-self showed up in the morning, with the impression that if I made a fire in the countryside, the forest rangers would see me, and of course in the afternoon nobody would care about my painting. After I destroyed all the different symbols and wrapped it all up in the blanket, I went looking for a distant corner of the Villanueva countryside. Along the way, I passed by a small group preparing to launch a hot air balloon. I saw it as a serious downside to my expedition. I then realized that this hot air balloon element I added at the end corresponded more to my father than to my mother. I finally found a corner to burn it all and contrary to my predictions, everything went smoothly.

Then came the step of cleaning and purification of the house. I vacuumed and cleaned all the rooms that I occupied, then completely cleaned myself with the lavender, lemon, and salt mixture. It was already three o'clock when I arrived at the park, and that's where the magic began. Car parked at the entrance to the park, a few hours of sunshine in a rainy week, a large stone bench in a rose garden that is both very calm and with a passage, but especially this feeling of loving everyone after these two days of total isolation, alone in my hell. I was happy to see them all.

I had barely set up my easel on the bench when a little boy rushed over and told me he wanted to see me paint. We chatted while I began painting. He was a small ten-year-old Romanian, Alejandro, who was with his mother and grandfather. He explained that he liked to paint, too, that he received an award at school for one of his paintings, but that on the other hand he failed his swimming test. He said all this with a lot of humor, which was good for me who was painting nervously because of the eyes of passersby. He asked what I was going to paint and as I told him that I didn't know yet, that something would come out of the colors, he began to describe what he saw. First he saw a snail, then fire burning a tree, and finally a stone surrounded by flames falling to the ground like a meteor. At the end he suggested that I paint a swan or a duck. I would have liked to give him the painting, but he had to leave too quickly. He came to tell me goodbye gravely, looking me straight in the eyes because it was forever. I had barely covered half of the sheet when a young woman rushed from afar to ask me if I was selling my painting because she was drawn to the colors. I told her of course that if she really loved it I would give it to her. She was touched and sat next to me waiting for me to finish. Her name was Nathalie and she was visiting from Bilbao. I realized later that her anxiety to have my paint- ing corresponded in all respects to my anxiety to give it to someone. I finished what could be described as a vague sketch of a background and I don't think I underestimate myself saying it wasn't great, but she took it happily. I could see then that it was not necessary to be a grand master to please and that I had something to give despite not being the best.

I was quite surprised by such a quick outcome, and obviously very happy, I began to put away my supplies when an old lady asked me for a plastic wrap for seeds she found on the ground. She mostly wanted to talk and sat down next to me. She explained to me that she was sad because her family who spent a week with her had just left. She was a dry little woman from Galicia, who, I think, had come to Madrid to be with her children. We talked a bit about everything and nothing, her family and her grandsons. Finally a young guy came to tell me it was time for me to go home, asking me to move my material because he wanted to work out on the bench. Having thus met three generations, I went home really happy.

The following Sunday I took an itinerary that I would respect the five other days: the train, the climb to the park, and the stone bench in the rose garden. Some days I had a chance to talk with people who usually were there before me on the bench, sunbathing, reading a book, or doing crosswords. I settled down and started painting until we got into conversations for some trivial reason, conversations which sometimes continued for a good part of the afternoon. I realized later that I had never before made contact with strangers. Some encounters were deep, others less, but in itself it was a radical change compared to my past. These were people who were going through a delicate moment in their life, a change of country, work, or perspective. One day I spoke with two men who had a real mirror effect on me. Another aspect was the succession of symbols that showed me the magic of life when you plug in. First of all, this hot air balloon on my journey on the third day. The symbol which came up again the last day. Then the little Alejandro who came to welcome me in the rose garden as if to tell me that I was in the right place. Next this woman to whom I offered a painting and who told me that her husband was called Grégorio Pintor and was getting out from the hospital after an operation and that my gift gave him even more pleasure. Or this man who came to tell me I should paint fabrics for modern clothing, thus associating my work with that of Catherine, my sister, a designer in New York, who uses hand-painted fabrics for her models. I could also feel how much the outside world unfolds exactly like my internal state: the eagerness of this young woman to take away my painting on the first day, the moment of delicate and difficult transition where some people who spoke to me in a deeper way found themselves, the poverty of contacts and difficulties in the day when I left with leaden feet.

Another drastic change was to have offered the result of my own work. To succeed I had to overcome my fears, my laziness, and my pride, but I could see that I could give something without being the best, and it is a result that encourages me a lot. I feel that this act plays out as a catalyst that allows me to launch into a positive, creative life full of very instructive surprises.

THANK YOU ALEJANDRO,
GREGORY

→ LETTER 67 ←

From Jaime (thirty-nine years old)

My first act is focused on my dad. The goal is to get rid of that *losing-horse* feeling induced by my father's devastating temperament and a Cronos aspect that continuously provoked situations in which he put me in a position inferior to him. To release myself from that programming that leads me to play over and over again the same dominant-dominated pattern.

From time to time, without warning, my father took me to participate in athletic competitions where I was set up to lose. This generated in me a feeling of deep frustration of not having lived up to my father's expectations, who cheered me on (and insulted me in passing) from the stands to beat all records as the "son of Augustus" that I was.

The living room of my house was presided over by a fake bullfighting poster which included the name of Augusto A., "The Bullet," along with two great bullfighters from the epoch. I was terrified of bulls. I felt humiliated and frustrated every time when I was in the village and he forced me to participate in the bullfights. I saw myself as a traitor by not being up to the circumstances. "The son of Augustus cannot be afraid." Situations like this deeply marked the path of my life, headed largely toward a caricature of my father, chasing the illusion to be accepted one day, to be able to exist in his eyes.

For this act, I'm going to run five kilometers a day for ten days in a sports stadium, from April 1 to April 10. I will wear a reproduction of Rubens's "Cronos" painting and a chronometer hanging on my chest. Each day I plan to improve on the time of the previous day. Every time I will win a medal with an inscription on the back that reads: "Race against Cronos, first prize, date XX-April-2003." I will fabricate bull-fighting posters with the name of Jaime A.,—"The Free"—that I'm going to hang in my room. Along with the posters, as a daily trophy, I will hang one medal, until all ten are there. After the ten days are up, I will take two eggs that symbolize an unused potential (a castration image) and create a mural with them, a collage, using the white as glue, the yolk as paint, and we'll see what to do with the shell. In this mural I will reflect a project, a plan of life that belongs to me. Then I will burn the image of Cronos, and I will dissolve some of the ashes that I will drink in a glass of champagne.

I start to feel stimulated when I go in search of the medals and bull-fighting posters. The two times I went to Madrid (I live thirteen kilometers away) for this purpose, both times I ran into a friend, Angela, practically in the same place. I want to see the original "Cronos" painting in the Prado Museum. I don't know Madrid well and to park always seems like a feat. When I think I'm close enough, I leave the car and what do I see before me? A stall of bullfighting posters. I take two. I go to the museum and while looking at the "Cronos" painting I get goosebumps. Both Goya's and Rubens's work awaken the same emotion in me. I walk around the galleries like a cold-blooded zombie. I feel determined to break this curse. I do not want to do this to my son! I buy two reproductions and leave. The same day I find a sports trophy shop, which was called "Alegre" (for a time the words happy and joy were following me). I ask for permission from the Municipal Stadium to go running every day. No problem, they explain: if it is to prepare for tests, I can use the track without having to be federated, pay, etc. It is, I think, a competition against being myself.

The rest was a solitary act. The stadium atmosphere pumped up my heart. Every afternoon I was practically alone on the track. I ran my thirteen laps religiously, minding my chronometer. It was all an internal fight between a skeptical voice that told me, "You can't, you are not fit anymore for these jogs, what are you playing at . . ." and another, that said with anger, "You are not going to eat me, I will run with all my strength so you won't catch me!" I started with a lot of energy and on the fourth day I couldn't even walk, climbing stairs was torture, my whole body ached. I was about to give up, the first laps were really excruciating. I took something for pain. Two days, by three and four seconds I couldn't beat the mark of the previous day. From time to time when I came across a young woman running in the opposite direction I used her as reference to resume the rhythm: the swaying of her hair, the lightness of her gazelle strides, the word happiness echoed in my head. Suddenly I had an impression of surfacing, of becoming light too. I realized just how stingy I am. I saw myself making minimal effort because I felt obliged to overcome myself. On the sixth day, it emerged as a revelation. What a way to live, always with the handbrake on! I told myself: "Jaime, are you doing it or not? Give it your all!" I started to act differently, passionate but with strategy. The first days I ran with nothing and only looked at the time toward the end to find out if I had to speed up or not. Now everything was different, the challenge was at every lap. I practically ran with the chronometer in hand and I felt powerful, much freer. What before seemed like an eternity turned in a moment. Between the first and last day I improved my time by six minutes. Every day I got home, exhausted but happy, I wanted to celebrate with a small party. I felt satisfied in front of my trophies.

To my surprise the hardest part was to answer the question: "What is it that I want?" When I started to make my collage my mind was blank. No inspiration, no aspiration. I couldn't find a soulful image. I told myself: what I want is to go out from there, from that defenseless learned apathy, that voice that tells me that whatever you do, nothing will change. I made a reproduction montage of Cronos in which Cronos was seen as giant, devouring another smaller one that in turn ate another one younger than him, and so on up to four. To the last of this series, I snatched the boy from his mouth and incorporated it into another frame in which there were some figures, as heavenly entities, who took some children by the arms to help them rise. The son of Cronos was there, now raised by those arms of love. With the egg yolk and my blood I drew a heart that I decorated with rose petals around it. As I was placing the petals, it felt like a warm caress, as if I began to pamper myself, to treat myself with consideration. I consider the mural unfinished, with lots of space available to add projects, goals, illusions. For a while after the act, I experienced a new sensation that was situated at the level of my chest: the feeling of being in the world, of doing things without the inquisitive look of the father.

Do them just because, for me.

JAIME

✣ LETTER 68 ✣
. . . .
From Jason (forty-seven years old)

Objective of the act: open up my heart to open up to others. Why? I am forty-seven years old. I have a wife and a daughter. I am a French teacher and a musician. Until now, I remained a prisoner of an ego and of enormous narcissism linked to emotional emptiness from my childhood. Despite the realization, through inner work, of the fact my parents did not like me at all, I continued to reproduce this emotional emptiness inside and could not open my heart or open myself to others. So I wanted this psychomagical act to get to the bottom of the problem and escape this prison.

Part one of the act:

1. On a piece of cardboard draw a heart. Inside, write "to our beloved son," signed "your dad" and "your mom." Tear this heart into small pieces. Place the pieces in a corset to wear on my belly under my shirt for twenty-one days. In the same corset, place notarized inheritance documents of my parents (they both died a few years ago), as well as the many letters that my father wrote to me and in which he expressed all his avarice.

2. Buy the cheapest possible clothes and underwear in a super-market, as my mother used to do for her children. Wear these clothes for the twenty-one days.

3. During these twenty-one days wear a Walkman on my head that constantly plays a cassette recording of my voice. This voice is concerned for me and asks me a lot of questions: "How are you? Did you sleep well? Did you eat well?" It encourages me to plan ahead: "Do you have everything? Have you thought about every-thing you need to do tonight, and tomorrow?" It also proves me right on everything I used to blame others for, in work or private life: "I am not seen for everything I do; no one recognizes my merits." Only remove the corset and the Walkman to give my lessons, lead the choir, or at night to sleep.

Part two of the act:

On the 22nd day remove the corset. Place the clothes in a box for donation. Make recycled paper with cardboard pieces of the heart, the notarized documents, and letters from my dad. Use the made sheets of paper as musical scores. Compose two songs, one in a feminine style and the other in a masculine style. Write the melody to these songs on recycled sheets of paper. Offer to sing for free at the wedding mass of a couple about to marry (I am a classical tenor and I sing regularly in marriage masses). Include both composed songs in the program.

Procedure of the act:

The clothes my mother used to buy were not only cheap, but also sad and tasteless. So were those I was wearing. With the Walkman on my head I cut myself off from others and enclosed myself in a sad, bland character, obsessed with his concerns about himself. The first week I felt a certain comfort in this isolation. I no longer had to make an effort to go toward others. I agreed with the voice of the Walkman. I also started eating whatever, whenever, and began to put on weight, like when I lived with my parents. Actually, I didn't feel very different from my usual state of mind. It was simply much more focused. I lived stuck in behaviors and thoughts that came back more regularly than in my everyday life. From the second week, this feeling of comfort had gradually given way to real hell. The will to cut myself off from everything and everyone made a nightmare out of every obligatory contact with others. Everyone annoyed me, as a rule. I thought: "What else are they going to ask me as I go home tonight? I'm sure it's me they're going ask to do this work. I've had enough. I'm tired. Why can't we ever be left alone? No one thinks of me."

At the same time, I couldn't help but observe this character in which I put myself. One day I realized that I lived only on the level of the mind and stomach. I was filling my stomach to devote most of my energy to digestion, but also to calm anxieties and tensions. I was using the mind for the same purpose and to live things that others experience on another level. For example, I bought pornographic magazines again, something I did in my youth when I had problems with physical contact with my partners. The emotional engine was completely in breakdown. I was much sicker than I thought. Childhood memories returned and I reentered that totally emotionless world, the way my father, my mother, my sister, and I lived side by side like juxtaposed beings, without any meaningful interaction.

I felt as if I were in my father's skin, in his fears, his cowardice, his avarice. I was him and he was me. The fear was very strong. At the end of the twenty-one days, I was fed up with experiencing the world as a permanent aggressor. Moreover, I was bored in my bubble, fed only with potato fries and mayonnaise. I took off the corset and the Walkman with contentment, but little more. I felt that I had opened a way to operate differently, but that it was now necessary to take it and gradually change my whole way of being. When my mind and the anxieties subsided, I put myself in a state of receptivity to compose the songs. I received the male melody in a dream. The female melody I had received in a dream twenty years earlier, but until now I had done nothing about it. This time, in a state of inspiration, the lyrics and the musical arrangement arrived. At the same time, I rediscovered the pleasure of artisanal manual work through the art of the paper recycling. I visualized the church where I was going to sing at the moment of the conception of the act. I explained to the priest that my wife had been very ill and that I had made a vow that if she recovered, I would offer my voice to a couple for their wedding. He was moved and helped me find the couple in question. On the appointed day, I hired—and of course paid for—an organist to accompany me, and I sang my songs. I was excited to read this music on sheets that contained the entire family universe, a universe that had always prevented me from being a real artist . . . and these songs really have strength and emotion.

In the weeks that followed, there were strong temptations to return to the mind, into the stomach. I feel that I can't tell myself any more stories and that it's up to me to choose one way or the other.

JASON

→ LETTER 69 ←

From Jessica (thirty-five years old)

The objective of the act was to break free from the frenzy of power that contaminates my whole life. It's an aspect of identification with my mother.

For three days I would dress like my mother, Miss Rottenmeier* style, with a very tight bow that I would wear day and night and a

---

*Miss Rottenmeier is an authoritarian, perfectionist character from the 1881 children's novel *Heidi* by Johanna Spyri.

photo of my mother at my chest. After the three days I would cut a lock of hair that would symbolize my desire for power, and I would burn it along with the photo. I would keep the ashes in the belly of a doll. On the first of January I would dig a hole where I would bury the clothes and the little doll with the ashes and, on top, I would plant a tree.

My appearance totally changed with the bow and clothes. I scared myself as the features of my face looked so similar to those of my mother. At first I played the role in an exaggerated way, believing it to be more efficient. But actually it was a protection in order not to feel. When I started to internalize, I changed entirely. It was very hard. The act also coincided with Christmas and being surrounded by the closest people whom I love the most. Little by little the character of my mother materialized in me, until I became her completely. She hated everyone, despising men as much as women, with corrosive criticism. I wanted to attack, to make others pay for my discomfort, to destroy my surroundings. Nevertheless I felt above everything and everybody. I was unable to communicate. I didn't want to either! I could not stand that anyone was or had something better than me. My contempt for Life was total. I became more and more rigid; on the other hand, my head worked at full power, like a madman who talks to himself. My whole being was hate, and I came to emanate something so negative that even my dogs barked at me like at a stranger on the last day.

What later struck me the most was realizing that I lived those days totally inside my madness, identified as my mother, and that I would have been able to leave, to abandon all the people who love me. When the end of the three days came I panicked. What would happen when I took off my costume? I had the impression that the hatred and frenzy of power was the only thing that filled my life, that there was nothing else. I was moved when my friends came to meet me without my costume, because it was as if they were telling me that I was someone else and not just what I had just experienced, which for me was still my only reality.

It also came naturally to dig the hole to plant the tree. The soil was so wet and hard that I had to dig it with my hands and with great effort (also night fell and I had to finish in the dark). But the effort cleansed me. After the act was over I felt very well. On the other hand, I was more aware of all this negativity in my daily life, and in my relationship with others, and this made me suffer. Only after a month I started to feel that something had changed.

Jessica's second act:
Objective of the act: I'm sick of always living in maternal need and being unable to give to others.

I would model a doll in clay that would represent me as a child, and for thirty-five days (corresponding to my age) I would take care of her as a mother, giving her everything that I had not received. I would paint an elephant that would symbolize the positive maternal function, and I would carry it with me for the whole act. At the end of thirty-five days I would take the doll to a church to give it to the Holy Virgin. I would put her clothes in a small suitcase that would be taken to heaven by balloons. I would burn her bed, mix the ashes with water, and with it I would water my two olive trees. In the end I would throw a party for the children of my friends.

This act was magical from the first moment. I totally invested myself in the role of the mother. I felt her need for love and I wanted to give her everything, everything that my mother never gave me. But little by little a deep sadness began to invade me. I realized that she was blocked as a mother, that she was incapable of love. I also felt the girl's fear of being abandoned. Plus a clay arm broke. I experienced this as a sign. I started to make her talk. I realized that she was the best in the class. Then I understood why her arm broke. All her actions (her arm) were dominated by the desire for power.

I explained that was because her mother never loved her. To my surprise her reaction was very violent against me. She affected me a lot because I realized that she was capable of anything in order to convince herself that her mother loved her, and I became aware that this is the case with my psyche, that I don't want to betray my mother.

I decided to model a new arm and make a psychomagical act together with the old one.

We would go to a place to leave the arm inside a glass until the rain dissolved the clay. Then we would mix it up with clay from where we live, and we would model two hearts, one for her and one for me. So we did. It was surprising for me to discover that the ideas "appeared" to me; they flowed alone, as if they showed me the way. For example, news on the radio reminded me of a childhood event that marked my negative view of sex. So I did what my mother should have done: explain to me the miracle of life. I didn't imagine it would affect me so much. It had a cleansing effect.

Also, all her complexes began to emerge, and I began to see a girl marked by obligations, always judging if she is right or wrong. It occurred to me to put on a music tape randomly and we started dancing and shouting. I felt the energy that was unleashed, all that was contained by the rules. So we kept on dancing every day.

We did a lot of activities together (singing, playing the piano, painting, horseback riding, walking); everything took on a special dimension and I felt very present in everything we did. It coincided with the day of our birthday. I made beautiful things for her and a party. Besides, my partner was with us. I wanted my girl to have another vision of men, different from that of my mother, full of hate. There were also times of crisis. And every time I reacted imaginatively. I realized that something was changing in her; she was full of anger because her mother did not love her. We went to a lonely place to shout out the rage. It took effort because of the intensity of all the rage of an unloved girl coming out.

I was completely disarmed the day I prepared a puppet show for her, because I felt overcome by a huge inexplicable girlish emotion. Another important event took place when she started asking me about God. I realized how dramatic and traumatic the experience of her First

Communion was. Her mother scolded her while leaving the church because she didn't ask God for anything, and she told her that she was already too late, that God would want nothing to do with her (I remembered that I got sick, so big was my disgust). I thought of reliving the day of my First Communion. I sewed a white dress with a veil and flowers. We held a real ceremony. My girl talked to God; she asked for what she wanted. It was very emotional. When the time of the farewell came I explained I was going to take her to the Great Mother, that she would always take care of her. But first we would have to forgive our biological mother. So we went to her symbolic tomb and the girl forgave her. I was happy with everything that we had lived together, of the bond that had been created between us. I also felt that I could go now.

Since I had trouble finding a church open in the morning, I headed to the cathedral. It was full of tourists but they pointed me to a chapel reserved for worship. I came in and it made an impression on me: the Virgin was there with the Child in her arms, on top of an impressive altar. But the access was closed. As I felt that this was the place. I looked around: a few faithful praying in silence and a man cleaning the candelabra. I walked up to him and said I had an offering for the Virgin. I think my emotion was such that he could not refuse. He opened the passage for me and I went up to the altar. I was overwhelmed. I felt something immense, the profound greatness of the Great Mother and of Life. She welcomed my unloved girl forever. I sent her stuff back to heaven with the balloons and burned the rest. I scattered the ashes beneath my olive trees.

The next day I prepared the party for the children. It was again an explosion of my imagination and I managed to create a magical evening for them. I felt rich, creative, and capable of giving. A month later I found out that just that day I was ovulating and conceived: I am pregnant.

THANK YOU A THOUSAND TIMES,

JESSICA

✦ LETTER 70 ✦
....

From Joy (thirty-one years old)

The months before the birth of my son Robin, I had very violent dreams that showed me that I didn't want children, and even less a boy. In reality, my refusal to live motherhood again was clear and suffocated me. On the other hand, I did not feel this opposition toward having a boy.

The first dream I had after his arrival was that my chest was made of soft flesh filled with waste that I had accumulated since the birth. I had no breasts, so nothing to feed him. My act was destined to come out of this state where I felt that "motherhood is a nightmare, a horror, and I have to live this once more." I needed help for him, and for me.

The first part of the act was to make a baby out of foam and paint it black. Put two papers against it: on its front write, "boys are trash"; on the paper behind write, "I hate motherhood." Wrap that baby in a piece of a garbage bag and wear it for three days and three nights on my belly, attached by a length of umbilical cord. Then go into nature to shout out my rage and my anger at having to be a mother again, to feel this refusal with my entire being. Then go see my mother, and give her that black hated baby with the words: "I'm giving you back what you gave me." Explain to her what it means to me and tell her about my sadness regarding her reaction after my birth.

For the second part of the act, every day I will wash one piece of Robin's clothing (over the number of days that have passed since his birth) and soak them in water with honey. The last day, I will also wash the clothes of Brigitte, my daughter, which I will also soak in water and honey; I will have her wear them for a day. On that day she will also have in the lining of her clothes two large photos of her parents—one of Alexandre (her second father, but the one she considers her real father) and the other of me—and she will wear them all day.

As for Robin, on the same day I will put a onesie on him on which I will have drawn a big red heart on the front (Alexandre had drawn one for me on my belly just a few days before Robin was born to welcome him) with the words "You're a boy," and behind it the inscription: "You have a father and a mother" (since my other big problem is that I don't want my children to have a father, since I didn't have one). During all those days that I wash the clothes, I will wear a red velvet heart on my belly.

When it's all over, I'll massage my companion with honey in order to put some sweetness on both a man and the father of my children, then I will draw a red heart on his sex to transform the thought: "He's the one who planted this horror/that child in the womb."

I start the act by making the little baby in foam but I have no emotion in me. I'm empty as if I were a working machine. Then I color the baby in black and there this waste of a baby begins to come to life. A wave of sadness washes over me. I feel very bad. I made the baby rather small because it's a big shame for a mother to feel this for her child. I embrace it and decide to keep it this size. I tie it to myself and again I feel that I cut myself off from what it moves in me. In the evening, when my partner arrives, I feel bad because when I move, you can hear the sound of the garbage bag on my belly. I feel dirty . . .

I'm tense and I especially want to be alone. The first evening Robin has a fever. I'm scared, very afraid because I have the impression that if I cut myself off from the violence of my feelings, it is he who will suffer. The next day when I wake up, I realize that I forgot to put the two inscriptions on this baby; I open the piece of garbage bag and slip the two messages against the child. . . . There I burst into tears because it is too strong. I feel a deep shame to live with that on my belly, in my belly. Everything is unleashed in me and I feel very bad. Facing Alexandre, his father, we don't talk about it! I have trouble embracing this baby-horror when I am by his side because he is experiencing the opposite. His is a big heart beating to the rhythm of the children that surround him. He really loves them and I don't. . . .

The third day: I really think that my life is useless since I am a mother. I consider it worthless.

It takes over my entire being. Be a mother and nothing else . . . a daily nightmare. I go for a walk. . . . A word knocks in my head: CONDEMNATION. This is how I live this life as a mother. I am full of rage, I'm fed up. It's as if I have to fight maternity. I start to shout: "I've had enough!" I have images of a violent dream with my mother, with this heritage against motherhood and against boys. A hateful voice comes out of my throat, I hit the trees, I am in rage against life that allowed this to happen to me. I'm going home. I'm going to see Viva, my mother. Seeing me arrive, she has already understood. She is very tense and says to me: "I imagine that you will give something back to me?" I nod. I feel the situation is more difficult than I imagined. I thought she was going to simply collaborate, like two adults who undo a knot . . . but it doesn't seem to unfold that way. I tell her, "I am giving you back what you gave me," handing her the small package that I ask her to open. I explain that I want to get out of my hell and be done with these generations of mothers who hate their sons. I add that contrary to what she would like to think, my second delivery went very well, my companion helped me and welcomed his son with joy, and that this birth will remain very important for me. My mother takes this waste child but I feel that she is not really getting it. It wasn't easy at all.

Second part of the act: in the beginning, carrying the heart takes so much more out of me than carrying the trash baby! It's absurd but I have a feeling like I'm going to forget it all the time (after showers, and so on). I wear it day and night for twenty-five days. . . . The sensations evolve. . . . Little by little I'm starting to feel good about this heart against me. I like to feel its softness, its warmth, and the few minutes a day when I take it off, I feel naked. I heat it with my hands in the evening before going to sleep. As for washing clothes, I take it a little mechanically at first, then it becomes a kind of ritual that I appreciate, linked to Robin.

One night, following an evening where I feel very aggressive toward Robin, even violent in my gestures because I'm tired of this gift twenty-four hours a day, I dream that Robin dies and that I am given his little body in a trash bag, still warm but already inert. . . . I feel that I'm losing it because it's unacceptable, and above all inconceivable. I can't live with this within me. . . . I wake up sweating, take Robin in my arms, and cry for a long time, the being that I am. . . .

Concerning Brigitte, my daughter, the day when she must wear a clean and softened outfit . . . it's Carnival! The one and only day of the year when she does not wear her own clothes since she is going in disguise! I'm desperate . . . I'm counting days again . . . and in fact it's the next day. I regain energy. I sew the photos in the lining of her jacket, and curiously she who always is too hot spends the whole Madrid–Seville trip in the car (we were leaving for a week) with her jacket on. When she is offered to take it off toward the end of the trip (Alexandre doesn't know anything), she replies: "No, I'm fine with my jacket." I smile internally. This is the last day I wear this velvet heart on my belly and removing it takes a real effort; I don't want to part with it, I feel good with it against my belly.

In the evening I offer Alexandre a massage. He gets it immediately . . . and remains silent. I want to cry while my hands coat his body with honey. I feel very touched, but it is not sadness. It's more of a happy ending, even if it moves me deeply. As I draw this red heart on his sex, I think back to this dream where I made Alexandre responsible or guilty of the conception of the child. . . . I want this heart to help me see things differently, and I take my time to draw it.

The value of this act is precious since I see that I experience things differently. I do not feel completely caught up in this negative motherhood anymore, unable to keep my head above water. I live with that in me . . . and I feel stronger. Although other waves of negative motherhood have returned since then, I have experienced them with more lucidity.

Joy's second act:
After completing the first act, I find a certain balance but I continue to live my motherhood with difficulty. The dream with my dead son still haunts me. I'm looking for motherhood to nurture me instead of being something I endure.

For this act, I will draw milk from my breasts once in a while, when I feel it necessary, and I will use it in preparation of desserts or other sweets, made for me . . . and only for me. This motherhood will nourish me and make me better and more generous as a woman, as a mother . . . as a being.

The first few weeks I get the milk out with no problem, but the very first time, I have a very strong feeling of guilt, as if I do not deserve to offer this to myself. The following times it doesn't come back. I make pancakes and pour this milk into the preparation. I see myself as the protagonist of the Mexican film *Like Water for Chocolate*. It is a kind of witchcraft, but used for positive purposes. This act fills me with joy simply because since the birth of Robin, my son, I hadn't really done anything for myself anymore. All my attention goes to my children and to my partner, Alexandre.

I eat these pancakes alone, with a hot drink. It's a huge sweetness that fills me little by little, like a kind of love that I receive from God or more precisely from Grandmother who would watch over me. . . . It's hard to explain with words. I feel loved from Above, as if I am getting the energy/the milk of a great warm celestial breast, and that completely moves me. For a few moments, I don't know what really happens to me. I make some pancakes several times, sometimes a cake, and when I don't have time, I just pour some of my milk in a drink. The effect is always the same and never tones down. Often I close my eyes to better fill myself with this wave of love that invades me. . . . It is extraordinary.

For a month and a half I can no longer extract my milk because I have less of it. It makes me despair because "I need it." In hard times, if I eat one of my magical preparations, I re-center, I immediately find balance.

I abandon the idea of continuing . . . and visualize this milk which nourishes me. The effect is very similar although still weaker. One day I come up with the idea of taking advantage of the strength of Robin suckling to pull some milk for myself. That works! I restart the act and enjoy it before weaning begins and puts an end to this extraordinary food.

Joy's third act:

The objective of this act is to re-stimulate my libido because since the birth of my son Robin it is much lower. I have the impression that I spend my days having to answer to the continual requests of my children, of my surroundings, of my work . . . and the sexual expectations of my partner are experienced as additional needs to meet, no longer as fun to share.

For this act I will write a passionate love letter to my partner, describing to him everything that I like when we make love. I will put it in a condom that I will wear in my vagina for a day or more. . . . I can also write short erotic stories (including us both, for example) and carry them within me, in the same way.

The idea made me laugh but I liked it a lot because I felt an imbalance in my relationship and I wanted to find a dynamic sexual life with Alexandre, as this had been the case before Robin's birth. I started writing this letter in one stroke, including in detail the most erotic caresses! . . . Just to think of it, I felt my body wake up and wish for night so I could see my partner. I carried this letter with me all day and on several occasions very warm thoughts came to me!! I couldn't wait to make love to him that night. I prepared the room with desire to welcome him in this renewal. . . . We had a very indulgent night of fun . . . it had been a long time since the last time that happened to us!! I loved the experience and I will do it again . . . with some erotic stories perhaps . . .

JOY

✦ LETTER 71 ✦

From Liseby (forty-five years old)

I am the sixth in a middle-class family with seven children. My brothers and sisters were all bright, curious, and cultivated. Me, lazy. I didn't want to do anything and settled in a false marginality gilded by hatred and the criticisms I addressed to them. And so I wanted to do a psychomagic act to get out of my laziness, my parasitism, and my hatred toward them.

I will wear a very heavy necklace with photos of my six brothers and sisters, with the inscriptions of their respective diplomas (I had planned a stay with my parents soon, and by then would already be wearing this necklace). I will go begging in a wheelchair for five days (none of the women in my family circle ever worked and I always knew my maternal grandmother in a wheelchair because she was paralyzed by multiple sclerosis). Every night I will wash the clothes that I wore to beg. At the end of these five days, I will go and bury the necklace and burn the beggar's clothes. I will keep some ashes that I will put into the base of a cake that I will offer to six friends (representing my siblings). I will send a pink rose to each of my brothers and sisters.

The act went as follows: I wore the necklace the entire stay with my parents. A few memories came up. Seeking not to cause conflict I cast myself into the family mold. For me it's like being completely asleep, and the underlying hatred transpires in every sentence. I rented a wheelchair that I put in my car. Every time I had to park and sit in my chair I was very uncomfortable, afraid of being seen and taken for the cheater that I am in the end. But I realized that no one was paying attention.

To find myself in a wheelchair without being able to move was actually not very painful for me. That's what I do most of the time: wait for someone to push me, enduring life. So I started to beg, to complain that it was too hard to work, that I couldn't, that I needed help. I did it with no shame, no self-love. Someone bumped into my chair and I was furious—a disabled person deserves some consideration after all!

But the first coin fell, surprising and shocking me, so I must look pitiful. A man whom I found very handsome came by and gave me a coin. So here was the image that I gave off, my permanent attitude toward men, how I would try to seduce them. The gaze of others reflected to me the image I projected: a poor little thing to be pitied, who can't do anything, an unnecessary burden. My performance must have been strong since the second day someone wanted to take me to a social worker. On the third day someone called the police but my story was ready, and finally they left me alone. A man offered to push me, but very quickly he left me there like a bulky package. That evening, remembering the scene, it was my mother whom I would have liked to see in the gutter; I was acting in response to what she did to me. But for the first time I knew that behind this hatred there was a very strong desire for love. The gaze of the children was hard to bear, them being so alive in the face of this zombie. Obviously they didn't understand what I was doing here, like that. From the corner of my eye I think I saw a child with a limp—what an image of himself I was sending him! I thought of the example of their mother that I gave to my children. A beggar myself in front of them, I gave them nothing.

A man lay his half-helpless wife next to me, saying, "You'll be fine there in the sun." It was my turn to see my reflection. I, who have never given anything to a beggar, found it hard to understand the generosity of people. Sometimes I had the audacity to notice that I only received five coins; other times I was all too happy to receive these five cents. Great, easy in the end, but a life of five cents, what is it? Is this what I want? Little by little, shame overcame me; how dare I agree to take from this elderly woman, obviously poor, who really limps but who is still smiling? I saw many old or handicapped people passing on the arm of a young person who sacrificed their life for them. Off the back of how many people have I lived?

I couldn't stay very long in the same place in my chair (it was winter, people didn't understand what I was doing here alone) so I ended my day by dragging myself around the city, limping, reaching out, but it was even more painful than the chair. I felt much heavier. . . . I came across other beggars, young people who obviously preferred to beg than work; here I was facing my theft. Gradually, I saw the workers in a different light. I admired the garbage collectors. To work, to take advantage of our qualities, our hands, our legs, is to have dignity.

In the evening I washed all my clothes one by one. First the hat—the mind of the one who tells herself that she is nothing, that she can't do anything. The sweater—the emotions of this little girl in maternal need, who hates everyone, my heart of stone. The gloves of the one who dares to stretch out her hand, to steal. The pants of the one who refuses to stand, to walk. The little panties of the whore who would sell herself to be supported, would do anything to be noticed.

On the last day I went to a train station. The atmosphere was horrible, heavy, very low, stinking of sweat. To beg, I went to those people that I reproached, but it was I who was much lower than them. I went to bury the necklace, pushing it into the ground with a hammer to release my hatred. Then I burned the clothes of the beggar. Forty-five years of begging, how quickly it can burn.

When I came back to my car, I realized that I left a part of my beggar's clothes in the trunk. I went back to burn them. Night fell. I stayed a long time, impossible to get off the dirt road, the car was bogged down and stuck. I understood that as my inner beggar telling me that I could not get out of this situation. As I had a small shovel in my car, I acted in order not to be defeated. I had to win this time, I got down to dig, to put branches under the tires—but during a new test the engine stalled. I went to get help but there was no one in the only house in the area. I gave up and called for rescue. When my friends arrived the car came out on the first try—it was definitely me who convinced myself that I was not capable. Now it was much clearer to me: I managed to more effectively cut off this mind, altogether paralyzing; I wanted to make my inability work.

Finally, I offered the cake to my friends and sent the roses. One of florists who delivered is called "The Green Meadow," the name of the residence where I lived for twenty years with my family. It was therefore a debt that I was settling with them.

THANK YOU,
LISEBY

→ LETTER 72 ←
....

From Veronica (forty-one years old)

During my analysis I came to the point at which I saw that my professional failure corresponded to my father's path. My ingrained Oedipus complex contributed to my staying committed throughout my life to this pattern, therefore allowing that *he would* stay the best. I am a violinist, following my father's wishes, but as a woman I didn't have a right to be a *great violinist,* a role reserved in his (and my) psyche for a man. I also saw that my father wanted me to be like my mother (a penitent), something that I also followed faithfully.

Finally, my attachment to these patterns, my fidelity to my parents and to the world where I was born, Pamplona, made me think about a psychomagic act to be able to free myself and grow.

For this act I had to fully satisfy my father's need to be the best. My father died years ago, so I made enlargements of three photographs and I placed them in a triptych on a kind of altar. With a child's violin I would play every day in front of him, continually making mistakes, saying that I am incapable, that only he could have played this instrument wonderfully. I would dress as a nun to be like my mother and would carry a huge globe covered only with photographs of Pamplona tied to my foot like the ball of a prisoner. I would do this for ten days and then I'd burn the photos. I'd drink some of the ashes in wine, I'd bury the rest with the violin, the habit, and the globe, and I would plant an apple tree over it. On that spot, with my current violin, the big one, I would play, elegantly dressed as woman artist.

Carrying out this act represented a sort of return to the moment when I decided to be faithful to my father, but I also noticed that in the present it suited me to stay in this pattern (of a girl). To begin with, I felt completely safe inside my nun's habit. I even found myself beautiful: "Dad, do you like me, am I pretty?" What comfort not to think about what you are going to wear, not to put on makeup, not to take care of the mundane world. Little by little the costume began to weigh on me, until one day I noticed that when I was with others I remained totally isolated, I didn't hear anything with that cap, and if I wanted to intervene they had to repeat things to me. . . .

I kept seeing nuns on the street. I ended up feeling gray, dull, with an immense rage at not being able to live. The ball that I carried by my foot turned all my movements into an ordeal. It even hurt my ankle. At first I kept looking at it like a fool. I almost always ended up in my mother's neighborhood. It was a pain. I was filled with sadness for having chosen to live that way, so limited and small, for having rejected my feminine condition, for being so afraid of losing those protections, to live. She was my mother. The sadness turned into rage.

On the other hand, each day I dedicated an hour to play for my father. The amount of feelings that came up was impressive. Sometimes I wouldn't stop crying while playing all the pain that I could. At first I remembered the melodies that I studied as a child and listened to my father making corrections, but I would perceive him as kind and affectionate. I looked at him fixedly in the eyes; it seemed that the photo looked back at me, and there was a lot of complicity (he admired me for doing what he could not do). I cried and said that it was very difficult for me to manage. When I started to play more complicated things I noticed that I wanted to continue getting that same attention, that he was more and more demanding (I started to be clumsy). So when I said: "Daddy, you would play it very well yourself, but I don't have your talents; besides, I am no more than a poor woman, not a strong man like you," I was totally convinced that it was so. At the same time I felt a lot of contempt for my abilities, a lot of resistance to growing and doing well, to stop sustaining my father's gaze even if it was to be criticized. I also had physical pain (hand and back) that have been constant throughout my life as a violinist. The last days my hand got used to the little violin and could play it in tune, but I kept making mistakes, stopping, praising my father . . . so that he would be happy. But I already knew that it was an act of will to change things. I knew I could now, accepting growing and embracing my capabilities, put aside the opinion and the judgment of my father (and others). I burned the photos and drank some of the ashes. I bought nice clothes. I still had to overcome an unfounded fear of burying everything in the field, of getting arrested by the police . . . unable to dig without being discovered. I finally did it and it was very easy. I got rid of the little instrument, of my father, of the nun and Pamplona. I felt a lot of emotion and a lot of responsibility for the future.

Interestingly, four days before finishing my act, I received a call from the opera house to play in the orchestra in the opera *Faust*. This was followed by *Valkyries* and other concerts, which meant opening a professional horizon closed until then and the daily possibility of overcoming my fears and complexes, vibrating with the music. MAGICAL.

A few days after the funeral I returned to the place to see if the apple tree was growing. I was surprised by the change in nature, I did not recognize anything. I didn't find the apple tree, but in its place I found the arms of a broken doll. I took it as a sign. I went back to the car to leave; in the middle of the road right in front of my feet I tripped over two wooden clogs, practically new, the size of a nine-or-ten-year-old girl's foot, perfectly placed side by side. I thought it was a sign that completed that of the broken doll and I took them.

I think that with this act I managed to break what made me "the doll" of my father and that from now on, the girl I still am has to start walking alone and become an adult woman.

THANK YOU,

VERONICA

⇥ LETTER 73 ⇤

From Jean-Stéphane

Dear pascALEjandro,

I was finally able to discover your film *Psychomagic, A Healing Art* that I was waiting so much for. I must admit that it totally upset me on several levels. Intrigued, I watched this work of Alejandro that I didn't know well. I am familiar with the art therapy that I practiced with child sol-diers in Liberia, during the film *Johnny Mad Dog*. I immediately found fascinating the notion that it was easier for the unconscious to understand the dreamlike rather than rational language. And I followed with pas-sion the different cases that you explore, all of which are amazing. This is exceptional. I was enlightened by this brilliant idea of a symbolic staging of the body to find the keys to the trauma that needs healing. In the end I don't know why but I wondered what my psychomagic act would be. And I came to the conclusion that for some unknown reason I had to put on clown makeup, like I did when I was at the circus school of Annie Fratellini and Pierre Étaix. I was at that time in full possession of my body through acrobatics, tightrope-walking, juggling, and dancing, as well as dressing up as a black and white Auguste clown.* Then a trauma marked my childhood. I was raped at that time, to which I responded with brutal and physical violence toward my attacker, almost killing him. After that I stopped the circus and turned to the movie theater. And I gradually went onto the other side of the curtain protecting myself behind my camera.

During this confinement, finding myself alone, I managed to com-plete a fictional screenplay that I carried in me for a long time about this trauma and my life since. It's called *Addicted to Violence* and it is the story of a photographer who travels to try to understand the vio-lence of the world by encountering people who suffer from it and are in its sphere, also filling a certain addiction that he cultivates for danger and extreme situations.

To understand your own violence through the violence of others. During this writing I discovered the work of Dr. Salmona on sexual violence and how in the face of extreme stress the brain breaks, mak-ing a traumatic memory that resuscitates only in violent situations, cre-ating a kind of addiction. I completely found myself in this scientific explanation of this particular trauma. Not only because of having been

---

*Auguste is a type of clown that entertains audiences with exaggerated expressions, slapstick com-edy, and pranks of all sorts.

raped but also in having realized that I was capable of killing, and how it caused this addiction that until recently I struggled to explain to myself. And that has nourished my writing as much as my own therapy. Awareness of this trauma was good for me and, somehow, released me. And I was finally able to complete this script.

If I'm telling you all this it's to return to your movie. The day after viewing it I decided to take action and put my makeup back on as a clown, like I had always felt the need, but never had the courage, to do. That same night, I believe, something clicked, as if suddenly finding myself as a clown, as I was before my trauma, allowed me to resume awareness of my own body. To realize that in response to rape I had decided to reject it, to ignore it. That there was not only my brain that split, and the psyche which had been affected, but also this body that I was so in harmony with in the circus that betrayed me. It was not only wounded, but was capable of killing. It had to disappear, so it would never again inspire the desire that would generate violence and reactivate this traumatic memory that I preferred to keep buried. Finally this attempted psychomagical act revealed real logic to something that unconsciously has been bothering me for so many years. I thought I had resolved trauma with psychological understanding without realizing that one piece of the puzzle was missing: my body. And I believe it's going help me to finally make peace with myself, my demons, and above all to regain possession of my own body, which I started more than a year ago with meditation. I know there is still work, but I see the way and it brings me a real serenity. I could never thank you enough. Thanks to you. Thanks to your film.

I LOVE YOU AND SEND KISSES.

JEAN-STÉPHANE

Dear Jean-Stéphane,
We are very happy that you liked the film and that psychomagic could resonate within you, and help you in a certain way to advance in your personal journey. Your act is right and very moving.

Alejandro suggests extending it into a more precise act. He invites you to put on the makeup (as you did) and dress up as a clown and live like that for three full days, including in the street. These three days symbolize the death of Christ and his resurrection three days later. Then he invites you to choose a child, find out what he would like, and offer it to him. In order to avoid problems and the risk of misunderstanding, you can choose one of your friend's children and explain to them that it is an act of healing. If you decide to do it, we would be happy for you to write to us what happened and what it provoked in you.

For my part, I also learned something about myself reading what you wrote. I too was a victim of sexual abuse when I was a child. I was very young and in my case this did not go as far as rape, but it went far enough to create a trauma that I concealed for a long time. But what was characteristic is that I had a form of rejection of any physical activity: I did not like sports, I didn't like to dance, I hid in my clothes, obscuring every sexual attribute. I thought that it was part of my personality but thanks to you I just realized that it came from there.

WE EMBRACE YOU VERY MUCH,

PASCALEJANDRO

Dear pascALEjandro,

Your email means a lot to me and I thank you wholeheartedly. I like Alejandro's idea of living three days as a clown and I will of course take his advice and do it . . . I have to find myself a costume! And about the child, I guess I have to give him the gift in person. My question is to know if it can be done with a child in France, remotely, via Skype for example, or is it preferable to have a child here in New York?

And I'm glad to hear that my "revelation" thanks to your film may also give an explanation to your own experience, Pascale. It's true that like you I have always felt this inability to dance, the rejection of sports at school, etc. . . . amazing . . . as if by realizing all this thanks to psychomagic, suddenly indeed everything made some sense. And what also surprised me is that I have unconsciously put all these elements in my screenplay, *Addicted to Violence*, including the fact that the character says he doesn't like to dance but is forced to under threat, which happened to me in Colombia, or even a freak-out during a strip poker session, etc. . . . And the film also opens on the character's voiceover explaining that violence will remain embedded in your body forever unless you lose your memory. This film is the journey to get to the bottom of it, and ends with the character saving an Afghan child, taking him out of the abuse that he undergoes from adults through his body, for them a sexual object. I can see here an analogy to that gift that Alejandro suggests to give to a child.

Dear Jean-Stéphane,
To answer your question regarding the gift to the child: if you do it remotely that would correspond to continuing to put your inner child at a distance, so it would be better if there is no distance. A child in New York would therefore be preferable because that's where you are.

Dear pascALEjandro,
Once again thank you very much for encouraging me to carry out this act and opening this door for me. Since this first step, this first psychomagic act, I've been overwhelmed by several signs and "revelations," as if suddenly everything has meaning, both on a personal and professional level. I feel that the act totally unlocked something buried within me for a long time, and look forward to spending these three days as a clown to fully and artistically close this chapter. I think I will do this next weekend to be able to be quiet and not too disturbed. I'm preparing for it. This morning I cried and apologized to myself without even being able to control the drive. This voice came out of my depths like a word that was liberated, that was finally being heard. It moved me. In this spirit I offered my friend's daughter a gift. They live a little outside New York in the forest so I thought it was a propitious place to offer her this gift and complete the act. She just sent me a photo of a smiling and

happy little girl doll that she would like. And I realize how important the end of this act is. Alejandro, you really are a genius, and you allowed me to reveal yet another thing to myself. Since the death of my mother, shortly after my rape, I never managed to give or to receive gifts. I have always avoided and rejected this idea, under the pretext that my mother left us during Christmas, when I was thirteen. She had prepared all our gifts, for my brothers and sisters and for me . . . but death took her before she had the time to give them to us in person. So after her death, we gave ourselves our gifts. Without her. And since then I have never wanted to receive a gift or offer one to anyone. . . . I was still embarrassed by this act. To give this doll to that little girl I saw being born will for sure be an important moment. And the only thing I want today is to share with others, to offer to others what you gave me, which is priceless. Can't wait to share all this with you verbally.

BIG KISS,

JEAN-STÉPHANE

Dear pascALEjandro,
I hope you're doing well.

I did my psychomagical act last weekend, a week ago. It was such an upheaval I needed these few days before I could write to you, the time to understand, integrate, think about what this act could have awakened in me. The first day was much about childhood, the circus school, learning to juggle again, getting back on the unicycle, mourning my mother, from laughter to tears. Then the second day was about trauma, sexuality, washing the naked body, purifying it, pouring hot wax on it, putting blood on it, making it up in white, making it breathe. And the third day, going outside. Confronting the clown on the outside, in the world, to receive the smiles and kindness of others. Then upon my return, allowing myself to paint, too. And finally last Monday I took the train to go to the Hudson Valley to offer my gift, this smiling doll for Eagle, my friend Rachel's daughter. Every step was exhilarating, guided by this inner child with whom I finally felt reconnected, found after so many years; I let myself be guided freely. I broke down barriers. The routine. Habits. And went to the most inner depth of my being. It was, I must say, intense, each day going according to its imagination, allowing myself to be carried by what he seemed to want me to say. And hanging out with him was an anticipated moment as well, but it happened to be a release. And then the first evening we saw *The Holy Mountain* again and the last evening *The Dance of Reality*. The only films possible to see in this state were yours, Alejandro. Which resonated all the more during the act. Glad to not have been disturbed by the outside world during these three days, with no telephone and emails, to stay alone with this inner child. In this cocoon. This reconstructed child's room. My house transformed into a play area. He also explained to me many of the questions I had been asking myself for years and years, shed light on gray areas, occasional misunderstandings, giving suddenly a clear meaning to my life until then, as if all that my unconscious had set up suddenly made sense, became clearer. Whether it's regarding my daily life, settling here in New York, every object that I was able to bring into my house to create my universe, or my previous films, my ongoing scenarios that also began to make real sense in light of what this act may have caused. All that was beautiful, magical, sometimes disturbing because it arrives like a euphoric flood. Today I want these revelations to keep moving me forward, this child to grow within me, to keep infusing me with his strength and creativity. When I wanted to offer the girl the doll that she wished for, something unexpected also happened. She curled up into fetal position, at first refusing to open the package. Then, her mother came and offered to open it for her. Eagle is struggling with autism, she's seven years old, and I think at her birth her mother also abandoned her inner child, her life as an artist, to become a mother. She feels that since then she has no longer been herself, which sometimes makes a relationship with her daughter difficult. I had the feeling that this doll, strangely resembling Eagle's mother, was also an unconscious way for the child to make her aware of *her* inner child and finally find her necessary peace. Then I came home and I also analyzed and understood many things about my relationship with my parents. Made peace as well with the early death of my mother. And realized that facing the relationship with my father which I considered appeased since then, my inner child felt a real anger at him for having rebuilt his life so quickly, for letting me become an adult perhaps too early. Because it is since then that I had shut this child inside me. But I am so happy with today's reconciliation. That's what I could feel, although all this has provoked obviously much more, but it would take too long to report on that, because once again it sheds light on each of my actions until now.

BIG KISS,
JEAN-STÉPHANE

↯ LETTER 74 ↲

From Philip

I had just returned from my honeymoon and I went with my wife to have dinner with Alejandro and Pascale in Ireland. While we were speaking at the start of the meal Alejandro observed that my lips were tight and mentioned it to me. He said it was OK to speak with him, that he was there for me. He then observed that my left eye was stronger than my right eye. The left eye was the feminine eye and the right eye was the masculine eye. He said that I was seeing the world through my mother's eyes and that my lips were tight around him because I wasn't comfortable speaking to men. Although Alejandro wouldn't have been aware of this, my parents had separated when I was three years old and I had lived with my mother, who had held much resentment for my father up until her death. I had been strongly influenced by my mother and other feminine figures such as aunties and my grandmother who helped raise me. I have always felt uncomfortable with men and more comfortable in the company of women. I thought what he had told me was interesting. The conversation continued and moved on to the art exhibition he was currently showing in. Some of his artworks on display were tarot cards. While we spoke about the tarot he offered to read my wife's cards. During the reading he said that one of the cards represented me, my father, and my brother. My brother and my father were talking to each other and not to me because there was a problem between us. I confirmed this was correct: I had gotten married a month previously and long story short there was a miscommunication and my father didn't get to recite a poem at the wedding, which he had planned to do without telling anyone. They thought that I had blocked him on purpose from doing his speech, which wasn't my intention. At this point Alejandro suggested that I wear an eye patch over my left eye for five days and only see through my right eye, and that this psychomagic act would resolve the problem. From speaking with Alejandro, it felt like he was genuine and that I should follow his advice.

The next day I bought a black eye patch and wore it for five days. The first day wearing it I spent at home, however that weekend I had a trip planned to London with my wife to visit an artist. Of course that meant going through the airport and London city with a black eye patch for three days. Although I looked like a bit of a James Bond villain people were surprisingly receptive to me with the eye patch, particularly in London. I remember being in a small boutique café in Kensington. I had stopped there for a coffee. I was the only person in the café and the waitress came over to talk to me and gave me a piece of cake as a gift. I had never been offered free cake from a waitress before; she was being really friendly and talkative with me. I noticed that around London wherever I went people were very friendly. When I arrived at the Groucho Club, which is a private members club, they didn't ask me who I was with and just let me walk in. When I visited that artist's studio with my wife, everyone thought I was some mysterious character of great interest. After a few days of wearing the patch, I felt super focused. My mind was clearer and my inner dialogue changed. Normally it would have been quite judgmental and I would have had critical thoughts about other people and myself running through my mind. That basically stopped for those days. Although I had spoken to my brother before wearing the eye patch,

I hadn't spoken to my father since the wedding. My brother had just been relaying secondhand information to me of his and my father's anger and disappointment over me blocking his speech at the wedding. However, when I got home, with some encouragement from my wife, I decided to send him a friendly text message to see how he was doing. He texted me back and then that was it, the drama was over. The wedding has never come up again as an issue. Since then my relationship with my father has improved a huge amount. All this happened around three years ago, and today as I write this message, I have just returned from visiting my father and am happy to report that we had an enjoyable afternoon together. Over the past years I've healed a lot of negative views and opinions of my father and have come to accept him as he is, not for what I want him to be. This has improved our relationship and helped me reconcile parts of myself that up until that point I had disowned, particularly my masculine side. I now feel more whole and complete, balanced and centered. I can trust men now and even most importantly I finally feel that I can trust myself. I needed to take a leap of faith and take an action that would help me fix my family problems and reconcile my relationship with my father and men. This psychomagic act catalyzed a change in me for the good and for that I am immensely grateful. Thank you Alejandro, may God bless you with health, happiness, and good fortune

⇸ LETTER 75 ⇷

From Yolande

Hello Pascale,

After our conversation when I was sharing my foot problem, precisely the front of the right foot, you shared with me and explained with benevolence the way your spouse Alejandro directed me to use psychomagic. So I took his advice to best get rid of this pain.

It was about taking soil, holy water (whether or not you are a believer), liquid honey, and mixing these ingredients, then keeping my foot in there for ninety minutes. And after these ninety minutes, while taking out my foot, I immediately felt almost total disappearance of my pain.

And since then, I walk much better even if I have to remain vigilant and rest my foot as much as possible. This experience is just indescribable, coming from me who is rather Cartesian.

SINCERELY,

YOLANDE

→ LETTER 76 ←

From Lusi

Dear Alejandro,

thank you and Pascale for your interest and endless inspiration. You both definitely influenced me and my life in a very positive way! Unfortunately, I never had an opportunity to do a "proper" psychomagical act, although I would love to. We spoke only for a few minutes on the street in front of your hotel on October 29, 2016, in Granada, where I had traveled all the way from Prague to meet you and get a psychomagical act. I told you that I was afraid to speak in public (because I am an anthropologist and I have to do speeches, lectures, and presentations). You answered: "You need to get naked in front of the public." There was no time to talk more. I took this advice both literally and metaphorically. When it came to literal fulfillment of the act, it was a challenge, because I always had a big problem with my body. I was shy to get naked even in front of my partners. The first step was getting naked the very same evening in Granada in front of my friends. Step by step, I started to get naked more, in front of other friends, my parents, public places, where it wasn't too controversial, etc. . . . It went hand in hand with consciously working on liking my body and feeling less shy. I also thought about the metaphorical meaning of exposing myself and I understood it as being authentic, real, without pretending, hiding, lying, holding secrets. . . . In this context I realized that there are three topics in my life I don't like to talk about and about which I am not authentic. Although it may seem very marginal and absurd: being an only child. I have no rational explanation why, but every time someone asked me, "Do you have any brothers or sisters?" I was ashamed to say, "No." When I was younger I would even lie, saying I did. Second, my parents' disabilities. They both have polio and met during medical treatment. My mum is in a wheelchair and my dad walks with a limp. It always made me feel very uncomfortable when people asked me, "What's wrong with your parents?" Lastly, my sexuality. I feel totally bisexual and I was always afraid to tell my gay friends that I also like men, and my straight friends that I also like women. I felt like I belonged nowhere and I was pretending to be gay or straight depending on the social group I was hanging around with. After Granada I started to talk more about these three things, when it became relevant. First, it was extremely uncomfortable for me, but now I have almost no problem with it. Both the literal and metaphorical "exposure" started to do wonders. I have absolutely no issue now with speaking in public, although I was paralyzed before. I feel almost excited and I love the feeling afterward. It's like I have faced a big challenge. Thank you for the inspiration.

WITH LOVE,

LUSI

→ LETTER 77 ←

From Rachel

Two psychomagic poetic acts—do you believe in the power of magic to heal, to transform, to manifest miracles in these times? I have to say I have witnessed this with my own eyes and life. Through the psychomagic poetic acts kindly given to me by Alejandro and Pascale Jodorowsky, my life has been transformed. Here is my story. . . .

Up until I met with Alejandro and Pascale, my life was full with an arts career, but I was missing the emotional part—I had a deep yearning for a child. I had read and learned about Alejandro Jodorowsky and Pascale. I learned they are pioneers of art, spirituality, and life, creating such great work that is original and inspiring for the world. When I went to see them in Paris I was received with kindness and good humor, such fun and smiles from both of them, a great beautiful energy of life and love around them. I have met many artists, shamans, priests, doctors, academics, poets, and such, but only Alejandro and Pascale's way, that of the intention, the power to transform for good, was the path that I found for myself. It was also a portal to true wonder and an understanding of the past and present. The experiences they gave me were a blast of all legacies, family trees, and all potential combined in one tarot reading. This is the only way I can explain this miracle. I still am in awe to this very day. I told them that I wanted a child but felt it was not possible. I was in my forties, I had a husband and we had tried for a child, but nothing seemed to work. I was giving up on this dream. It was a hope but I was also aware it was quite impossible due to my age. Most doctors told me it had a very low success rate and not to be disappointed. During the reading, which consisted of only three tarot cards, Alejandro suggested, "Why not have a baby, everything is possible, you could have a baby, who is saying no? It is up to you. But first we must look at what is happening in your life." This encouraged me greatly, and then he gave the first of many psychomagic acts and a journey that I'm on in my life, as I have opened my eyes to seeing the world in a different way.

I was told to write during a full moon the names of past lovers' initials with my menstrual blood on a small piece of paper. I was to tie the paper to a red balloon and release it into the deep, dark night sky. I did not question this as I duly carried out this act. The full moon in the depth of winter on an Irish night, I walked out alone in the darkness, into a muddy country field and carried out the instructions. At first it felt strange but I knew I had to follow through on this ritual. In the inky blue of the cold night the red balloon with the string carrying the paper was set free, until it was caught by branches of a tree. I released the balloon again, and it blew into the depths of the wintry night, smaller and smaller it seemed to blow away until I could no longer see it. Unfortunately, days and months went by and this did not work. Yet, as luck would have it, I went to see Alejandro and Pascale again, to gain an understanding, or accept this was not meant to be. Our paths crossed as I was in Paris for work and once more they kindly received me. It is also important to mention that as a woman I wanted to be both a director and a mother, but thought that was impossible too. How can you have both in life? And how could this happen to me or what was my fate? I told them the balloon act did not work. They listened intently and then I had a second tarot reading, which had a great psychological depth. It concerned my own family history. Alejandro explained that my mother (as my parents were divorced when I was young) had overcompensated and become a male and female figure to me. Therefore I required balance of the male and female in my life. He then showed me a small intricate figurine from his mantelpiece, a figurine of a beautiful Madonna with a rounded belly. And then a figurine of a masculine cowboy with a gun, who looked like a spaghetti western hero. It reminded me of a character from one from his films. He said I would have to combine the two elements, the mother and the male boss, to become one and be both in the world.

Alejandro then gave me a second psychomagic act and this one needed more courage—but I was not to tell my husband or anyone. It was to be kept a secret until the baby was born. I was to go to a sex shop in Paris and buy a fake penis, but it had to look real. I was to put it in a pink bag and then inside my handbag (so no one could see) and carry it with me to work and during my daily routine. It was strange and scary going into the sex shop in Paris and I felt I needed courage, so I pulled myself together, heart beating faster and faster. I found one and walked in. I was going into this shop as a rite of passage and it was surreal. I had to ask the shop assistant to show me which was the most realistic. I was shy and a bit embarrassed. I bought the object and placed it inside a pink bag and then in my handbag. I told no one! The bag went everywhere with me, it was at work, traveling and always hidden away, and very soon I forgot what was in the pink bag inside my bag. Months later, I could not believe it: I was pregnant and had a baby boy, and he is now growing into a happy toddler! It truly was a magical miracle—we are so grateful and happy that this has happened. I believe in magic and the psychomagic act from Alejandro and Pascale. Our lives have transformed in such a wondrous way and I am also understanding my past and looking forward to my future.

⇢ LETTER 78 ⇠

From Angela

October 2, 2019

Dear Alejandro,

Time has passed: we met at the Téméraire Café in 2007 and that was when you gave me a psychomagical act. At the time, I felt great emptiness and a feeling of not being embodied.

I didn't put it that way but you offered me a chance to work with one of your students. Which I did. And I came back to the Téméraire Café so that you could give me this act, which I also accomplished.

It involved going my grandmother's grave with a picture of the Virgin Mary and a two-kilogram stone. I had to take some milk in my mouth and spit it on the picture of the Virgin Mary by exclaiming: "Ectoplasm get out of me!" Then I had to plant a comb in the ground on the side of the grave saying that my grandmother's spirit could no longer reach me and that I was no longer called Marie-Pierre. You told me to change my first name, which I did. From then on, I told everyone that they should no longer call me Marie-Pierre but Angela. It happened without any difficulty. I lived like this for eleven years, asking to be called by this first name, which was not on my ID. During these eleven years, I developed many projects, both artistic and professional. I began to incarnate myself, to exist by myself. I felt like "me."

Recently (very recently, in January 2019), I decided to go further and to formalize this first name that has become mine, and inscribe it on my birth certificate and my identity papers.

Since that moment I have felt a unity and real alignment, allowing me to fully embody what I have to do here. What I haven't told you yet is that before you told me to change my first name, I went to speak with my mother, asking her why she had named me Marie-Pierre. She answered that when I was born she felt guilty about calling me that and thought that if I was not happy, I would change my name.

Very unhappy, I then asked her to give me the name that she had never given me. A few months later, we had another discussion on this subject and I told her how I felt about the first name, "Angela"; she replied that it was the name she had thought of for me.

I did the psychomagical act a few months later.

My dear Alejandro, thank you for the deep sympathy with which you accompanied me on the path of my being. Currently, I continue on my way. I feel like I've been resurrected or been born for a second time. I feel the alignment of my identity in relation to my being and the world. I am free of the impression of not existing, of having no place or the right to go out in the world.

THANK YOU INFINITELY,

ANGELA

⤳ LETTER 79 ⟵
. . . .
From Valerie

July 24, 2000

Hello Alejandro,

In September 1999, during a workshop on the Family Tree that you led at Nîmes, I told you that I always felt excluded and that I wanted to end that feeling. You then asked me what the relationship between my parents and what my relationship with my father were like. I answered that my parents hated each other and that my father was my god but at the same time very cold and very distant, an inaccessible god. You made me notice that I was still hesitating between one and the other, which is the case in many decisions in my life.

You prescribed the following act for me: Fly in a hot air balloon and throw three hundred copies of my photo overboard. Then put the ashes of a photo of my father in a glass of wine covered with a condom and drink it up. Throughout the act, I had to carry on me the XXth card of the tarot.

I was very happy when you gave me this act but gradually, as the days passed, I started to worry. I ordered my hot air balloon ticket in December 1999 and we had to wait until July 2000 to be able to fly because of the weather. But throughout this wait the angst continued. Finally, the weather conditions being ideal on July 21, I was able to do the act. I climbed into the hot air balloon, anxious. For the entire afternoon, I had a very bad neck and shoulders, especially on the right side.

We were seven passengers, plus the pilot.

When we started to rise in the air I felt very dizzy and I wondered if I would hold out. But the hardest part was yet to come: getting out the three hundred copies of my picture and throwing them one by one overboard in front of the passengers and the pilot. I got the package out of my bag and held it for a moment in my hands. I asked my neighbor what time we had left and what time it was now. It had been twenty-five minutes since we started flying. So I had about thirty-five minutes left to do the deed. I began. One of the passengers watched me, amused. I told him that I had made a bet that I had to keep. I kept throwing pictures one by one. Eventually, all the other passengers and the pilot noticed. Then the comments started. Some funny, like: "Are you appealing to your boyfriend?" Others less funny (especially those of the pilot): "Don't throw away too many, I'm going to get yelled at." In short, I still had at least eighty when I heard the pilot say we were going to land soon. Depending on the altitude and speed of the hot air balloon, some photos were flying over the balloon, which made the passengers laugh. Then the balloon picked up speed and the pictures were below us. It was ten minutes before landing. So I took my courage with both hands and I said to the pilot: "I have to go until the end of my bet—it doesn't matter if I throw them over a forest," and I accelerated the movement. I threw them one by one quickly. I had time to finish and as I prepared to pour the ashes of my father's photo in the glass of wine that I had in my bag, the pilot told us to get into landing position. Two minutes later we were landing. It was

244 Psychomagical Letters

very quick and almost harsh. When we were able to get out I rushed away and quickly put the ashes of the photo of my father in the glass of wine, and drank it all in one go (me who doesn't drink). I thought it would make me drunk, but in fact it made me feel good. Then the pilot brought out champagne. I drank a glass of it, without getting drunk either.

Two nights later I had an interesting dream: I dreamed that my father and I were entwined like lovers and we kissed like lovers. In my dream we were the same size (in reality, he is significantly taller than me). The following week I was extremely tired, moved. But something sweet and peaceful settled. There you go. I thank you for giving me this deed. I take advantage also to thank you for having the courage to work on yourself and for your precious help for a number of years.

BEST REGARDS,
VALERIE

→ LETTER 80 ←
....
From Fabiola

Dear Jodorowsky:

Last week, on Wednesday the 26th of March, I was in the Téméraire, where you read the tarot, and you recommended me two rituals: one for my relationship with my father and one for my relationship with my mother. I dressed like my father that Saturday, just a week ago today, and I covered my face with his photograph. I prepared the bag with fake blood and tied it to my stomach. As my father, I stuck the knife in the stomach bag. Several thoughts came up, but one with special force. You told me that sticking a knife in the belly is an action that has to do with the mother. I don't know much about my father's relationship with his mother, but when he was six years old he went to live with his sister, who was already married, had no children, and I think was a widow. It must have been painful, having been separated from his mother, away from home. It seemed that the belly, wounded entrails, and bleeding out reproduced this pain. And perhaps also felt relief when they emptied themselves of that pain and life.

I made a package with everything. I poured honey. The next day I made the trip to the cemetery, which is near Santiago. I had not bought flowers. In Paris I had seen flowering cherry branches and they seemed to me a beautiful symbol. Just before reaching the cemetery I found a flowering apple tree by the side of the road. I stopped to help myself. I thought it was a good idea to introduce it all in an abandoned pot I found, cover it with honey and soil, and plant the flowering twigs of the apple tree. At the same time I freed my cat. The beauty had been with me for three years, but in the last three months she was painfully restless. I believe that was because I kept her from the opportunity of meeting males and she had given birth twice. I refused to spay her but made her more invisible. She symbolizes my wild side and since I have already lived in the countryside, I decided that it was time to set her free. I opened the box. It smelled really bad. I said goodbye to my father and my cat. She and I, we've been around, each into liberation, a way of life.

That was on Sunday. I thought Wednesday or Thursday would be a good day to perform the act with my mother, but the truth is that at the start of Wednesday I did not feel very much like doing it. I had gotten up late, and I put a movie on, which happens very rarely. A friend lent it to me months ago. At the end of the film I wanted to kill myself. I felt a great frustration in my life. I have not realized all my wishes—what great suffering. I cried. It wasn't the first time I felt like this. I felt it even before my mother committed suicide. It was the moment of the ritual. I looked for her clothes that I kept. I chose a skirt that she wore for the last time shortly before committing suicide, and a black polo that I have used on many occasions, since it's my size. I prepared the place of the fall on the other side of the window. In the city where I live, there is a window that overlooks a porch. Once everything was ready, I opened the window and sat down, as she might have done. Some thoughts came to me that I imagine she could have had. I didn't jump right away. It was when I closed my eyes that I felt the emptiness that was opening before me and inviting me to throw myself into it. And so I did. I stayed a while lying down. I cried a little. A little lost. After a while I felt that I split, that my mother stayed on the ground and I got up. I got undressed and poured the honey. The next day I planned to go to the cemetery, an hour away from where I live.

After taking off both my mother's and my father's clothes, I took a shower. The one after the act for/with my father was longer as I needed more time in the water. The shower after the act for my mother was shorter and more serene. The next afternoon I bought some white daisies, which are my favorite flowers and bring me joy. I added the three branches from the flowering apple tree for my mother. I took the car and I arrived at the cemetery where she is buried. There I found a big pot for flowers. I removed the earth from it, I buried my clothes, I planted the daisies on top, a cyclamen, and the three apple tree branches in blossom (one for each of my brothers and me). I added the honey, fresh soil, and chocolate that I bought. My mother had a sweet tooth and was Mexican. (Now I realize this was the 3rd of April and it's on that day in 1971 that my parents got married.)

I feel like I left the part of my mother that had to go, that I have my space and more energy for my life and my self-realization.

The pot was really pretty.

Thanks for the tips.

I wish you the best and hope to get a chance to meet you again.

I LOVE YOU,

FABIOLA

⤙ LETTER 81 ⤚

From Martin

When I arrived in France I had a lenticular wart on the sole of my left foot, which kept growing. I asked the dermatologist, who said that it would take months to fully heal. When I told you about it, you interpreted that wart as the product of guilt I had for leaving my mother in Chile. To heal me, you suggested to take a picture of my mother, photocopy it ten times, and make compresses with them and green clay, which I would put on the wart every morning—and so I had to walk stepping on the photo of her every day. After the first eight days without seeing fundamental change, on the ninth day the wart had completely disappeared. During an appointment a few days later the dermatologist who treated me was surprised, and he thought it wasn't me, but my twin brother! Since that day I haven't had warts on my foot.

→ LETTER 82 ←

From Anne-Claire

Three years ago I told Alejandro Jodorowsky of a powerful sensation of an internal blockage preventing me from fully becoming a woman and an author. I also explained many painful episodes that marked my life for these last eight years: a succession of four miscarriages, the birth of my son in 2006, reoccurring attacks of hypomania once a year. The first one triggered at the age of thirty-six (late for this kind of symptom) followed an encounter with highly emotional effects.

In addition, in the fall of 2018, during a family dinner in our house in the countryside, a presence came up from a well in the cellar. This house was built by my great-great-uncle and my great-great-aunt, who were never able to have children. The painted portrait of the latter, very loved by those who knew her, figured prominently in the living room and is revered by the women in my family like a religious icon. Sharing the anecdote of the well, seemingly without importance, with Pascale and Alejandro first aroused a strong reaction in Pascale, who perceived an obvious link between this grandmother and me, whose name I share.

Alejandro validated this interpretation and deepened it, then prescribed me the following.

1. Mix some of my blood with holy water, and throw it all in the well under my great-great-aunt's house.
2. Carry a bag of soil as heavy as possible to her grave, deposit it there, and leave, all in the presence of my son. To thank this ancestor aloud, and express to her that I was giving back what was hers. Then clean her grave.

3. Have a business card printed with a name other than mine.
4. To confront my father, converse with him dressed as a man.

These acts involved the gathering of elements step by step, which was a small initiatory path in itself.

It was not easy to find holy water; all the churches where I went had only dried up fonts. I ended up taking some from a cathedral with the feeling of committing theft. Scenes of my act have burlesque vibes: while trying to be discreet and estimate the inevitably astronomical number of germs in these few drops of water, I tripped on a protruding slab when leaving the building (but the vial, well closed, remained intact)!

After vain attempts to play Sleeping Beauty pricking herself with the spinning wheel I had the idea of using my period blood—what seemed to me symbolically appropriate, since it's about the release of feminine energy.

Then I had to wait for an opportunity to go to the family home, which is far from where I live. I performed this act twice. The first time was at a funeral. There were many people around and I had to find an excuse to go to the cellar, where I threw the water into the well a bit too hastily for my taste (access to this well is all the more difficult since it is screened). The second time, during the next, more peaceful journey, I took a moment to make a little ritual by talking to my ancestress and thanking her once again. I had a great feeling of liberation and joy in the gesture and in the sound of the water reaching the well. I also found the act playful, and it seemed to have reconnected me with my child spirit.

The act at the cemetery took place without issues, thanks to my cousin who drove me from one mall to another in order to find a large enough bag of soil. Carrying this load to the cemetery was a bit laborious, and we had to take breaks on the way under the cautious gaze of my son, to whom I had of course explained the meaning of the act. When I left the bag in front of the grave, I also felt a sense of great release. This symbol of the burden that is returned to its owner seemed very powerful.

The cleaning of the family tomb following this gesture and the little speech that accompanied it had a very calming effect. I also realized that day that it was important to take care of our deceased, and that it could be done even more concretely than just by a thought or a prayer.

In this act it seemed to me that everyone found their rightful place, as if something could move on the side of the dead in the same moment in which healing happens on the side of the living. There was a little readjustment, rebalancing, harmony to restore. I cleaned the graves with care, taking my time. I wished for the absent members of my family to navigate their dimension with grace.

The act with my father prevented me from sleeping for several nights, because I dreaded his reaction. But curiously, it was not so complicated to perform. During one of my father's visits, I dressed as a man, with suit, tie, and the only pair of masculine shoes that I own. I also drew myself a discreet pencil mustache matching the color of my hair. When I opened the door to welcome him my father said nothing. It was only later, in the middle of our conversation, that he asked me: "Why this outfit?" I mentioned a bet with my friends, not knowing if it was an appropriate answer, but that's what came to me. And I felt relatively comfortable throughout our conversation. For now, I can't tell if the act carried out with my father bore its fruits, but last April, striking dreams made me understand that this unconscious work was on the move.

As for the business card, this act took me the longest to carry out: I was struggling to make up my mind about a first name. Then one fine day I stopped looking and opted for the first name that came to mind. I placed an order online after having carefully studied the design from the menu. It's to Pascale and Alejandro that I gave the first two. Following the advice of Alejandro, I give them to close friends, telling them that it's to free myself from the unconscious ties that my first name carries with it.

Overall, these acts were made in joy and have engendered a movement of my inner cogs that gives me the feeling of evolving, of freeing myself gradually from my shackles, and moving toward greater authenticity. I trust this process and I let it act today outside my awareness.

I still hear the voice of Alejandro giving his advice. I thank him infinitely for his absolute kindness.

ANNE-CLAIRE

Second letter from Anne-Claire:

Dear Alejandro,

In October 2021, we conversed and I told you that my hearing was seriously hampered by water stagnant in my ears for months. Moreover, for several days, tension in my lower belly would not leave.

You made me draw two cards from your tarot deck. Strength and The Lovers showed up. After making me describe these images, you pointed, with a brilliance that grabbed me, to the central family issue: my mother, in order to satisfy her father, who was very attached to his lineage and his name, wanted to have a son. But she ended up with two girls like he did. The person who gave birth to a boy in this family is me. You thus hypothesized that my mother interferes in my relationship with my son, acting unconsciously as if he were hers, and does not recognize me in my own role as a mother. You suggested I carry out the following act: present myself to my mother dressed in my son's typical clothes in order to embody her unmet desire and thus speak to her unconscious.

During this exchange with you the persistent tension in my lower belly dissolved, bringing me a certain relief. I put into practice the act that you prescribed me the very next day, as my parents had invited my family and me to lunch.

I borrowed the hoodie that my teenage son wears all the time, his jeans, his sneakers, and I tied up my hair. My husband and my son became accomplices of this psychomagic act, which I refrained from explaining, so as not to over-intellectualize the process. I had to make an effort not to anticipate my mother's reaction and on your advice, take confidence in the present of the act.

To our surprise, while welcoming us, my mother, although very observant, did not seem to spot my costume, so different from my style. During an aperitif, I sat opposite her: she saw me thus from head to toe. Not only did she not make any comment, but she was more cheerful and relaxed than usual. Also at the table, no word was uttered about my disguise.

During this joyous lunch, suddenly we touched on the subject of our ancestors. My mum shared with us information new to my ears, relating especially to my maternal great-grandmother. The romantic charge of her story led her to leave the table and come back with a bag of archival handwritten seventeenth-and-eighteenth-century manuscripts found in my grandfather's attic in Dordogne, which she had prepared to return to the administrative authorities. She had never before mentioned in my presence the existence of these old documents of fascinating calligraphy. Everyone seized these birth certificates and other scriptures to study the details before they returned to their source. An intense energy won the room.

When leaving my parents' home to get to an appointment, my mother joined me, and I decided to get changed in front of her. It was at that precise moment that she noticed, amused, that I wore the outfit of my son, pointing out that his favorite sweatshirt fit me well. I replied that it was his clothes, indeed, and that now I had to find mine. My mother made no further comment relating to my appearance that day and seemed to be lifted by a sparkling mood till the end of our talk. Would her unconscious capture something from this show?

I left this lunch in good spirits. It was a significant act, of which I still feel the benefits today. As if something was moving from the depths of me—and as a consequence in all of my family tree—toward a form of reconciliation, gradually setting me free from my invisible chains.

A recent dream of striking eloquence confirmed to me that I had crossed an interior stage. This act is its working primer. My hearing has been gradually improving since then, and the tension that bothered me at the time of our exchange did not come back.

For your attentive listening, your generosity, and your advice, thank you from the bottom of my heart, dear Alejandro.

ANNE-CLAIRE

✣ LETTER 83 ✣

From Alexandra

On September 3, 2020, the long-awaited, unexpected event happened. Walking down Rue Vieille-du-Temple, I bumped into the teacher Alejandro Jodorowsky, whom I admire so much, whose work I read, saw at conferences on YouTube, watched in movies, etc. Like a magnet I approached him and said I was excited to see him, since I admired him deeply. I told him that recently I had invented psychomagic acts myself.

With sweetness and familiarity he asked me to sit down. I went with Ruby (my adoptive daughter at heart) and my dog Chi. Ruby kept talking and Alejandro asked me if she was my daughter, and I told her that "she has become my daughter." Her mother died, and I was her father's partner. With total tranquility Alejandro asked me what was happening to me, if I wanted to speak, which became a quick summary of my current situation and where I came from . . . I am forty-five years old, at two months I lost my father in a car accident, my two-year-old brother and I became fatherless, and so we remained. My mother never remarried or had any loving and stable relationship (at least that we knew about).

At the age of twenty-seven, I came to Paris to marry the man I loved back then. The years passed and my desire to become a mother and start a family grew. But my ex-husband wanted to delay the process, pushing it off for thirteen years, and when we finally decided to have a child, my body rejected the possibility. Fibroids, perhaps, made it so two difficult attempts came to nothing. I did not want to insist anymore because I think there are processes in life that can't be forced. I thought of adoption because we had all the requirements to be able to adopt, and once again my ex-husband told me to wait, including even talking about this possibility. A year passed and it was impossible for him to take the time to talk on the subject, just for enjoyment, building, and discussion. Everything turned increasingly difficult and our relationship was that of two roommates without much more.

For years I had been aware that I was not satisfied as a woman, not only for not achieving maternity, but also sexually. And because I have always believed that in a couple you find a partner with whom to enjoy even the smallest details of daily life. So after a lot of reflection, insomnia, etc., I decided to separate.

I spent two and a half years trying to understand why it had come to this, heartbroken because I thought I didn't deserve a man with whom I would get along one hundred percent and start a family. I did therapies and all: spiritual searching, oracles, astral themes. I've known of Alejandro Jodorowsky for a long time and he was always a strong inspiration.

In June 2020 I met Thierry, eighteen years my senior, with his daughter of four years and ten months. The attraction was direct and undeniable, our relationship took an accelerated and firm path, and Ruby reacted positively. It was she who began to tell me that I was her new mom. Quickly but with no rush we began to live a relationship full of good things, until the family of her late mother began to tell Ruby that I could not be her mother. This created conflict between us occasionally, but especially within me, not feeling legitimate, jealous of the deceased because she managed to be a mother and I didn't, and above all feeling that with all my gynecological problems and Thierry's age, I would never get the chance to be a mother. But my greatest grief is not being unable have biological children, but that I don't feel legitimate in this relationship. I feel like less than Ruby's mom, almost like a spare woman.

Not to mention that my mother was not happy at first that I was with a man much older than me, and once she could digest it, her communication was limited to the incessant questions: Does he love you? Want you? Does he still love you? Does he fancy you? Do you put makeup on? What does he think? Do you seem intelligent to him? What does he say . . . ?

With this, I realized that my mother did not believe in me, did not believe in me as a woman, nor in my intellect, and I did not realize that, in fact, I doubted myself as much as she did.

This was all summed up to the teacher Alejandro the day I met him, and he asked me straight away: Do you know that all of your problems are because of your mother?

My answer was yes, because despite not yet having a complete image of the causes of why I was not able to be fulfilled as a woman, and still can't, now that I have everything, I sensed that it had something to do with my mother.

Without beating around the bush Alejandro told me to take a nude photo with my partner, the girl, and my dog. Then to send it to my mother with the following caption: "So that you know that I made it" . . .

Once I said goodbye and thanked him for this great gift, this key, this magic potion, this therapy, I walked toward my house and a whirlwind took over my body and mind. Before taking the photo the work started to manifest: I felt powerless, I was scared. I felt a kind of internal revolution, an excitement. But above all I did not feel able to take this photo, not out of modesty, but feeling that it was going to seem a brutal aggression toward my mother. And I was horrified at the idea of writing this phrase.

I talked about it with my partner who seemed most excited and did not understand why I was so terrified of the possible reaction of my mother. He saw it as natural and beautiful. There was no doubt that I was the only one who had a problem with it. I discussed it with my brother who unsurprisingly reacted like me. Although a year older, he still had not found a woman, given that he wanted to get married and build a family. Obviously we have the same problem. And my spiritual sister, a friend with whom I share many things and who coincidentally is also single and whose greatest wish is to find someone, shared my concerns. We thought alike: this would give my mother a heart attack. I couldn't even digest it, and that's where I began to understand that I had made a moral contract with my mother, not to be happy with a man since she had not been. How showing her the nude photo with this phrase capturing my victory was to show her defeat.

Weeks and weeks passed. I was able to understand many more behaviors and comments without being aware that they had marked me deeply and made me feel *not worthy*. . . .

So this was when I pushed myself and, with all the enthusiastic support of my partner, we took a beautiful photo with his phone, and *voilà*! My man, my girl, and my dog with me naked. I did not want to wait any longer, especially because I felt that the inner work had been done. I sent it with the phrase. . . .

And unexpectedly my mother said: "What a nice photo." What??? I could not believe it. Forty minutes later she sent another message (of course I forgot to say that my mother lives in another country, and this communication was by phone) to ask: "But what does this photo mean, you know that I'm very stupid?" Well, nothing stupid about it, she knew it wasn't the kind of photo I usually send her, and above all the force behind that act could not be just for fun. I told her that was it, I managed to have my family, and I wanted her to know it.

Maestro Jodorowsky, I am neither a writer, nor the best at summing things up, but what happened from the moment I saw you—the time it took me to perform the act (which for me was the strongest, because I wanted to and felt I couldn't)—to this day has been so transformative. Because this act, taking the photo and sending it with the phrase, even though it was done in minutes, has been a reactivator of my healing. I feel privileged, blessed to have had this miracle of meeting you. I don't know if I told you, but the morning before we met, I screamed alone in my room how sick I was of feeling like this!!! I needed for this to change, and hours later I found you with that beautiful wife of yours, and I am very grateful for your time, listening, support. May your life be full of blessings.

WITH ALL MY HEART,

ALEXANDRA

⇥ LETTER 84 ⇤
....

From Pascale

I had a happy childhood. The youngest of four children pampered by loving and attentive parents, I lived among adults who surrounded me without ever being stupid with me. I felt protected. Yet this childhood was marked by a secret that I concealed for a long time.

I don't know exactly how old I was, probably between seven and eight years old: I was the victim of sexual abuse, without knowing, without understanding it immediately. It happened without violence, almost gently and without penetration. But although I was very young and did not quite understand what was happening to me, I felt that these caresses were not appropriate and were far from being innocent and a manifestation of healthy affection. I pushed back my attacker during his advances, which fortunately stopped short. But the damage was done. My body acted like a shield and I only realized as a teenager that my vagina closed up so that no one could penetrate it.

I carried the trauma like a ghost that prevented me from going all the way in any romantic relationship.

I lived neither as a recluse nor fearfully, but I protected my interiority like a sacred temple. I nurtured an ideal of life, art, and love at the peak of all possibilities.

I didn't live like a clinical or neurotic case but I knew with a quiet certainty that one day a man would manage to open me and that everything would open with him. I knew that I would recognize him. I waited for him, and while waiting, I nourished myself with art, the absolute, desires, ideals, dreams. . . . I constructed myself, art anchored to the body like religion.

I waited for him, and while waiting for him I had significant encounters, like signs on my way to him.

Perhaps fate or chance led me one day to you, Alejandro, whose name and work I didn't know. You read the tarot for me for free in a café in Paris for the whole world, for people who knew you by word of mouth.

That day there were plenty of people waiting for their reading. You were focused on the person in front of you, seeing nothing else around. Except when you lifted your eyes with a strange and inhabited gaze. It was only on the third time that I understood that it was me you were looking at, indescribably but with depth and without seduction.

When it was my turn you didn't have to turn over the cards to know who I was. And my life changed almost instantly. I recognized you and I cried with emotion. During the months that followed, we were linked, then united, definitively. The first time you touched me, I let you discover without telling you anything that I was closed, and in fact a virgin. Without astonishment or questions, you were an example of gentleness. Step by step, with measured and precise gestures, over the weeks, you lifted the barriers, awakened my body that I locked like a fortress to you. With patience and infinite tenderness, you waited for the door to open to let you in me. And you never got out. Only you could do it with so much safety, with strength and love, without hurting me and without risking traumatizing me again and in an irreparable way. You are the being that I had long awaited.

I had unconsciously transformed this trauma into an intimate mythology to which only one being would have the key to save me. No one could have it except you. Because it took your wisdom, your strength, your knowledge, your intelligence, your experience, and your infinite love. And because the universe wanted it that way. That which was locked up inside of me gradually freed itself into a fulfilling sexuality, which has continued to develop over the years of metaphysical communion, because the union of two bodies that love each other is a sacred union.

Could we say that transforming a traumatic sexual assault by way of supreme love is psychomagical? What I can confirm, however, is that our life together is an act of psychomagic, since everything has indeed opened up.

Despite our forty-three years of age difference, we allowed ourselves the possibility of having a child, without forcing anything, and having faith that everything would be for the best. The child didn't come and you were afraid that I might take it badly. But to live our love with or without children was stronger than anything, and finally everything has a reason to be or not to be.

You then offered that we transform the biological child that we didn't have by creating pascALEjandro, our symbolic child who carries the fusion of our two first names, holding in its center the last three letters of my first name, which are also the three first letters of yours, which again, the universe willed that way.

This is the act of psychomagic that allowed us to brave the fact of not having children, to create it symbolically, this artist with four hands, two brains, two souls, which is neither one nor the other but which would not exist without both.

We feed it each with what we are and it grows having its own artistic autonomy. He will outlive us, like a fusion of our beings and our souls, which is for us, as an artistic couple that is separated by forty-three years but united by everything, even stronger than if we had a child.

According to the ancient alchemy book *Mutus Liber* the alchemist cannot accomplish the great work until he has found true love. The great work is done by two, two complementary beings, two individuals which feed a third entity. Ours is pascALEjandro. It's the most beautiful act of psychomagic that I have achieved thanks to you, with you, for eternity.

Thank you Alejandro, for absolutely everything,

from the depths of my soul,

Pascale

The Psychotrance Process

INTRODUCTION TO PSYCHOTRANCE

"To advance a kilometer, you have to take a first step," said Laozi. Psychotrance in this book is just that first step.

I was born in a toxic home. During my childhood I had no tender relationship with my father, nor with my mother, not even with my sister. Because I was the son of immigrants, no other child granted me their friendship. Emotional loneliness made me read, between the age of five and seven, all the books in the meager library of Tocopilla, a port located in a desert area of northern Chile. In that parade of letters, what impressed me the most was an anatomical engraving of a split-open human head, exposing the brain. My childhood imagination transformed that brain mass into a turtle without a shell. For a long time I lived anguished, believing I had a loquacious animal feeding on my blood inside my skull. Being invaded by foreign ideas made me doubt myself.

"Is my brain mine or am I his? If he thinks and I don't think, what am I? An ape swallowing strange words?"

At the cost of efforts beyond my young age, I forced myself to distinguish, in the jet of words that the turtle vomited, those that were mine. By gradually developing self-awareness I freed myself from those childhood fears.

"My brain is not a parasite, but a viscus; that is mine just like the heart, liver, or kidneys. Its task?

Grow the seeds of consciousness with which all human beings are born, until we manage to turn it into an immortal soul."

Later I permitted myself to inform my inner child that we do not reach the world with a seed of consciousness, but with a fully developed awareness.

"Our main task is to release the awareness of its outdated ideas. Underneath the confusion of words a sacred silence extends; under the confusion of feelings extends a holy peace; under the confusion of desires extends a sacred ecstasy. . . . But our family, society, and history lock us up in a cage of racial prejudice, religious beliefs, political fanaticism, and economic woes. In view of these limits our brain hides in its vast unconscious immense capabilities that will only be possible to use when the body transforms itself into an organism capable of communicating by telepathy, of overcoming terrestrial gravity, of producing changes in matter, of projecting an astral body, of traveling through time, of extending our life thousands of years."

My inner child came back to harass me with questions.

"If what I call 'I' does not exist and a viscus cannot create thoughts, who creates them?"

Without any scientific proof I told him that the brain is a receptor of thoughts, not their creator. *Kabbalah* in Hebrew means "what is received." For the rabbis, the Torah is not a book written by human beings, but a series of messages received from a divine plane.

The psychiatrist Carl Gustav Jung asserted that the individual unconscious is attached to the unconscious of all others, thus forming a collective being. Jung may have known the teachings of Helena Blavatsky, one of the founders of Theosophy. Inspired by Hindu mysticism, she used the Sanskrit word *Akasha* to name the invisible aura spread around our planet. In this Akashic library there is inscribed, by means of sounds, all human thought—past, present, and future.

I allowed myself to accept these theories by freeing my imagination and taking them as far as possible.

The collective unconscious remembers the past and future, not only of humanity, but also of the Cosmos, from the moment it emerges from Emptiness, until the moment when it dissolves into unthinkable nothing. Our memory spans millions and millions of years, so many that it is impossible to imagine its quantity.

Can we then know the Truth? Is what we call Cosmos not one but a great swarm of universes? What's in the impenetrable heart of the planet on whose surface we are born and die? Are we born or are we matter that assumes a new form? Do we die or are we a set of elements that disperses in a space-time of which we don't know either its form or duration? We don't know what is after death, we don't know what life is. Scientific truths change as new qualities of "matter" seemingly without mass are discovered; the microscopic world can be infinite.

Are we very far from finding the depth of the matter? Are the Whole and the Emptiness two aspects of the same mystery? Is being a part of any? Is the intangible part of the corporeal? If All and Emptiness are one thing, there is no interior or outside, no center or surface, no right or left, no up or down, no far or near, no beginning or end. The All-Empty—shall I call it God?—is neither big nor small, neither simple nor complex, neither pure nor impure, neither bad nor good.

The humble philosopher Socrates (470–399 BCE) confessed: "I only know that I know nothing and I am not even sure of that." Moses Maimonides, physician and theologian (1138–1204 CE), in his voluminous treatise *Guide for the Perplexed* concluded: "God is that of which nothing can be said."

Ludwig Wittgenstein, mathematician and philosopher (1889–1951 CE) in his book *Tractatus Logico-Philosophicus* said: "Whereof one cannot speak, thereof one must be silent."

Aware of logical thinking's profound ignorance, many therapists look to Indigenous cultures for the Truth that civilization has taken from them: union with the world of dreams, of the dead, of the spirits that populate sea, sky, and land. Helped by psychotropic substances, they discover that everything that exists lives, speaks, feels, and wants.

Would that deep trance allow them to assimilate the wisdom of their ancestors? Will we finally find the Truth? Can you eliminate your Self, as Buddha advised? The artificial I, Ego, can be eliminated . . . but not the authentic Self, Essential Being, necessary to unite with other Essential Beings. The Voodoo adepts from Haiti do the same. During religious ceremonies, they receive gods in a trance, whom they dress up as characters by giving them a name, a suit, a melody, some symbolic objects, and a particular behavior. Ogu, fierce warrior, threatens his enemies with a machete; the Baron Samedi, Death, with the bleached face, exhibits a wooden phallus; the beautiful Erzulie wears three wedding rings, one for each of her husbands. These ancient characters, plus a hundred others, are similar, to some extent, to the numerous archetypes that, according to C. G. Jung, are universal symbols, passed down through generations and present in all cultures.

The Mighty Father imposes family life with absolute authority. The Mother-Virgin instills behaviors related to motherhood without sexual pleasure. The Persona is the public image that you want to share with others. The Shadow is everything that is kept secret. The Trickster violates the laws to prove how vulnerable they are.

The collective unconscious is made up of this set of archaic characters, as is Voodoo and other religions, which maintain power thanks to prizes and punishments. Believers can ascend to heaven or fall into hell based on prehistoric terrors like fire, cold, darkness, wild beasts, natural disasters, enemy tribes, loneliness.

Our family, if it is toxic, creates a false perception of ourselves. We grow up without seeing reality objectively. The artificial self rejects any changes. Every time that we wish to "sin," our archaic memory makes us fear that if they discover us they will punish us by expelling us from the clan to the fierce outside, where wild beasts or tribal enemies will devour us.

Human beings realize themselves by not rejecting changes. The Cosmos has created a mysterious goal for us. We must face the future and expel the myths that have built up in the brain, until we reach the ultimate consciousness, where we stop watching ourselves think, feel, desire, or act. It is a challenge to the mind. There is no separation: it is not subjective or objective experience, but a union in which thinking, feeling, desiring, and acting are harmonically integrated. The future requires us to live in the present, without prejudice or religious dogmas, or political fanaticism, or homelands with artificial borders, or perceived restrictions that can accompany our age, or unjust social classes, and no sexual definitions, no desire for power, glory, or money. . . . Our inner child tells us:

"Because my body is just a loan, I will cease to confuse being with having. To be born is to change, to live is to change, to die is to change. I'm not what I think I am, nothing defines me, nothing limits me, nothing is mine alone that is not everyone's, what happens to others happens to me. Being the All, in no case am I something of someone, nor is someone something of mine. I only am when I am nothing. My intellect has learned to die."

Psychotrance is not a possession similar to the one described in this prologue. It's a search without disguises, magical rites, superstitious symbols, or inexperienced beliefs, where we allow feelings and sensations into our limited perception of ourselves, which enrich us without turning us into something other than what we really are: inhabitants of the future.

✳ 1. Sensory Imagination

Our unconscious accepts everything we imagine as real. That allows us to capture aspects of reality that the intellect cannot perceive. Analyzing a flower, in a way, is the autopsy of a corpse. To get closer to what it vitally is, we need to feel that we are that flower. He who observes the other without putting himself in its place cannot know it. The words bring us closer to things, but are not the things. A definition never defines the totality of what is to be understood. Because of our mental, emotional, sexual, and bodily limits we do not live as who we really are, but as who we think we are. This concept of ourselves changes our perception of the world, imposing the limits that our mind manufactures. All that we identify with brings qualities.

✳ *2. Skin, Meat, Blood, and Bones*

I'm going to jump the literary barrier to work directly with you. If I tell you "Cleanse your mind of the parasites that harass it," I mean the cackling of thoughts, feelings, desires, and needs that never cease to resonate in your mind. Like a baby mounted on a wooden horse, you spin and gyrate around your ego. Get off that carousel. Let it spin without identifying yourself with its cackling. Clear your mind. Get naked!

Regarding the skin that envelops your body, you perceive it as a border that separates you from the "outside," believing what you really are is only locked inside it. Your unconscious covers you with a shell made of what disturbs you: failures, rejections, fears, guilt, inferiorities, dissatisfaction, hatred, envy, anxieties about dying. They compress your body, preventing you from enjoying the happiness of being alive.

To free yourself from that shell that isolates you from reality, you must scrape, with a hard soapy toothbrush, every inch of your skin, imagining that you strip it off its negative experiences. Once you are finished scraping—which done conscientiously can last more than an hour—take a cold shower. Then, without drying off, stand straight for ten minutes, feeling that all your pores are clean. You have expelled from your skin what you think you know and what you think you are and what you think you have.

After this pause, rub your hands together with olive oil mixed with a drop of essential lavender oil until you feel them as bright as two fireflies. You can start the massage of your dark "interior."

You grant the luminosity of your hands to each muscle, massaging it tenderly back and forth, though at the beginning you will feel like a wary animal. When your mind accepts that your muscles gleam, sink your fingers deep inside your body, like opening a beautiful chest closed for centuries. Pressing with loving attention, like a good mother, you will transmit the light to your throat, your heart, lungs, stomach, intestines, kidneys, liver, and pancreas. Every organ appreciates your luminous caresses sharing ancient well-being with you.

Next, sliding your hands up your chest, feel them penetrating into your heart to immerse yourself in the blood that it circulates. Open, like fish swimming in a stream current, your hands sail, slowly spreading their light counterclockwise until you reach the heart again. There you stop to catch your heartbeats: they are the song of life! Everything vibrates to the rhythm of your heartbeat: the "inside" plus the "outside," the city, the country, the planet, the galaxy, the endless universe. . . . But not your skeleton, because you have identified it with death from childhood. Those bones filled with vigorous marrow are not those of a foreigner, however—they are your true homeland!

Rub and press each of your bones. Wake them up, make them breathe, treat them with respect as if they were jewels. Feel their extreme sensitivity, perceive the love with which they produce that marrow that is the food of your soul. Start dancing, not thinking that you move a skeleton, but feeling like you're a skeleton moving the rest of your body. Let your bones express themselves, accepting strange positions, movements, and rhythms that you do not know.

Dance without any limits, emitting shouts, melodic sounds, mysterious words. Do all this feeling that you are not your immaterial ego, but a concrete body expressing itself freely.

✳ 3. Primary Energy

The light that fills you and the Cosmos is the product of an eternal energy, countless times more powerful than the simultaneous explosion of many atomic bombs. Let yourself imagine and feel that every cell in your body, beginning with the marrow of your bones, contains this terrifying force. Feel it circulate through your spine, let it enter your skull, dissolve it in your blood, make it circulate through your arteries and your veins. Strength! Strength! Strength! Like a gigantic primordial wave, energy invades your limbs, viscera, muscles, eyes, tongue, and sex organ. Huge waves, dazzling waves, lightning bolts, hurricanes that arise through the pores of your skin. You join the power of the land, of the seas, of the air, and beyond.

The energy of the moon, sun, planets, and herds of stars. All that gigantic power nests in every cell of your body, as well as in each particle of universal matter. Now that you know, it is yours. Imagine and feel that you dominate it. You transform into it. You collapse into yourself; you are the core, immaterial force. You are going to take over the space filling it with your energy. Continue expanding as far as possible, further and further, infinitely further, to stop where your imagination can no longer reach. Later do the same but the other way around. Then do the same to one side and then the other. And finally, do the same ascending and descending. Start becoming a sphere that contains everything. You are energy, neither good nor bad. You build, maintain, destroy. Nothing and no one can stop you. From the central core absorb yourself. Return into your body.

❊ 4. Recovery of Freedom

Family traditions, the dictatorship of rational language, fallen morals, enslaving activities, patriotic fanaticism, insane criticism—all prevent us from using all our possibilities. As soon as you try to act freely, you're taken for a dangerous madman. Trained from childhood like obedient circus animals, our greatest limit is the fear of freedom. Enough!

Right now you're going to start freeing yourself from slavery. Feel that you are locked up, from head to toe, in steel armor that squeezes you, suffocates you, immobilizes you, embeds you in a pile of soil. Realize that you live buried in the anguish of a prisoner on death row.

With the desperation of a castaway that holds on to a small cork, close your eyes. Supporting you in the security of existence they give you, descend to your feet. Penetrate into the heels, feel them as two spheres of living bone, capable of crushing any obstacle. Imagine you are breaking the links of a thick chain with them, reducing it to dust. Penetrate your insoles, feel their extreme solidity, kick with them bigger and bigger rocks that soar high, until you imagine you are throwing a mountain into space that turns into a comet. Penetrate the arches of your feet, bridges between a lost past and future death, prisoners of the fear of change, of advancing. Reach the toes that try to cling to the present that slips away. With monumental force disintegrate your shoes of steel! Let your feet acquire the lightness of birds! From your ankles to your head, disintegrate the rest of your metallic bark! Take a deep breath, feeling free. Go outside. Imagining yourself weightless, walk for an hour, reciting two phrases, each divided into three steps:

I am of you!
I trust myself!

When you finish the walk, lean your back on any wall, and without worrying about the people passing by, close your eyes and start asking yourself questions and giving yourself answers:

Who am I?
(You are what you are and not what others want you to be)
What am I tied to?
(You are tied to the consciousness of your Awareness)
What don't I have?
(You do not have a personal Self)
What do I aspire to be?
(You want to be the spirit of your matter)

With your eyes closed, feel that you have roots that reach the center of the Earth. Open your eyes. Observe with childlike eyes the world you believed you belong to.

✳ 5. Sacred Madness

For three days leave the character that you appear to be in daily life. Break every habit. Hide your mirrors and your clocks. Dress in very large clothing, paint a red circle on the tip of your nose. Surrender to life without knowing what you are. Avoid being imprisoned in definitions. Every time someone gives you an order, respond, smiling, "I'd rather not." Don't accept advice, models, owners. Do whatever you feel like. If someone tells you something serious, laugh. If someone says something funny to you, make a sad face. Let the words pass in front of your conscience like an alien herd. Be free to imagine the heinous, be free to imagine the sublime. After those three days go back to being who you've always been, but keeping the red circle on the tip of your nose one more day.

✳ 6. Awareness of Consciousness

What do we call "Consciousness?" It is one thing to be aware of something, another thing to be aware of Consciousness. "I am aware when among other bodies I am present in this body. I perceive the movements of my hands, my heartbeat, the rhythm of my words. I perceive with all my senses at once, what happens in me and in the world."

That's a limited description of a conscience, anchored in the "I" and in "Mine." We are used to seeing ourselves as something separate.

"My ego is something separate, my body is something separate, my parents are something separate, my partner is something separate, my car is a separate thing, my money is something separate, each being, each thing is something separate."

When we try to reach the top of our Consciousness, we crash against "something separate."

If I try to observe "My" awareness, I split into observed consciousness and observing consciousness.

If "I" want to observe that observing consciousness, I divide once again. If I don't get rid myself of the "I," that action never ends. The only thing which is not separate is the Whole, the absolute union of the multiple. Each being, each thing is a fragment that contains a multiplicity. If we say "dog," we mean an animal of precise form, which changes as we try to imagine a dog similar to all dogs. We realize then that our dog is a summary of all the dogs we have seen, plus the dogs modified as our mind adds or removes them: a gigantic dog, a dog of the size of a flea, etc.

It is enough for us to invoke the unconscious so that it answers by multiplying and transforming things and beings. Every individual is a parade of an endless number of different selves.

Being a marriage of unity with the multiplicity, you are the infinite space, eternal time, the still center of the present in constant transformation. A harmonic Cosmos where each part, no matter how small, vibrates in the ecstasy of a perfect moment, absolute union with no aspiration to be better or have more: an "I" without something!

That Consciousness, which cannot bear to be described or classified, which was never born and never dies, is in you watching you grow, live, reach the moment of your extinction. Hallelujah! You dissolve into Consciousness, just as all living beings will dissolve into the entire Cosmos. She will re-create another, and another, and another, each time different. What you really are, you have always been. If you suffer, it is because of an illusion that does not relate to you.

Let go of past disappointment or the anguish of the future.

✳ 7. Intra-Instant

When you dissolve into Consciousness, its energy drives you with a faith devoid of fear. It's like a boat waiting for you next to the pier. If you do not embark, you are a memory or a prognosis, never an awakened being. If you get in, it takes you without you knowing where. For you, arriving is going.

✳ 8. The Symbolic World

In your home, take a handful of white labels with "NO" written in black ink, and another handful of black labels with "YES" in white ink. Paste those affirmations and negations on what you own: your bed, table, chairs, furniture, photos, books, clothes, crockery, etc. . . .

Pile up on the street the things on which you have left a NO, so that anyone can take them. Arrange objects on which you left a YES in a harmonious way. Lie down on the floor on your back. . . . Your body calms down, your mind calms down, your memory calms down. Anguish does not poison your hope, no misery threatens your dreams, no disease tarnishes your conscience, no ambition eats away at your liver, no prejudice rots your freedom. . . . Take a deep breath, fill your belly with air, and expel it vigorously imagining that you are disintegrating the immense rock that was crushing you without you realizing it. Rid the words from your mind. . . . Silence spreads like a lucid cloud. Little by little you lose weight. You fly without knowing where or what you are looking for. Soon you're lying on the floor of a cramped hotel room. It's hard to breathe. You understand that you have always lived feeling like a prisoner in a meat cage. A tremor seizes you, spreading across the floor. You fear that your head will evaporate, your heart will stop beating, your body will explode. Slowly furniture, walls, the seedy building, the streets of your ruined city, the whole world begins to melt. You are floating in front of a gigantic sun. Its flames take the shape of your face. "I am the treasure you have always sought. Quiet your mind, empty your heart, tame your sex, expel from your image of yourself your memory."

The face of flames transforms into a mirror. You realize that you don't see your reflection in it. You are not two, you are one. Shining like a lamp you float in the center of a limitless space.

Breathing, memory, the spill of seconds and minutes all calm down. All your images of yourself were false.

With sighs of relief you begin, as slowly as possible, to take off your clothes as if you would tear peels stuck to your skin since childhood. They made you believe that you were an empty form. Convince your brain, your heart, your sex, your set of cells that reality is yours! If you do not join the Whole, you drag about a soul in agony. . . . Enter your navel and dig deep to your oldest memory: that sublime period in which the umbilical cord poured the same energy that nourishes the Universe into you. Love, love, love, your heartbeat expanding like an aura integrated with the beating of the Earth, to later dissolve into an ocean of galaxies. Your mother cuts the umbilical cord with her teeth. You are born. Like two avid flowers your lungs open. You are gripped by an infinite desire to absorb the air of that planet-cradle that crosses the space nourished by the sun. But the prejudices of your family, made up of parents, grandparents, and millions upon millions of great-grandparents, cover your heart with a crust of myths, orders, and prohibitions. You feel like you live caged inside an alien personality.

Fighting to regain your authenticity, you turn the darkness into light, evil into affection, selfishness into generosity, the error into lesson. If you perceive yourself in a new way, the world will offer opportunities that agree with what you improve in your mind.

✳ 9. Be Without Appearing

Lock yourself up for a week without seeing anyone, keeping your mobile, your computer, your TV, your CD player disconnected. Resist loneliness without hearing music, without watching films, without swallowing news, without reading newspapers or magazines or books, without writing, without drawing, without smoking, without drinking liquor or eating unhealthy foods (only plain water, nuts, and fruits), without speaking out loud, without singing, without masturbating. If you are able to let go of what you are not to discover what you are, at dawn on the eighth day you will open the door and you will enter a world as changed as you are.

✳ 10. The Twilight of Words

If we suffered abuse in childhood, instead of growing normally we remain imprisoned in the age when it happened. Victims of a memory that martyrs us or which unknowingly blames us, we hide it by falsely forgetting it. Intellectually we behave as adults, but emotionally we are still children. When we manage to understand that the way of life we have adopted does not correspond to what we really are, we face a difficult choice: either we bury that traumatic memory in a fake oblivion again, or we free ourselves from relationships and activities that do not satisfy us, to move toward ourselves.

The roots of the fragrant lotus flower sink into a fetid swamp. To get to the sublime we must immerse ourselves in the depth of our darkness.

Lie down on the floor and pretend to be dead. First get rid of all identification with your bodily sensations: erase the images of your body. The constant river of words that endlessly floods you emerges from a character that you are no longer. Without masks that define you, without being divided into an actor and a spectator, be like a mirror that does not define or judge what it reflects. "A grain of sand, floating in the blue of the noon, darkens the whole sky." Perceive the silent energy that accumulates under what you think. Without giving them importance let the words come and go like clouds driven by the wind. If you fight, trying to eliminate them, your efforts will multiply. Do not identify them with reality. They are just maps of what you call "reality." When they dissolve, you, free of definitions or prejudices, of age, of beginning or end, can finally capture the sublime beauty of what you truly are: a being that contains everything, stretching across space-time like an infinite dawn.

✻ *11. The Essential Being*

Stop your thoughts. You're already like a forest that simply grows, with nothing to prove. You don't know who you are, but you know how you feel. You have nothing to ask of anyone, you do not demand anything of yourself. Imagine the color red while you relax your feet. You let them live their own life. Red! You relax your legs up to the knees, while imagining the color orange. You let your thighs relax up to your sex, while imagining the color yellow. You allow your sex to live its own life, while you go up to your belly and your chest, imagining the color green. Release your arms up to your shoulders, your back, your anus. You immerse yourself in the color blue. You loosen your neck, the nape of your neck, your nostrils, your eyes, your ears, your lips, and your tongue. The blue turns purple. Relax your forehead. You have an intensely smooth face. The entire skin of your body shines like a rainbow. In this sacred moment, your whole being lives its own life. On the inside of your navel a dense ray of light is born. That bright line runs up your spine, pierces your skull, stretches toward a cloudless sky. It is a maternal extension with which you unite.

Traversed by the luminous axis, you begin to spin, rising to the center of the sky. A gentle wind picks you up and carries you away, floating, toward a landscape that delights you. What it's like? Lush? Deserted? Is there a sea, a river, a lake, forests, mountains, animals? You walk through that lovely landscape and you get to the place you always wanted to possess. In that land you see your palace grow, or your temple, or your castle, or your rustic cabin. In short, the beloved home in which, one distant day, you would like to die. What is that building like, what shape, what size? Fly around to see it entirely, then walk into it. Through a door, through a window, through a skylight, through the walls? Wander inside. Where are you going, what obstacles do you face? How do you beat them? At last you find the treasure or the prize that you deserve! That place that you built with your imagination will be your refuge forever.

Anything you want to create, you will create it there. Any God you want to see, you will see it there. Any gift you crave, you will find it there. You could talk with your dead. . . .

You return to your cloudless sky, where you wait for the shaft of light. Descend toward your "real" body. You will discover there what you really need.

THE UNCONSCIOUS ACCEPTS EVERYTHING THAT WE IMAGINE AS REAL.

Index

About the Author

Alejandro Jodorowsky was born in Tocopilla, Chile, in 1929. During his career as a tarologist, therapist, author, actor, theatrical director, and director of cult films (*El Topo, The Holy Mountain,* and *Santa Sangre*), he developed psychomagic and psychogenealogy, two new therapeutic techniques that have revolutionized psychotherapy in many countries. Psychogenealogy served as the background for his novel *Where the Bird Sings Best,* and psychomagic was used by Jodorowsky in the novel *The Son of Black Thursday.* Both of these techniques are discussed and explored in his books *Psychomagic* and *Manual of Psychomagic,* in his autobiography *The Dance of Reality,* in *Metagenealogy: Self-Discovery through Psychomagic and the Family Tree,* written with Marianne Costa, and in his most recent film, 2019's *Psychomagic, A Healing Art.* He has also written two books on the therapeutic application of the tarot: *The Way of Tarot,* written with Marianne Costa, and *Yo, el Tarot* (I, the Tarot). In addition to his books on spirituality and tarot, he has written more than thirty comic books and graphic novels, including *The Panic Fables: Mystic Teachings and Initiatory Tales,* the complete series of his spiritual "Panic Fables" comics translated into English for the first time. In 2019, Alejandro Jodorowsky was cited as one of the "100 Most Spiritually Influential Living People in the World" according to *Watkins Mind Body Spirit* magazine. He currently lives in Paris.